ALL ABOUT DOLL HOUSES

Also by Barbara L. Farlie

ALL ABOUT

Doll Houses

by Barbara L. Farlie

with CHARLOTTE L. CLARKE

PHOTOGRAPHS BY OTTO MAYA

DRAWINGS BY JAIME IRIBARREN

BOBBS-MERRILL *Indianapolis/New York*

ISBN 0-672-51976-3
Library of Congress Catalog Card Number: 75-513
Typography by Irving Perkins/Layouts by Helen Barrow
Manufactured in the United States of America

First printing
9 8 7 6 5 4 3 2 1

FOR MY HUSBAND
WILLIAM NEWMAN FARLIE, JR.

"Love is an act of the will"

Contents

Foreword

Almost everyone is fascinated by dollhouses and their furnishings. Once regarded as the province of little girls, dollhouses are manufactured today for both sexes and all ages of people—in the form of houses, houseboats, apartments, and campers. I have discovered that men are as interested and active in the hobby of dollhouses as women, and are capable of making exquisite miniature furniture.

One of the nicest things about an involvement with dollhouses is the people you're going to meet. Miniature enthusiasts are among the friendliest individuals I have ever known. And because of their complete willingness to share trade secrets, they have made miniature construction and collecting into the third largest hobby in the world. Another pleasant feature of dollhouses is the fun you can have within the family. Decorating and redecorating a dollhouse is an ongoing hobby that engages each and every family member; as is true for life-sized houses, when the last room of your dollhouse is finished, it will be time to start all over again with the first.

When I decided to make dollhouses one of my own hobbies, I thought I would buy a truly antique dollhouse and furnish it with authentically antique dollhouse furniture. But when I discovered that the houses and furnishings are extremely scarce and expensive, I undertook the creation of a dollhouse that would look like an antique. Though I was certainly no dollhouse expert, I enjoyed crafts and knew a lot about antiques. Hopefully, I could combine these interests and produce a credible, even elegant dollhouse.

I knew that two heads were better than one. I was not a skilled builder, and so Charlotte Clarke entered the picture; not only was she a miniature enthusiast, she had built numerous scale models with her son. Our collaboration was a huge success, for we built three dollhouses—the ones that form the heart of this book.

Ironically, our biggest problem was figuring out how to make the smaller items for the dollhouses—the accessories. We visited toy stores and studied miniature furniture catalogs, sighing over wonderful little tea services and the like, but refusing to buy them because we wanted to make everything ourselves. Finally I hit on liquid solder as a medium for bonding metal to metal, and thus a teapot, sugar, creamer, and a host of other accessories were born.

A dollhouse becomes a showcase for your own creative talents and should be displayed prominently—in living room, dining room, or family room. I keep one dollhouse in the front hall and another in an upstairs sitting room. You'll be surprised how much enthusiastic comment your dollhouse will generate at your next party. Inevitably, a party guest or two will stop by the following day with some tiny treasure to be crafted by you into a dollhouse accessory. If you're just beginning to furnish a dollhouse, a party is a sure-fire way to acquire useful and fascinating trinkets.

This book has been designed for the amateur crafts person, who will discover in it a world of crafts, including stencilling, decorative painting, antiquing, rug hooking and braiding, furniture finishing, needlepointing, and others. Only the simplest and least expensive tools and supplies are recommended. Later on, when you become more proficient, you may decide to work in basswood or mahogany instead of balsa wood; similarly, you may decide you want a jig saw instead of a manual saw, or a lathe instead of metal files.

Many hobbies evolve into extremely profitable at-home businesses, and dollhouses are no exception. Certainly, as the demand for quality dollhouses and furnishings continues to exceed the supply, more and more hobbyists are turning professional.

The hobbyist can benefit by studying pamphlets about certain famous dollhouses: Queen Mary's Dollhouse at Windsor Castle in England; Sir Neville Wilkinson's Titania's Palace, which is exhibited around Europe though mostly in England; Colleen Moore's dollhouse (see the book entitled *Colleen Moore's Dollhouse,* Doubleday, 1971); the Bradford Dollhouse at the Smithsonian Institute in Washington, D.C. What helped me most, however, was not a single dollhouse but rather a collection of 97 magnificent miniature rooms given to the Chicago Art Institute by Mrs. James Ward Thorne. "The Thorne rooms," as they are popularly called, present a history in miniature of prominent European and American interior design styles. A lover of dollhouses, Mrs. Thorne traveled widely to collect the finest articles for the rooms, but she also made many of the pieces herself. I urge anyone reading this book to write the Art Institute for their catalog on the Thorne collection; cost, including postage, is about four dollars.

I would like to thank the people who made this book possible: Charlotte Lamson Clarke, who contributed enormously in ideas, time, and energy; her husband Tom, and children Fred and Pammy, for their interest and patience; my husband Bill, my children Lisa, Billy, and Craig, and my parents Blanche and Herman Leitzow, all of whom made their own special contributions. I am also deeply indebted to: Catherine B. MacLaren, editor and publisher of *Nutshell News,* one of the best publications on miniatures, who gave me vital leads; Mrs. Dunbar B. Abell, Mrs. George B. Brockel, Mrs. William C. Dinkel, Mr. and Mrs. Chester N. Hopper, and Mrs. Theodore Merrill, and Mr. and Mrs. Truman Moore for generously sharing their time and talents with me and for permitting me to photograph their dollhouses and miniature rooms. Finally, special thanks to: Mr. and Mrs. Donald Black, Mr. and Mrs. Anthony Cardone, Mrs. Harry Clarke, Miss Anne Duchen, Mr. and Mrs. Anton Hauser, Mrs. J. Harris Lamson, Mrs. Peter Sloan, and Miss Elizabeth Zenorini.

BARBARA L. FARLIE

PART I Basics and A Brief History

Before you begin to build a dollhouse or to furnish a miniature room, you should ask yourself these questions: Who will be using the dollhouse—you or a child? Will the dollhouse function as a showpiece or as a toy? The answer will determine the amount of time, energy, and money you put into the project. If the dollhouse is to be a child's plaything, you will probably fill the window openings with clear plastic acetate instead of six-over-six-pane Colonial windows; build a trestle table and bench instead of a pedestal dining room table and chairs; paint the ceilings instead of putting beams on them. On the other hand, if you are creating a prize dollhouse to be the envy of your peers, and if you're a stickler for detail, you will undoubtedly work painstakingly on it over a long period of time.

TO BUILD OR NOT TO BUILD

Your first decision is whether to build a dollhouse shell from scratch; or to purchase a prefabricated dollhouse kit; or to furnish a few rooms instead of building a whole dollhouse (see chapter two on unusual dollhouses). Typical floor plans are given in chapter three for Colonial, Georgian, and Victorian dollhouses. But if you are unsure of your abilities to build the complete dollhouse, or if you do not want to take the time, we recommend buying a kit; these can be customized to look exactly as if you'd built the entire house yourself, yet the effort is minimal.

The kits we like best are manufactured by Yield House and My Uncle. Both companies advertise nationally and are extremely reliable. In addition, their dollhouses are amply sized, sturdy, and weigh considerably more than those of competitors. Popularly priced, they range from about 50 to 75 dollars, including shipping. All assembling and decorating are left up to the buyer.

Yield House specializes in saltbox and townhouses made of high quality pressboard. For a free catalog, write: Yield House, Department 108, North Conway, New Hampshire 03860. The My Uncle line includes a townhouse and soon will add a small Cape Cod dollhouse; the houses are made with a newly developed plywood that has layers of tough plastic bonded to its surfaces for smoothness and sturdiness. The company will send a flyer or pictures on request if you write Mr. Albert S. Eaton, President, My Uncle, 133 Main Street, Fryeburg, Maine 04037.

SOURCES FOR IDEAS

The best way to start ideas flowing vis-à-vis your dollhouse is to pore over catalogs of life-sized furniture, department store catalogs, home-oriented magazines, and books on period architecture, furniture, and interior design. Our favorite inspirational source is the Williamsburg Craft House catalog. Most furniture catalogs give the dimensions of the furniture being advertised, which makes it easier to convert the life-sized measurements to miniature, if you decide to copy a piece.

You should also pay close attention to the furniture and accessories in your home and the homes of friends. Visit antique shops and fairs, village and single house restorations, and museums that contain rooms of period furniture and design.

SOURCES FOR
DOLLHOUSE FURNISHINGS

The best places to pick up odds and ends for a dollhouse are: church and school fairs; rummage and garage sales; thrift shops; craft shops;

supermarkets; hardware, upholstery, wallpaper, and electrical supply stores.

Of course your own home contains numerous items for a dollhouse. For example, after-shave caps make beautiful vases, teapots, and tureens. Other useful caps are on bottles of detergent, eyedrops, perfume, liquor, and champagne (yum, yum). The list of household discards to save for your dollhouse projects is relatively endless: small pocket mirrors, fabric and trim scraps, odd bits of yarn, buttons, open cans or jars of good paint, and broken jewelry, to name a few. Be sure to tell friends and relatives to save their discards for you, too.

One reason for spreading the word about your dollhouse needs is that a friend or relative might happen to have a box of really old fabric scraps tucked away in the attic, or perhaps an old petit point purse or beaded bag in disrepair; such valuables can be turned into rugs, tapestries, curtains, or coverlets for your miniature rooms, and render them more authentic. Whenever we had a choice—and particularly when working on the more formal rooms—we achieved authenticity by using scraps of old fabric, fringe, or lace donated by friends or found by us. Other authentic touches: a pair of tiny antique lead soldiers borrowed from a boy to place on the fireplace mantel in the Colonial bedroom (page 68); the door of the spice cabinet in the Colonial dining room (page 68), which is made from half of a broken Victorian daguerreotype frame.

But don't imagine that such authenticity is necessary. For the soldiers, for instance, you could easily substitute tiny figures from a cake decorating set, from craft shops, and from shops that carry small plastic figures for model train sets. For the spice cabinet you could achieve an almost identical result by using a balsa sheet for the door and embellishing it with embossed paper before staining or painting it. No attic discoveries of ours made possible the patchwork quilt in the Colonial bedroom (page 68) or the elegant damask-covered walls of the Georgian bedroom (page 69); both were made with recently purchased fabrics.

For those pieces of furniture or accessories that you don't want to make yourself, look in the pages of *Nutshell News* (1035 Newkirk Drive, La Jolla, California 92037) or *Hobbies Magazine* (1006 South Michigan Avenue, Chicago, Illinois 60605). Both magazines carry the advertisements of dollhouse, dollhouse furniture, and accessory suppliers. (We're not including a list of suppliers here because it would not be accurate a year or two hence, whereas the magazine ads are current.) *Nutshell News*, an outstanding quarterly, is the authoritative source for the miniaturist in all areas, and *Hobbies* has had a small, but excellent section on miniatures for years.

Also helpful are the following publications:

Creative Crafts, which is a bi-monthly magazine devoted to crafts, often has informative features on miniatures. Write: Carstens Publications Inc., P.O. Box 700, Newton, New Jersey 07860.

Miniature Gazette, which is a quarterly devoted to collecting and making miniatures. This publication is put out by the National Association of Miniature Enthusiasts. Write: N A M E, P.O. Box 2621, Anaheim, California 92804.

Mott Miniature Workshop-News is a wonderful single issue publication that offers patterns, plans and technical tips and advice on all phases of miniatures. Write: Mott Miniature Workshop-News, P.O. Box 5514, Sunny Hills Station, Fullerton, California 92635.

Paul A. Ruddell's free catalogue lists a great variety of publications and books on dolls, dollhouses and miniatures. Write him at: 4701 Queensbury Road, Riverdale, Maryland 20840.

Northeastern Scale Models' catalogue of inch to the foot, ready-made moldings, trims and architectural details. For catalogue, sample moldings and price list, send $1.00 to: Northeastern Scale Models, Box 425, Methuen, Massachusetts 01844.

THE IMPORTANCE OF ARTISTIC LICENSE

Early on, we decided that this book would be for the amateur crafts person; thus, it seemed wise to take artistic license when the results would not be affected detrimentally. For example, you will notice the absence of electric lights in our dollhouses, which would indicate candles, gas lamps, or whatever. They were omitted because electricity is hardly a beginner's undertaking.

We also took a bit of artistic license with the historical periods to which our dollhouses belong. For instance, the keeping room in the Colonial dollhouse (page 68) appears as it would have in the early part of that architectural period, while the bedroom is late Colonial, with a canopy bed instead of a simple cot or trundle bed. We did this because the canopy bed has more visual appeal and is more popular to make. Similarly, the kitchen in the Victorian dollhouse (page 69) contains an icebox, which is a very late Victorian piece; yet other decorative and functional aspects of this particular dollhouse would have appeared earlier in the Victorian era.

Artistic license, when exercised judiciously, encourages you to create a dollhouse that is a personal dreamhouse instead of one that epitomizes historical accuracy. Nevertheless, you should strive to have your dollhouse be fairly representative of the architectural period you choose to duplicate.

THE BEGINNING MINIATURIST

If you have never before made any miniature furniture, we recommend you choose projects at the outset that consist of no more than ten pieces. Also, stick to projects that don't require beveling, or have cabriole legs.

CHAPTER *2* *Unusual Dollhouses*

If you do not have the time or inclination to build the shell of a dollhouse, you can convert a piece of furniture into one. Or if you don't have the appropriate space in your home for an entire dollhouse, you should consider the creation of a single miniature room. Some of the nicest displays of miniature furniture we've seen have been built into cupboards, chests of drawers, bookcases and desks. Some delightful examples are described below, and shown in color on the following pages.

1. CHEST OF DRAWERS

This Georgian townhouse is in a built-in chest of drawers, but could also be in a free-standing chest or in a bookcase. A small hand saw and an X-acto knife were the only tools used in the making. The facade is one piece of ¼"-thick plywood attached to the house with tiny screw hooks, making it easy to remove to display the interior. Balconies and grills are gold embossed paper; fanlights are gold foil doilies; street lights are made out of lamp finials and Christmas tree balls.

2. CUPBOARDS

a. A peaked roof and chimneys were added to an unfinished cupboard to create this fine example of a dollhouse for children to play with and love. Windows and doors are all fool-the-eye decorative painting, so there are no panes for small hands to break or doors to come off the hinges when opened repeatedly. When not in use, cupboard doors are closed.
b. This dollhouse in an antique pine cupboard is typical of the ingenuity of Valentine and Chester Hopper, widely respected collectors and makers of miniature furniture who supply stores and other collectors all over the country.

3. SECRETARY

Rooms in this dollhouse are defined strictly with rugs and furniture so as to not alter or mar the handsome secretary. The neutral setting highlights the exquisite furnishings, with much decoupage, this talented miniaturist's trademark.

4. CLOCK CASE

These settings for miniatures were created by Carol Dinkel, whose clock case rooms are owned by several fortunate people across the country. The small area inside a clock requires a working scale of one-half inch to the foot.

5. SCALE CASE

This miniature room setting in an antique glass scale case was made with minimal effort. Lacking such an antique, you can establish the same effect with a shadow box, a lantern, a lucite cube, or a glass box made with identical squares of glass glued together and covered on the edges with gold embossed paper trim.

6. CHRISTMAS WREATH

To make a miniature setting for the holiday season, select an artificial wreath at least four inches deep, with a center opening of 10 to 12 inches. The room container is one half of a child's overnight suitcase, or a metal fruitcake tin, but it could also be a round plastic dishpan; either way, the container should fit snugly into the wreath. When decorating is completed, hang wreath on wall with picture wire.

1. Chest of Drawers (Barbara L. Farlie)

2a. Cupboard (Vivian M. Abell)

2b. Cupboard (Mr. and Mrs. Chester Hopper)

3. Secretary (Gini Merrill)

4. Clock Cases (Vivian M. Abell, Dorothy L. Brockel)

5. Scale Case (Mr. and Mrs. Chester Hopper)

6. Christmas Wreath (Barbara L. Farlie)

Colonial Dollhouse
(Charlotte L. Clarke)

Georgian Dollhouse
(Barbara L. Farlie)

Victorian Dollhouse
(Miss Rebecca Moore)

CHAPTER *3* *Colonial, Georgian, and Victorian Architecture*

Choosing an architectural period for a doll-house is an intensely personal decision. If you prefer the simple things in life, you will undoubtedly be drawn to creating a Colonial dollhouse. If you appreciate elegance and formality, perhaps you'll want a Georgian dollhouse. If you're an incurable romantic, you may be destined to work on a Victorian dollhouse. To help you decide, we are going to discuss the most notable characteristics of architecture and design during Colonial, Georgian, and Victorian times. Keep in mind that this brief history refers to human-sized houses, not just dollhouses.

COLONIAL HOUSES— THE 17TH CENTURY

The period in America between the building of the first cottages at Plymouth and Jamestown and the year 1700 can be called "Colonial" or "early American." We prefer the "Colonial" label because it clearly distinguishes 17th century architecture from that of the 18th century, which is called "American Georgian" or simply "Georgian." (The looser term "early American" is often used to describe everything up to the Victorian period.)

In general, Colonial houses were compact, sturdy, and spartan. These small dwellings of the earliest settlers appeared secure and warm but not at all luxurious. Life was hard then, and so exterior and interior design was dictated by necessity.

THE EXTERIOR

The earliest Colonial homes had only one room, called a keeping room, which served as living room, dining room, kitchen, and bedroom. Later, a parlor, or foreroom, was added, and from this nucleus grew a house around a central chimney. Eventually, the two-story house, or "saltbox," emerged, which was the predominant form of American architecture at the beginning of the 18th century.

All Colonial homes had significant features, including oak frames and beams, clapboard or shingle facades, shingled roofs, and dormer windows with unleaded panes. The earliest Colonial windows were made of oiled paper, but soon glass was commonplace. Almost without exception, the two-story Colonial home had eight or nine windows on the front of the house; the first floor had the door plus four windows, the second floor had four or five windows. The original small diamond-shaped window panes of one- or two-room homes gave way to rectangular sash window panes in popular combinations of six panes of glass over six panes below. Other popular combinations were eight panes over eight, nine over nine, and 12 over 12.

Many exteriors were left unpainted. If a home was painted, the color was usually white; if there were shutters, they were often painted green. Facing clapboards were very short, usually four to five feet in length, and very wide.

The saltbox house was patterned after the cottages of 16th century England, but unlike its Elizabethan ancestor, which was half timber and half stone or brick, the saltbox's exterior was entirely wooden clapboard or weathered shingles.

The two-story saltbox was usually one room deep, with the kitchen appended to the back of the house. One large stone chimney, centrally located, served several rooms.

So named because of a resemblance to a salt container of early times that had a sloping top, the saltbox's sweeping high-pitched roof of hand-split shingles sloped down in the back to accommodate the lean-to kitchen.

Six-over-six-pane windows on the front of a saltbox were standard—four on the second floor and three plus the door on the first.

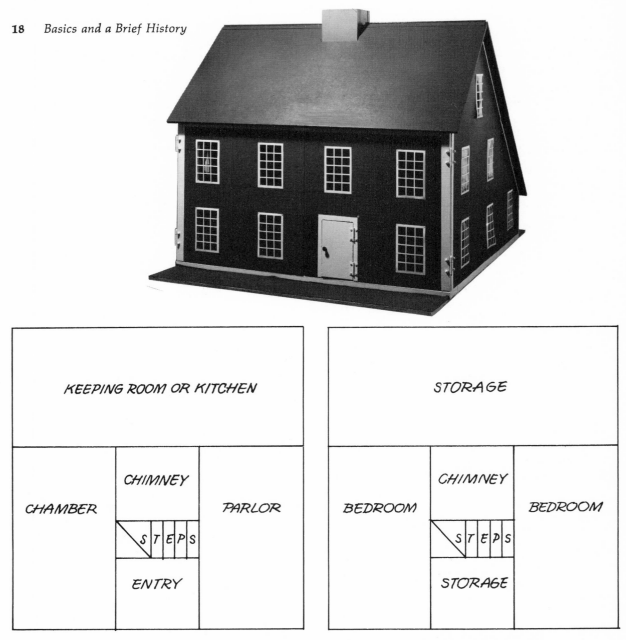

KEEPING ROOM OR KITCHEN

CHAMBER

CHIMNEY

S T E P S

PARLOR

ENTRY

FIRST FLOOR

STORAGE

BEDROOM

CHIMNEY

S T E P S

BEDROOM

STORAGE

SECOND FLOOR

Shutters were usually omitted. The exterior door consisted of several vertical boards joined at intervals with interior boards running horizontally or diagonally; hardware was hand-forged wrought iron.

The floor plan for a typical saltbox house would have looked like the above.

THE INTERIOR

The interior design of Colonial homes consisted, in the main, of various ceiling, floor, and wall treatments. Beamed ceilings, designed to support two-story houses, were a decorative as well as structural function. Simple, applied

moldings appeared around the ceilings; these were replaced later by a raised, or projecting, molding called a bolection molding.

The very earliest floors were usually constructed of random-width oak planks, often five to ten inches wide, which were secured in place with pegs. Floors were often painted, stenciled, or spatter-dashed in lieu of rugs.

The earliest Colonial walls were usually whitewashed or stained. One popular stain was blueberry juice. If whitewashed, the walls were offset by a contrasting color on the woodwork. Stenciling and marbleizing were devices employed to put pattern on walls at little cost, as were the crafts of embroidery, applique, and weaving. Wallpaper didn't exist except in the most prosperous homes near the end of the century.

Upon entering a three- or four-room house, one would notice a large wrought-iron hinge on the heavy front door, called a strap hinge because it worked like a strap. This, too, was decorative as well as utilitarian. There were no locks on doors until after the Revolutionary War. Interior door hinges were shaped like an H or L, said to stand for "heavenly love" or "Lord's house"; another interior hinge was shaped like a butterfly. Interior doors were composed of six panels (as they are in Colonial-style houses of today).

A two-story house had a steep, narrow stairway, generally located in front of the central chimney. Colonial stairways were nearly always made of planked boards, which concealed the sides of the stair treads and risers. Space under the stairs often served as closet or storage area covered with paneling.

The heart of a Colonial home was the fireplace, part of which was called a beehive oven because of a strong resemblance to its namesake.

GEORGIAN HOUSES— THE 18TH CENTURY

The Georgian period of architecture had its debut in England about the time George I ascended to the throne in 1714. The most famous architects of the day in England were Inigo Jones, William Kent, and Sir Christopher Wren, the latter being responsible for bringing Georgian architecture to America. Coinciding with the work of these men was the golden age of English cabinetmaking, the leaders of which were Thomas Chippendale, George Hepplewhite, Thomas Sheraton, and the brothers Robert and James Adam.

Georgian architecture in America flourished first in Virginia. Leading architects at the time were Richard Taliaferro, who probably designed Westover and Carter's Grove; George Washington, who designed the addition to the original cottage at Mount Vernon, which is the Mount Vernon we know today; Thomas Jefferson, who designed his home, Monticello, in

the Georgian manner; John Arris and William Buckland.

In the main, Georgian houses emphasized symmetry, were spacious, and possessed many details inspired by classical Greece.

THE EXTERIOR

In America the Georgian house was usually a detached, two-story structure. It differed substantially from the saltbox by being larger—two rooms deep, in some instances—and by having two big chimneys, at opposite ends of the house which served several rooms. The roof sloped more gradually than the saltbox roof, and had a flat deck on top, called a hipped roof.

The exterior construction material was brick, white clapboard, or stone-sized pieces of wood painted white to resemble stones. The division between the house's two floors on the exterior was defined by a projecting band course running horizontally across the length of the facade. A dentil molding spanned the top of the house just below the roof line.

There were usually five windows on the second floor front of a Georgian house, and four windows plus the door on the first floor front. The number of panes per window varied, but often was eight over eight or 12 over 12. Shutters with handsome wrought-iron latches were common. Double paneled doors replaced the simple one-piece Colonial door. All Georgian doors and windows were treated importantly, such as with the hooded triangular pediments and side columns seen in the middle photograph facing page 17. Such attention to classical detail was typical of a Georgian house, lending it a look of formality and order.

Most Georgian houses were shaped like an H, as in the floor plan on page 20.

THE INTERIOR

Upon entering a Georgian residence, one encountered a broad staircase with turned balusters.

The walls of rooms on the first floor were paneled or covered with fabric. Floors were often parqueted, and in the prosperous homes, adorned with Oriental rugs.

Windows, doorways and archways, and ceilings were trimmed with ornamental plaster work and intricate wood carving in classical designs. Interior doors had six graceful panels and brass hardware.

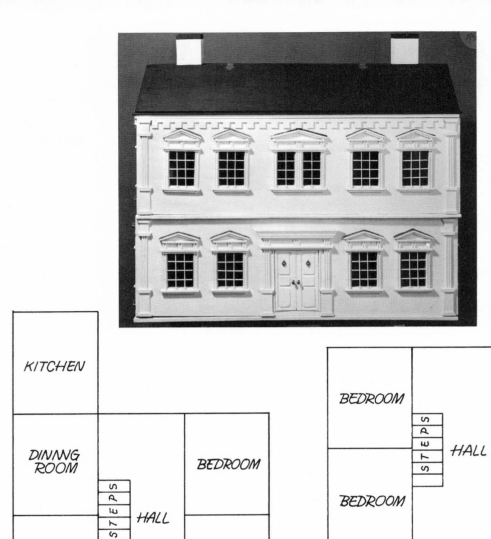

KITCHEN

DINING ROOM

CHAMBER

STEPS

HALL

BEDROOM

PARLOR

FIRST FLOOR

BEDROOM

BEDROOM

STEPS

HALL

BEDROOM

BEDROOM

SECOND FLOOR

Oak and walnut were the chief interior woods. Gilding was often used to highlight interior architectural features.

The focal point of a Georgian living room was a fireplace, often faced with marble.

VICTORIAN HOUSES— THE 19TH CENTURY

Named for Queen Victoria of England, the Victorian period of architecture was characterized by asymmetrical design, irregular outlines, and excessive ornamentation. Larger families required larger houses with staffs of servants to run them. An increasingly mobile society cre-

ated the need for extra bedrooms to accommodate guests. Bathrooms and other specialized rooms, such as smoking rooms and conservatories, appeared.

Leading architects of the time were Sir John Soane and Augustus Welby Northmore Pugin in England and Alexander Jackson Davis and Henry Hobson Richardson in America.

THE EXTERIOR

Victorian houses in England were often constructed of red or yellow brick or stucco cubes; in America, brownstone and clapboard were popular materials.

A mansard roof made with shingles or slate, and pierced by dormer windows, topped many Victorian homes, along with a fascinating array of gables, turrets, towers, and cupolas. Chimneys appeared here and there in no particular order or number.

Victorian houses were usually tall and nar-

row. The facade was interrupted by all sorts of porches, perhaps a porte-cochere, and the elaborately pierced, wooden ornamentation known by the nickname of "gingerbread." The facade was often painted one color, the trim and gingerbread another color, and the roof was a third color.

The small window panes of the Georgian period were replaced by great expanses of glass set into long, narrow window frames. Pointed arches and some stained glass panes were fashionable window treatments.

Few Victorian houses could be called typical, for they could be small or large, moderately plain or downright ostentatious. Most houses, though, were several rooms deep with haphazard interior partitions and corresponding exterior projections, such as in the truly Victorian floor plan here above.

THE INTERIOR

The look of Victorian interior design was crowded, cluttered, and busy. Pattern, usually floral, was everywhere—on walls, floors, furniture, and accessories. Paintings often covered walls as in a gallery. Rugs were laid on top of other rugs. Brightly colored tiles surrounded many fireplace openings. Books and knicknacks were in abundance.

Three styles of molding predominated: Roman, Grecian, and Gothic; all were wide and had an ogee curve. Ceilings rose to great heights. Interior doors were simplified to four panels. Golden oak was the wood of the time, though rosewood, ebony, satinwood, and walnut were popular. Wood in all its forms was often elaborately carved; in fact, some Victorian furniture

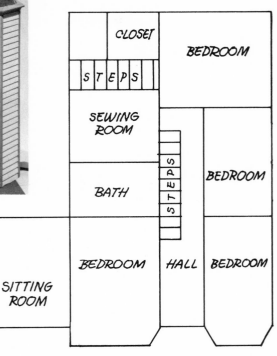

SECOND FLOOR

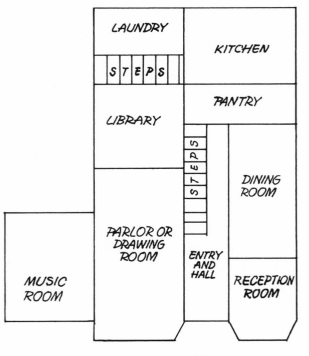

FIRST FLOOR

was carved to illustrate bestselling novels of the day.

Although illuminated by gas lights, Victorian interiors were dim because of heavily-curtained windows.

CHAPTER *4* *Principles of Interior Design*

Though we are not professional interior designers, we do know there are certain rules one must follow in both life-sized and miniature rooms in order to achieve pleasing results; these rules pertain to the elements of symmetry, balance, scale, color, texture, and pattern.

Each architectural period throughout history used the elements of interior design in distinct ways. For example, Colonial homes were usually small, so little attention could be paid to symmetry or balance; but symmetry was often an important design feature of the larger Georgian homes; and the Victorians were apt to defy the notion of symmetry in their decorating.

Scale is an element of design that is all the more crucial to the crafter of miniature rooms because he or she is accustomed to life-sized scale, and to seeing home furnishings in proper proportion to each other. But the rules of scale and proportion sometimes have to be broken when working with miniature rooms. For example, an actual Colonial room was not higher than perhaps seven feet, but if you made a dollhouse room seven inches high, you would barely be able to look into it. So you need to exaggerate ceiling height in a Colonial room, while creating the optical illusion of a low ceiling by the use of such horizontal devices as chair rails, wide moldings, and baseboards.

Scale is so vital to a crafter of miniature settings that we have included a special conversion table to insure an accurate translation of large into small. For in a dollhouse you cannot afford to miscalculate the size of room, architectural details, furniture, and accessories; they must all be in proportion to one another with relationship to the size of the room itself.

We must also consider the placement of larger furniture pieces. Fortunately, there are only two rules which have endured for several centuries. The first is that the dining room table should be placed in the center of the dining room, with the sideboard on a long adjacent wall or, if there is a fireplace, on the next largest wall. (In the Colonial keeping room, we took artistic license with the table placement in order to fit more furniture into the room.) Secondly, beds may be positioned anywhere in the bedroom, including the middle of it.

So let's begin our furniture placement in the living room, or parlor, where the family of yesterday entertained. The dominant piece of furniture is a sofa, or settee, to provide seating for several people. A tea table in front of the sofa and a small occasional table next to the sofa are proper. A second large piece of furniture, such as a highboy or breakfront, should be centered on a large wall adjacent to the sofa wall. A comfortable chair or two and a small desk finish off the living room.

As mentioned, the dining room has a table in the center, surrounded by chairs, and a sideboard on the longest wall of the room if there is no fireplace; two of the dining chairs can be placed on either side of the sideboard. There can be a small serving piece on the wall across from the sideboard.

A library should be furnished for studying and reading, with the largest piece of furniture being a desk placed on one of the walls; if the room is sizeable, the desk can run out from the wall at a right angle. Other library furnishings are a large bookcase or breakfront against another wall, a comfortable chair, and accessories such as books, a globe, a dictionary stand, and a family portrait or crest.

In a life-sized bedroom, the bed should be placed on the largest wall, if possible. However, if the room is small as in a dollhouse, don't bisect it with a big bed. Other bedroom furniture in position: a dresser on a short wall, a small table near the bed, a comfortable chair which does not interfere with traffic.

Color is regarded by many professional designers to be the most important ingredient in interior design, for it is the ingredient that unifies a room or a house and stamps the owner's personality on it. Color plays a vital role in authenticating the appearance of a dollhouse. Just as there are popular decorating colors today, such as orange and pink, so did the last three centuries have color preferences. The Colonists used mostly primary colors, and their lighter gradations, because of available dyes. The Georgians favored the neutral colors of white, beige, and gray, as well as the colors of natural wood. The Victorians were fond of dark green, red, brown, and mauve, all of which, when used in combination, produced a romantic if slightly chaotic mood.

The role of texture in interior design is more subtle than that of color, but just as important. Colonial textures included brick in fireplaces and floors, pegged wooden floors, planked or whitewashed walls. The more refined Georgian textures were marble in fireplaces and floors, fabric on walls, wall paneling, and ornamental ceilings in plaster. Favorite Victorian textures were flocked wallpaper, velvet draperies with lace undercurtains, marble and bronze statuary, and closely woven rugs such as Axminster and Brussels.

Finally, a word about the motifs favored in patterns during the three periods under study. Colonial motifs were few and simple, the tulip and sunflower being typical. Georgian motifs showed the interest in ancient Greece, as well as in the Orient and France; thus some favorites were shells, columns, and chinoiserie. The Victorians took their motifs from ancient Egypt, from the world they lived in, and from religion, and these included fruit, flowers, and ecclesiastical ornaments.

PART II

General Projects

Instructions

CHAPTER 5 *Wood, Tools, and Supplies*

When making furniture and accessories for your dollhouse, you will refer often to this part of the book. This chapter, for example, contains a list of the tools and supplies you should have on hand before starting most of the book's projects; chapter 7 has the directions for sanding and staining balsa wood, which you'll need to consult while in the middle of many projects. So read this part carefully now, but even more carefully later when actually working on a project.

BASIC TOOLS AND SUPPLIES

You should have the following tools and supplies on hand at all times to insure good craftsmanship.

cutting board or surface
metal-edged ruler
shirt cardboard
tracing paper
X-acto knife handle and #11 blades
wood stains
shellac
varnish
white resin glue
turpentine
single-edged razor blades
sharp scissors
curved manicure scissors
wire cutters
small saw
sandpaper (two grades)
emery board nail files
dowel sandpaper files
metal files
denatured alcohol
artist's paint brushes
0000 steel wool
paper towels
straight pins
round wooden toothpicks

masking tape (plain and double-faced)
liquid solder

BALSA WOOD

The chief ingredient for most projects in this book, balsa wood is inexpensive and easy to use. A dollhouse room with mahogany or basswood furniture can cost up to $1,500, whereas a typical dollhouse room with balsa wood furniture costs around $15 and looks just as elegant. To elevate balsa above the mundane, we have developed a finishing technique that makes a piece of furniture both beautiful and durable.

In addition, we have taken advantage of fool-the-eye devices, such as fake carving, turning, and drawers, so furniture detail not only looks expensive and elaborate, but it also requires minimal effort and skill to make.

Another of balsa's assets: Working with it requires no expensive power tools. Of course, you may prefer to use a finer-grained hardwood, such as mahogany, for your furniture; such woods can be cut with power tools, if you have them.

Balsa is a soft wood available in a wide variety of sizes at hobby and craft stores throughout the country. Sold in both sheets and strips, most pieces are 36" long, but occasionally you can find a piece as short as 22" and as long as four feet. You should buy quality balsa wood, choosing the grain and texture carefully.

Balsa wood sheets are 2" to 6" wide and $\frac{1}{32}$" to 4" thick; for miniature furniture, don't buy any sheets thicker than $\frac{1}{4}$" or less wide than 4". Look for sheets with the least amount of graining on them for ease and sharpness of cutting.

Balsa wood strips are precision cut to the right sizes for miniature furniture—$\frac{1}{32}$" to $\frac{1}{4}$" thick and $\frac{1}{32}$" to 1" wide. You need a variety of sizes of small square strips and narrow thin strips. These strips are made out of spruce wood, too, which you may use interchangeably with balsa; they also come in basswood.

You can also buy corrugated balsa, which is ideal for rush seats of chairs and rolltop desks, and scribed balsa (wood with tiny lines on the surface), which works well for cabinet doors where the effect of planking is desired.

Round wooden dowels are made out of hardwood, mainly birch, in diameters as small as $\frac{3}{32}$". Keep a supply of $\frac{1}{8}$", $\frac{3}{16}$", and $\frac{1}{4}$" dowels on hand.

PATTERN MAKING AND MARKING TOOLS

For making miniature furniture patterns, you need shirt cardboard, or oaktag, available at dimestores, stationers, and art supply stores; tracing paper to transfer patterns from this book to the cardboard; a sharp pair of scissors; curved manicure scissors, necessary for cutting around tiny, hard-to-get-at curves.

CUTTING TOOLS

Essential to the craft of building miniature furniture are a hard, smooth cutting surface and an X-acto knife. A magazine works as a cutting surface for a single project, but a bread board, especially one with a Formica surface, withstands repeated blade marks. A straight edge of a bread board that is at least 1" thick acts as a guide for sanding straight edges of balsa wood, and the Formica surface aids in the assembling of balsa pieces into perfect squares and rectangles.

X-acto knives are sold in most craft and art supply stores with a variety of interchangeable blades; the very best blade for balsa wood is the #11. An excellent supplementary cutting tool is the single-edged razor blade; sharper and thinner than the X-acto blade, it is used to make small, precise cuts. Available in hardware or paint stores, single-edged razor blades must be handled and stored carefully. Both X-acto and razor blades should be used with a metal-edged, or all metal, ruler only; never use them with an all wood or plastic ruler.

To cut wooden dowels you need a small saw

—coping, jeweler's, fret, or razor—available at hardware and hobby stores.

SANDING TOOLS

For making miniature furniture you should have two grades of sandpaper on hand. One is a grade called production sandpaper, or a flint sandpaper marked "very fine"; in this grade, never use anything coarser than #280 sandpaper. The other grade is an even finer sandpaper called "wet and dry," which is black and is graded in the 300's and higher; in this category, anything up to #360 sandpaper is all right for your work. If you are fortunate enough to find a sandpaper called finishing paper, which is gray, use any two grades of this numbered between 280 and 360 for all sanding.

Emery board files are excellent for sanding straight edges and some curved ones. For very precise curved edges, make two round sandpaper files by cutting and wrapping a small piece of sandpaper around $\frac{1}{4}$" and $\frac{1}{8}$" dowels.

A set of metal files, the kind used to make jewelry and models, are necessary for certain cutting situations. These files are about $5\frac{1}{2}$" long and can be found in craft and hobby shops and in some hardware stores. Their specific uses here are: Round file and half-round files curve edges and drill holes, rat-tail file drills holes, and triangle file curves edges.

STAINING SUPPLIES

For staining balsa wood, we recommend the Minwax line of stains because they contain a built-in wood stabilizer or sealer (also called primer), which will save you about ten to 15 minutes of working time. If you use a stain other than Minwax, you can buy a wood stabilizer (the most readily available being Minwax's Natural), or you can make your own. The formula for homemade wood stabilizer: Dissolve one tablespoon of Knox gelatin in about one cup of water; keep in a warm place or it will jell.

Stains come in a wide variety of woodtone colors and must be applied with artist's brushes, available at craft and art supply stores. Wipe off excess stain on wood with a soft rag or paper towel; toweling is preferable because it is relatively lint free. Stains may be diluted with turpentine to obtain lighter shades. Brushes should be cleaned with turpentine.

ASSEMBLY SUPPLIES

Whenever we tell you to use glue in this book, we mean white resin glue unless we say otherwise. And the brand of white resin glue we like best is Sobo. Perfect for balsa wood because it sets quickly, dries clear, and has the correct bonding strength, Sobo is found in dimestores, as well as hardware, craft, and fabric stores. Although the Sobo container has an easy pour-through spout, toothpicks are the best applicators for miniature work.

When assembling furniture, eyebrow tweezers are a good tool for picking up small pieces of balsa wood.

After gluing together two or more pieces of balsa wood, the directions often tell you to place the assembly under a suitable weight until the glue is completely dry. A book is perfect for this; but watch the size and weight of the book, as balsa is fragile. Put newspaper, wax paper, or aluminum foil between wood and book to prevent glue or stain marks on the book.

Balsa wood is soft, so unless directed otherwise, don't use clamps, elastic bands, spring-type clothespins, or metal hairclips on balsa when gluing pieces together.

FINISHING SUPPLIES

Both shellac and varnish should be used on miniature furniture in order to obtain a beautiful, durable finish. Since both products begin to spoil as soon as you open the container, always buy the smallest possible quantity, for in miniature work, supplies can last a long time.

Buy the white shellac, not the orange. Buy clear varnish only in semi-gloss, satin, or eggshell finish; the plastic varnishes called polyurethane, which are sold under various brand names, are the most effective. Apply shellac and varnish with clean artist's brushes and clean them well after each use, using denatured alcohol on shellac brushes and turpentine on varnish brushes.

Furniture should be sanded or smoothed with steel wool between coats of shellac and varnish. Actually, steel wool is better than sandpaper for a delicate shellac finish, even though it is full of lint, slightly messy to use, and prickly. Buy 0000 grade steel wool, nothing coarser.

Balsa wood can be painted with any commercial paint, but the small bottles or spray cans of paint sold in craft and hobby stores for model-making are a great savings in time and expense; we especially recommend Testor's model paints. Model paint comes in a wide range of colors, including several brown shades to simulate woodtones; these woodtone paints can be matched closely with stains if it is necessary to paint part of a furniture piece and stain the rest. Model paint has a lacquer base, which can be diluted with lacquer thinner or nail polish remover. Try to buy model paint in an enamel or gloss finish in order to omit the steps of shellacking and varnishing. If, for any reason, you have to buy paint in a satin, or dull, finish, you will have to shellac and varnish after painting if you want a high gloss finish.

Paint, shellac, and varnish products carry warnings on the containers regarding working conditions; these must be heeded!

HARDWARE SUPPLIES

Hardware for miniature furniture is available everywhere but hardware stores, namely, at craft, department, and fabric stores, and dimestores.

Half-inch straight pins make excellent nails or upholstery tacks for reinforced gluing. Regular straight pins serve as door hinges for cabinets or can be used to secure beaded drawer knobs in place. Large-headed straight pins, sold for beading purposes, are suitable for securing drawer handles made of wire.

Small $\frac{5}{8}''$ hinges sold in craft stores for decoupage projects are used on miniature furniture. And so are various sizes of beads. Pearl beads, ranging in size from the tiny seed pearl to a large $\frac{3}{16}''$ pearl, are the most suitable, as are small metal beads in various shapes and sizes.

The round, metal, four-pronged device that holds a rhinestone to fabric makes a keyhole or bed bolt cover. So do belt eyelets, and in addition, these make candle holders. Decorative plastic twist pins, designed to hold slipcovers in place, make curtain tie-backs, as well as woodcarving motifs.

If you don't have an old wrist watch to spare, a clock face can be cut out of a magazine or catalog, but be sure the dial is in keeping with the period of your dollhouse.

Carefully selected embossed paper will give you a myriad of drawer handles, drawer handle escutcheons, wood carvings and fretwork, brass galleries, and other furniture embellishment. Sold in long strips, or rectangular or oval picture frames, embossed paper comes in a variety of patterns, including shells and flowers. Many craft stores have excellent selections of this paper, but if you can't find what you need (and gold and silver embossed paper can be hard to find), write to N. Ginsburg and Co., 1313 West Randolph Street, Chicago, Illinois 60607, and ask for their catalog and a list of stores supplied in your area.

Decorative buttons imitate wood carving well, and so do some jewelry finders. Most carving on furniture is a floral pattern, but for the occasional scallop seashell pattern, use a button shaped like a shell or, in a pinch, embossed paper with shell motif. For faking rope molding on furniture, use heavy picture hanging wire.

The backs of screw-type earrings make good door knobs; so do map pins and men's studs from formal dress shirts, if they are round and simple in design. Junk jewelry is the best source for earring backs, or they can be bought at a jewelry supply or craft store. Small gold safety pins are cut up to make door hinges. Thin copper sheeting from a hardware store, or balsa strips, can be cut for door plates.

Unless your hardware comes in the color you want, you will have to paint it with brass, gold, or woodtone paint. Some hardware requires the use of wire cutters and two pairs of nose pliers.

UPHOLSTERY SUPPLIES

For upholstering miniature furniture you can use either regular upholstery fabric or dress fabric with a suitable thickness and pattern. The material must be fairly light weight and closely woven, the best being cotton, satin, rayon, silk, synthetic blends, antique satin, and thin brocade.

Avoid pile fabrics, such as velvet, velveteen, and corduroy; heavily textured fabrics; and loosely woven fabrics, which will ravel.

Fabrics with a pattern or design woven into the material are especially suitable for period furniture. Of course, the pattern must be very small. Appropriate solid colors for period rooms are soft shades of red, blue, green, and gold. Avoid overindulging in pattern, and strive for a harmonious blend of colors.

Don't buy more than ¼ yard of fabric; ⅛ yard is even better, but many stores won't sell such a small amount. You may need more fabric if you plan to upholster more than one piece of furniture in the same pattern or if you plan to make matching draperies. Be sure to allow for matching the pattern, if the fabric has one.

Cotton padding comes in a variety of forms and is necessary for any upholstered miniature furniture. Use absorbent cotton from the drug store or padding sold for quilting at a fabric store; the latter is preferable because it is thinner.

For miniature furniture welting, buy narrow soutache braid from a sewing supply store. This braid, which usually comes in white, can be dyed beautifully with permanent color felt tip pens, ink, or commercial vegetable dyes. Dip the braid in hot tea for a second to get a perfect off-white color. Tightly woven string dyed to match a fabric may be used in lieu of soutache braid, and so can middy braid.

MISCELLANEOUS SUPPLIES

Molds for shaping wet balsa wood are found around the home; drinking glasses, frozen orange juice cans, and cooking pots make wonderful molds. Other items to have on hand are a compass, a protractor, and a right-angle ruler.

HARD-TO-FIND ITEMS

If you can't find balsa wood, basswood, X-acto knife and blades, and metal files, write to Sig Manufacturing Co., P.O. Box 1, Montezuma, Iowa 50171. Other hard-to-find tools can be obtained from the Brookstone Co.; for a free catalog, write to 16 Brookstone Building, Peterborough, New Hampshire 03458.

CHAPTER **6** *Using the Book's Patterns*

For each furniture project in Part IV, the pieces of wood that are rectangles, squares, and circles are described by their dimensions only, which you will follow when cutting. The pieces of wood with curved lines, however, are given as actual-sized patterns, to be transferred to the wood in one of two ways. The first is to trace the book pattern onto tracing paper, and then transfer the tracing onto the wood, using carbon paper or lead pencil. The second way involves making a cardboard pattern of the tracing, and retracing this onto the wood.

The cardboard pattern method is easiest; the pattern can be made in one of the following ways:

1. Trace outline of book pattern onto tracing paper with a sharp pencil. Turn over tracing paper, place on piece of cardboard, and rub tracing with side of pencil point until pattern outline appears on cardboard.

2. Trace outline of book pattern onto tracing paper with sharp pencil. Turn over tracing paper, put on hard surface, and rub tracing with side of pencil point. Turn tracing paper back to right side, place on cardboard, and with sharp pencil, trace pattern outline onto cardboard. This makes a sharper line than above.

3. For an even sharper line, trace outline of book pattern onto tracing paper with sharp pencil. Place piece of carbon paper, carbon side down, onto cardboard. Place tracing paper, right side up, onto carbon paper and trace pattern outline.

Cut out the cardboard pattern with scissors, using curved manicure scissors for small patterns. Place the cardboard pattern onto the book pattern to see whether the tracing and cutting are accurate, which they must be, because even the width of a pencil line can add an unwanted fraction of an inch to a pattern.

It is sometimes helpful to make cardboard patterns for circles, but not really necessary if you use a compass.

Never use paper for patterns except when working with fabric.

MARKING THE WOOD

The grain of the wood is indicated in the diagrams of the curved line patterns, and the cardboard pattern should be placed on the wood accordingly. Mark the outline of the cardboard pattern onto wood with a sharp pencil, checking the dimensions of the pencil marking on the wood with the dimensions of the pattern in the book.

Dimensions for the width and length of rectangles of balsa wood are given with each furniture project. Mark the rectangle directly onto the wood with a sharp pencil and ruler. In general, the width runs crosswise, or against the grain, of the wood; and the length runs with the grain. Occasionally, the length is marked on the crosswise grain, and is so specified in the directions. Mark squares of wood onto the wood in the same manner as rectangles, though you don't have to consider the direction of the wood's grain with squares, or with circles, either.

Mark circles onto wood with a compass, or trace a household object with the same diameter directly onto the wood. If you use a compass, protect the center of the circle from the sharp end of the compass with a scrap of wood. Or you can make a cardboard pattern of the circle first.

DESIGNING YOUR OWN PROJECT

Though this book contains numerous furniture projects, you may decide you'd like to copy a piece of furniture from your own home for your dollhouse. You can do this with a ruler and the conversion table in this chapter; see diagram 1. The conversion table enables you to make a one-twelfth replica of a life-sized equivalent; worked out on a calculator, it gives the one-twelfth equivalent up to a height of 100",

CONVERSION TABLE
Scale: 12″ to 1″

Life size Miniature size

Life size	Miniature size
5″ =	7⁄16″
10″ =	13⁄16″
15″ =	1¼″
20″ =	1 11⁄16″
25″ =	2 1⁄16″
30″ =	2½″
35″ =	2 15⁄16″
40″ =	3 5⁄16″
45″ =	3¾″
50″ =	4 3⁄16″
55″ =	4 9⁄16″
60″ =	5″
65″ =	5 7⁄16″
70″ =	5 13⁄16″
75″ =	6¼″
80″ =	6 11⁄16″
85″ =	7 1⁄16″
90″ =	7½″
95″ =	7 15⁄16″
100″ =	8 5⁄16″

which is about the height of a highboy or secretary. (There is an inch-to-the-foot ruler you can buy from certain mail order dollhouse supply companies, which would preclude the need for the conversion table.)

To create miniature furniture, you must think in terms of inches rather than feet. For example, if the piece of life-sized furniture you want to reproduce in miniature is a secretary which measures 79″ high, 38″ wide, and 20½″ deep, the conversion table translates those measurements into appropriate miniature measurements. Although life-sized measurements on the table are given only for every five inches, you will still find the table accurate enough for your purposes. So, although 79″ is not indicated on the table, 80″ is. You would then refer to your ruler, and go just a fraction under 6 11⁄16″, or to the nearest eighth, which is 6⅝″, to obtain the height of the miniature secretary. Similarly, the width of 38″ on the life-sized piece falls between 2 15⁄16″ and 3 5⁄16″ on the conversion table; with your ruler, select again to the nearest eighth, which is 3⅛″. The 20½″ depth measurement of the life-sized piece comes close to 20″ on the conversion table, which is 1 11⁄16″; on your ruler this is just a fraction under the nearest quarter of an inch, so you would select 1¾″. Always try to work to the nearest eighth or quarter on the overall dimensions of miniature furniture, but you'll have to go to sixteenths when making a furniture detail, such as a drawer, and sometimes even to thirty-seconds.

Once your eye becomes used to the one-twelfth scale, you'll find you can pretty much use your own judgment on measurement, as you will have developed a keen sense of proportion.

CHAPTER *7* *Working with Wood*

The number of pieces of balsa wood required for a piece of miniature furniture varies from project to project. Most of this book's projects call for 10 to 20 pieces of wood; a few have 20 or more pieces. This chapter discusses how to handle those pieces of balsa from before they're cut out until after they've been assembled and are ready to be moved into your dollhouse.

CUTTING

Don't try to cut all the balsa wood pieces for a furniture project at one time, because you can get confused and even lose some pieces. Instead, cut pieces for one section of the project before proceeding to the next.

You need an X-acto knife for cutting pieces of wood with curved edges, and an X-acto knife and metal-edged ruler for cutting pieces of wood with straight edges. Make sure the X-acto knife blade is sharp (the thicker the wood, the sharper the blade must be). The cutting surface must be smooth so the wood won't get scratched, yet be hard to withstand the sharp blade of the knife and perfectly level to achieve neat, clean-cut edges.

The procedure for cutting straight lines varies depending on the wood's thickness. A single X-acto knife cut separates a $\frac{1}{32}$" or $\frac{1}{16}$" thickness of wood, if you hold the ruler firmly with one hand and draw the knife through the wood carefully with the other. For a thicker piece of wood, draw the knife through it two or three times, going deeper each time. The X-acto knife will cut lines of any length, but for lines $\frac{1}{2}$" long or less, use a single-edged razor blade; it is thinner and sharper and thus makes a neater cut.

The cutting of a curved line depends not only on the wood's thickness, but also on the arc of the curve. For a wide arc or sloping curve, cut directly on the marked line with an X-acto knife, unless the wood is over $\frac{3}{32}$" thick. For thick pieces of wood and for narrow arcs, cut next to the marked line—not on it—and then with emery board file or round sandpaper file, sand the wood down to the marked line.

A similar cutting and sanding technique is used for cutting a decorative edge with narrow S-shaped curves, but in addition to knife and sandpaper file, you need a triangle file. To make such a decorative edge, follow these steps:

1. Cut a straight line near the marked curves; see diagram 1.

2. With a $\frac{1}{8}$"-round sandpaper file, sand the small arcs, using lower numbered sandpaper first and then higher; see diagram 2. For a wider arc, use a $\frac{3}{16}$"-round sandpaper file.

3. With a triangle file, make a notch where the S-shaped curves meet in a point, and with emery board file, sand remainder of decorative edge down to broken line; see diagram 3.

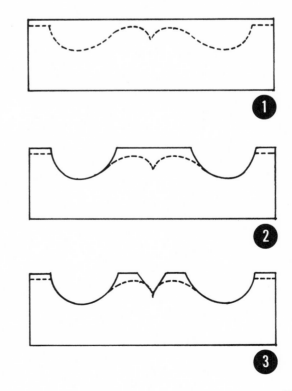

For cutting balsa wood strips, a single-edge razor blade makes the cleanest cuts.

Never use a saw on balsa wood except for cutting large blocks. You will need a small saw to cut dowels because they're made from harder woods.

All edges cut with the X-acto knife should be clean and smooth. When you begin to notice that the wood is not cutting smoothly, that the edges are crumbling or splintering, it is time to change the blade. If an edge is not too badly damaged, repair it with spackling putty or plastic wood rather than starting over again. If a piece of carefully curved and sanded balsa wood breaks, stain the broken pieces *first*, then glue them back together again before assembling.

SANDING

Although sanding is the most important and time-consuming activity in making miniature furniture, it is also one of the easiest.

Most wood pieces are sanded twice with two different grades of sandpaper. For the first sanding, use the production, or very fine, sandpaper. For the second sanding, use the finer paper graded in the 300's and higher.

You will save time by using emery board files to sand the straight edges of your wood pieces. To sand curved edges, make your own round sandpaper file with a dowel or pencil that is the right size for the curve you intend to sand; wrap the dowel with a small piece of the coarser sandpaper; sand and then repeat the sanding with finer sandpaper on the dowel.

The most important rule in sanding is: *Always sand in the direction of the grain of the wood.* If you don't sand with the grain, the wood will look scratched after stain is applied.

To sand a piece of wood, fold a workable size piece of the coarser sandpaper in half and sand both surfaces of the wood gently; too much pressure on the wood can scratch it or even alter the thickness. You may prefer to wrap the sandpaper around a small block of wood to make sure the wood surfaces are sanded evenly. After the first sanding, you can see and feel that many of the rough wood fibers have disappeared. The second sanding will make the surfaces completely smooth to the touch.

For the thin $\frac{1}{32}''$ balsa wood sheet, sand only once, lightly, with the finer of the two grades of sandpaper. Thin wood strips also need only one sanding with the finer grade of sandpaper. Hardwood dowels need only one sanding, too, with either of the two grades of sandpaper. The round wooden toothpicks used in some furniture projects do not need to be sanded at all.

It is not necessary to sand the straight edges of wood twice with an emery board file; one sanding with the finer side of the file is sufficient. The emery board also helps to straighten edges that haven't been cut absolutely straight.

Since many curved edges of the wood pieces have already been sanded once in the cutting and sanding technique described above, all these edges need is a second sanding with fine paper wrapped around the correct-sized dowel, or around a round file or half-round file.

When assembling a piece of furniture, it is often necessary to sand the sharp edges where the top and bottom surfaces meet the flat sides or thickness of the wood; this is called rounding the edges (not to be confused with beveling, described in chapter 8). Rounding an edge differs from a light sanding in that you shape the edge until it appears semi-circular.

It is helpful to sand two or more pieces of wood at the same time when they are supposed to be the same size or length. Because the legs of a piece of furniture must be absolutely equal in length, line them up on your work surface and sand the edges at the same time. Two or more curved pieces of the same size and design should also be sanded simultaneously.

The sanded wood is now ready to be stained. No matter how tempted you may be to do so, *do not glue the pieces of wood together at this point, unless you are planning to paint them, because stain does not penetrate glue.*

STAINING

If you do not use a Minwax stain on your wood, you must first apply a wood stabilizer or sealer; see directions on page 28 for a homemade variety. This process, known as priming, helps seal the wood's pores, thereby stabilizing the texture and allowing the stain to be absorbed smoothly. If you don't prime, the stain may dry unevenly and, worse, form spots or puddles. Apply primer liberally with a brush; wipe off excess and let wood dry for about ten minutes before applying stain.

Minwax stains, which we have previously recommended, are known as "penetrating," which means they penetrate wood fibers easily, and are clear and unmuddied by paint pigmentation. But if you prefer to use another brand of stain, be sure to prime the wood first.

A half pint of stain will finish many, many pieces of miniature furniture. For the most part, disregard any directions on the label, for they are geared to life-sized furniture. Although you will undoubtedly develop your own staining techniques, the following procedure produces excellent results.

Stir the can of stain to thoroughly mix in the small amount of paint pigment on the bottom of the can. With an artist's brush, apply stain liberally to both surfaces of the piece of wood.

While staining both surfaces at the same time saves time, it does present an absorption problem. If you prop the wood vertically, the stain runs off too quickly and doesn't penetrate properly. If you lay down the wood horizontally, the top surface absorbs the stain while the bottom surface lies in a puddle of stain. Both surfaces can absorb stain simultaneously if the wood is put on a miniature bed of pins. To make this: Push half-inch straight pins through a piece of cardboard, using as many pins as needed to hold up the wood piece. Then *very* gently place the wet, stained piece of wood on the pins. Wait five or ten minutes, remove the wood and then wipe off excess stain evenly with a paper towel.

The piece of wood is still not dry, so wait another 15 to 20 minutes before assembling. You can speed up drying time by placing the wood under a hot light bulb or in a low oven, but these steps can cause fading. Or you can speed up drying time by rubbing the wood with paper toweling and applying hard, even finger pressure; much of the stain will come off on the towel, but the wood can be darkened later with a second coat of stain. Rubbing the wood with paper toweling also prevents streaking and smooths the wood fibers, which rise when wet.

The stained pieces of wood are now ready for assembly. At this point you can apply a second coat of stain, if you wish, or you can

add a second coat after assembling, when glue has dried, by dipping a paper towel in stain and rubbing on the wood surfaces. A second coat doesn't darken the original stain very much, even when a darker color is used. If you want a lighter shade of color, use turpentine to lighten the stain.

Hardwood dowels do not take a penetrating stain as readily as balsa. To match dowels to balsa wood, use a darker stain on dowels, or rub the pigment at the bottom of a can of stain into the dowels.

ASSEMBLING

Assembling is the gluing together of all the carefully cut, sanded, and stained pieces of wood to make a whole piece of furniture. *But before you begin gluing together the pieces, you must always re-measure them to make sure of an accurate fit;* for no matter how carefully you cut out the pieces, you can easily be off by a tiny fraction of an inch. If the pieces don't fit together exactly, trim them until they do.

White resin glue is essential to the assembling step, and so is a flat, smooth, level work surface. Such a surface facilitates the job of gluing straight, even edges and perfect right-angle corners or T-shaped assemblies.

Unless your directions state otherwise, the pieces of balsa are glued so the grain runs vertically.

After re-measuring the wood pieces, apply the glue to the edges with a toothpick for a smooth, neat job. Though the amount of glue to use varies, too much glue will spill over the edges and too little glue will not hold the pieces together properly. Crosswise edges absorb more glue than lengthwise edges and so require more glue. You do not have to put glue on both edges that are going to be cemented; glue on one edge will suffice.

The most frequent error made during assembling is the incorrect gluing of edges. One incorrect butting (joining of parts) means that the remaining pieces of wood won't fit together properly. The error can be remedied whenever discovered, however; even after the glue has hardened, you can cut apart the butted edge with a single-edged razor blade, taking care to separate only the glue, not the wood.

Unfortunately, many edges cannot be glued together with any pressure other than human hands, which means you must hold the pieces of wood together with your hands for a short time until the glue begins to set; then remove pressure and let the glue dry completely. Glued edges often need to be propped while the glue is setting; use anything at hand except a prop that could scratch the wood. Once a glued edge begins to hold, another edge on the same piece may be worked on.

While the glue on a piece of furniture is drying, it is usually advisable to weight down the top surface of the furniture with a suitable object, such as a book. Your directions will tell you when to apply such pressure. Be sure to put some protective covering between the furniture and the weight.

Even though white resin glue has excellent bonding strength, some joints need additional reinforcement with half-inch straight pins. One way to reinforce with these pins is to place glue on both edges of the pieces about to be joined, then push a pin from the bottom surface of one piece of wood through to the other piece of wood; even the head of the pin helps support the glued pieces. The second way to reinforce joints is to make a hole in one of the pieces of wood with the pointed end of a pin. After doing this, cut the head off the pin with wire cutters, then put the flat, cut end of the pin into the hole, glue both edges of the wood pieces, and push the pointed end of the pin into the other piece of wood.

FINISHING

The two finishing procedures of shellacking and varnishing endow your piece of furniture with durability and beauty; on a more practical note, they prevent fading.

Disregard any directions on the container of shellac and simply mix the shellac with an equal amount of denatured alcohol in a clean can or jar. Paint on the shellac with a clean artist's brush just as you would apply paint. Let it dry 10 to 15 minutes at room temperature or, if in a hurry, under the heat of a light bulb (but never in an oven).

Now rub the piece well in the same direction with 0000 steel wool, being careful of corners because even light pressure can rub off the color of stain; also, exceptionally fragile furniture should be rubbed with great care so it doesn't break. Wipe or blow away any lint or grit, especially at the crosswise edges which seem to attract and trap lint or grit like a magnet. In fact, fine sandpaper which has been used a couple of times is far better for crosswise edges and hard-to-get-at spots. Don't be alarmed if the shellac seems to turn gray.

Apply a second coat of shellac; wait 10 to 15 minutes and then repeat the steel wooling procedure. For hardwood parts like dowel legs, or for fragile legs, one coat of shellac is enough.

Clean your brush with denatured alcohol. Always keep it clean between uses. It's smart to reserve a brush or two for shellacking only, and to do likewise with brushes for varnishing.

Varnishing gives a piece of miniature furniture the patina or luster of real furniture. Furthermore, it hardens the wood and gives additional sealing power to the furniture joints. Apply varnish with an artist's brush right from the container without stirring it up first. As you stroke on the varnish liberally, brush out any bubbles that form. Clean brush with turpentine.

Varnish dries completely in about 12 hours. You must apply varnish and dry it in a lint-free area because lint will ruin the finish. Also, the area should be fairly cool—no warmer than 75°—or the varnish will remain sticky; if you are varnishing in the summer, work in an air-conditioned room or the basement.

If you ever break a piece of wood while working on it, you can glue the pieces back together. Because balsa wood contains a lot of grain, regluing does not show, especially after the wood has been shellacked and varnished.

CHAPTER *8* *Simple Woodworking Techniques*

Professional cabinetmakers and carpenters use expensive hand tools and machinery for woodworking. Fortunately, the amateur craftsperson needs only an X-acto knife, sandpaper, and certain other inexpensive materials to simulate woodworking techniques.

WOOD TURNING—POSTS

The posts of a piece of furniture are often turned on a rotating machine to give them some decorative interest, but when turning is required for projects in this book, you will do it by hand. The curved tester and straight tester beds have four posts; the top half of each post is an artist's brush handle used as is, but the bottom half is a $\frac{1}{4}'' \times \frac{1}{4}'' \times 2''$ balsa strip which has been turned by hand. To do this, round each of the four corners on one end of the strip with an emery board file until a curve emerges across each of the four surfaces; see diagram 1. On the other end of the strip, sand $\frac{1}{2}''$ of each corner edge with emery board file until the sanding begins to round the square post; see diagram 2. Finish rounding and tapering the post with sandpaper.

For smaller turned posts, such as on the deacon's bench (page 157), the turning has been done for you because we use round wooden toothpicks already tapered at the ends. For a fancier small turning, such as on the davenport desk, a tiny bead painted with woodtone paint, or a small cube made from a balsa strip, adds interest to the post.

Posts or pedestals supporting a weight such as a table top are usually heavily and handsomely turned. A small brass lamp finial is a good substitute for such a pedestal; paint the finial with woodtone paint to match the rest of the piece of furniture. Directions for mounting the lamp finials are given with the projects in which they appear.

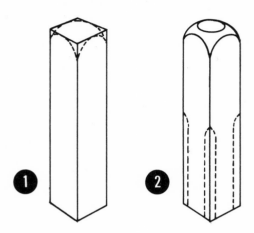

Spindle wood turning, often erroneously called spool turning, is faked with beads painted with woodtone paint; see the Victorian what-not.

WOOD TURNING—LEGS AND FEET

For a straight round furniture leg, sand the bottom edge of a wooden dowel with an emery board file until it looks rounded.

An S-curved leg, or cabriole leg, is more difficult. There are three types of cabriole legs in Part IV; the longest, most graceful, and most difficult is made from a $\frac{3}{16}'' \times \frac{3}{8}''$ balsa wood strip, as follows:

1. Place the leg pattern on the $\frac{3}{8}''$ side of the wood strip, and mark outline of pattern on wood with a pencil.

2. Cut away a rectangular section from the top half of leg, making sure a perfect rectangular section with straight sides remains; see diagram 3.

3. With X-acto knife whittle out the curve on upper inside edge of leg, then whittle out the curve on lower outside edge of leg; see diagram 4. With dowel sandpaper file, sand the two curves down to pencil outline.

4. Cut off corner of back inside edge of the

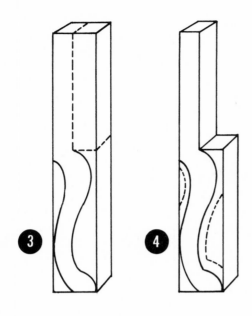

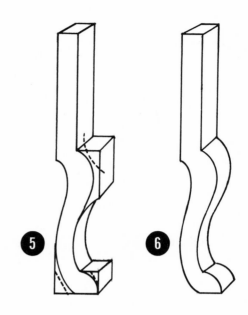

foot with single-edged razor blade and round cut edge with emery board file; repeat for front outside edge of foot. With X-acto knife whittle out the curve on upper outside edge of leg and sand curve with emery board file; see diagram 5.

5. With dowel sandpaper file smooth both inside and outside edges of leg to make one long continuous S-shaped curve on each edge; see diagram 6.

WOOD CARVING

There are many ways to simulate the look of real wood carving. One easy way is to use different thicknesses of wood, as on the drawer fronts of the Victorian bureau, commode, and serving board. For decorative furniture moldings, thick picture hanging wire is an excellent substitute. For openwork carving, called fretwork, embossed paper strips suffice. Carved wooden finials on highboys and grandfather clocks are made with a balsa wood strip, tiny wooden cubes, a round bead, and an oblong bead. For carved floral and shell designs, use buttons, embossed paper, and the decorative heads of twist pins. All substitutes are painted with woodtone paint to match the piece of furniture they enhance.

BEVELING

A beveled edge slopes at a 45° angle. Which kind of beveled edge is used in a furniture project depends mostly on the thickness of the wood. There is about a $\frac{1}{16}''$ allowance made for beveling in all the patterns, except where directions indicate otherwise.

The first type of beveled edge, called a straight bevel, has a flat edge; see diagram 7. It is the only bevel possible on the thin $\frac{1}{32}''$ drawer fronts and door panels. To make a straight bevel, line up the side edge of the wood piece to be beveled with the side edge of your work surface. Holding an emery board file at an angle, sand the edge slantwise, using the work surface edge as a guide as well as your fingers; smooth and finish with a piece of fine, folded sandpaper. The important thing to remember when beveling an edge is not to destroy the straight line of the edge itself while working on it.

On thicker pieces of wood you can make a curved bevel. Begin this by making a straight bevel first with an emery board file, then switch to a dowel sandpaper file and sand the slanted edge until an even curve is formed along the edge; see diagram 8.

A round bevel is achieved by first making a straight bevel. Round the sharp top edge of this with an emery board file, then switch to a

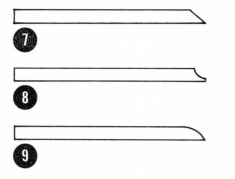

fine, folded piece of sandpaper and round the remainder of the edge; see diagram 9. A round bevel is not to be confused with rounding an edge, which is a sanding operation that creates a semi-circular edge, not an angled one.

MITERING

A joint cut at a 45° angle is called a mitered joint. Although used on certain pieces of furniture, mitering is more commonly found on picture frames, room moldings, and around fireplace openings. The directions for mitering are as follows:

1. Measure the total length of wood you need and cut a strip of wood or molding to this length; for example, if your picture frame is to be 2″ × 4″, you need a total of 12″ of wood.

2. Divide and mark the top edge of the wood strip into the correct lengths of the pieces of picture frame, molding, or whatever. At each mark make two slanted guide lines down the side of the strip—one line to the left of the mark and the other line to the right—and make a slanted line at the beginning of the strip from the corner top edge to the right, and another at the other end of the strip from the corner top edge to the left; see diagram 10. Now cut along each drawn line.

You can use a protractor to draw perfect 45°-angle lines, but if you're going to do much mitering, we recommend buying a miter box from a craft store. This inexpensive instrument contains slots that guide your saw at exactly the correct 45° angle. Place the wood strip along the back edge of the miter box so a mark on the top edge of the strip lines up with a slot on the back edge of the box; which slot you line up with which mark depends on the direction you are cutting, to the right or to the left. A miter box is almost essential for wood strips of any thickness.

3. Glue the cut, angled edges together to form a perfect right-angle construction.

Usually, a strip of room molding is three dimensional in shape, which might confuse you. Simply determine which edge is the top edge and make marks and guide lines as directed. Since most dollhouse rooms have only three walls, you will be measuring and marking for three pieces of molding.

If you want to make a mitered joint on a single wood strip, place the strip facing you vertically and draw a square at the top; the size of the square is determined by the width of the top edge of the strip. Draw a diagonal line, which is automatically 45°, from either of the top corner points to the opposite bottom corner point; see diagram 11. Cut on the guide line. It is important, of course, when cutting several pieces of wood strips in this manner to determine ahead of time in which direction the angle is to be cut.

DRILLING

For putting the tiniest holes in balsa wood, use a straight pin. For larger holes, use a rattail file. Whenever you have to cut a shape into the surface of balsa, drill a round hole with a round file and then continue enlarging the hole with the round file or an X-acto knife.

MOLDING WOOD

Balsa wood can be shaped by wetting it in warm water and securing it to a mold until dry. Directions for molding are given with the specific projects requiring this process.

SCORING WOOD

Scoring is a useful woodworking technique for indicating fireplace bricks, a rush chair seat, or lids for a cast iron stove. Scoring wood means marking it with indentations, which are made with a toothpick or the pointed end of a brush handle. Wood scores best when indentations are made in the same direction as the wood grain.

HINGES

The easiest kind of hinge mounting is a straight pin hinge made, naturally, with a straight pin and applied to miniature doors. First, you must figure out which way the door is to swing open. In most cases, as you look at the door in front of you, the hinges will be on the left side of the door.

To put the hinge into operation, push a straight pin through the top of the door frame down through the door that is being hinged as far as the pin will go; before pushing, center the pin in the corner of the top edge, then push straight so the pointed end of the pin won't break through the surface. Repeat the procedure with another pin through the bottom of the door frame up through the door as far as the pin will go.

You should always leave a tiny bit of space between the side of the door and the door frame, so when the door is opened, there is some place for it to swing into and go back slightly.

When there is a pair of doors, such as on an armoire, breakfront, or secretary, door hinges are on the left of the left door and on the right of the right door, as you look at them.

Though not the strongest hinge, the straight pin hinge withstands repeated openings of a door.

Sometimes you need decoupage hinges, particularly where there is no door frame to which to hinge the door from top or bottom. To secure them, you can use either the tiny screws that come with the hinges or straight pins. But first, you must trim decoupage hinges down to about ⅜", a size in proportion with a piece of miniature furniture. Use wire cutters, scissors, or saw and cut away any excess part of the hinge not needed for the screwing operation. To add extra strength to the hinge, coat the larger part on the underside with glue before screwing in place.

If you want the decoupage hinge to be inconspicuous, you can "blind" hinge. Make a small incision with a single-edged razor blade in the wooden frame and bury the flat part of the hinge; if you put a little glue on the flat part, you don't have to use screws. Then carve out a slight recess for the round part of the hinge on the surface of the wood you are hinging so the hinge is almost flush with the surface.

DRAWER HARDWARE

For Chippendale handles, take two pair of pliers and pull apart sewing loops from a hook-and-eye package with equal pressure until they are open enough to resemble miniature handles. For Victorian handles, pull apart sewing loops and bend into a slightly triangular shape. For Hepplewhite handles, use sewing eyes just as they are. String these handles on a thin stiff wire, propped between two frozen juice cans or some similar support, and spray them with gold or brass paint. Save time by spraying a lot of handles at once. Attach the handles to drawers with beading pins (if beading pins are unobtainable, use straight pins) by pushing pins through the ends of the sewing loops or eyes. There is no need to shorten the pins because only the pinheads will show. Touch up pinheads with gold paint, using a tiny artist's brush.

Map pins make excellent drawer knobs. First, stick them in a scrap of balsa wood and paint their heads with woodtone brown, gold, or white; when dry, insert them in drawer fronts with a little glue. If you can't find map pins, mount any small, smooth-surfaced round bead onto a straight pin or beading pin with a little glue; then proceed as for the map pins. For very tiny knobs, use the head of a pin by itself.

Victorian drawer pulls are made from narrow embossed paper strips in a leafy or floral design to resemble wood carving; cut them to size and glue in place after painting with woodtone paint to match the furniture stain. Narrow embossed paper strips are also used for escutcheons (rectangular drawer handle plates) for the triangular Victorian handles made with sewing loops.

DOOR HARDWARE

For a Colonial doorknob, use the entire back of a screw-type earring (this means everything except front decoration). Make the doorknob plate from a ⅛″ balsa sheet cut to ½″ × 1″. Cut the door hinges in an H or L shape from a ¹⁄₁₆″ balsa sheet. Knob, plate, and hinges should be in proportion to the door. Paint them flat black and glue in place.

For a Georgian doorknob, use the entire back of a gold screw-type earring or a small stud from a man's formal dress shirt. Make the doorknob plate from a thin piece of copper sheeting or plastic acetate cut to ½″ × 1″, or from a metal box clasp for a necklace. Door hinges are made from cut-off straight pieces of small gold safety pins. Paint Georgian hardware gold —whatever isn't already gold; or to be more authentic, paint it brass. Glue hardware in place, or apply with liquid solder.

Make a Victorian doorknob from the entire back of a screw-type earring, or from a plastic twist pin used in upholstering; paint white to resemble china or decorate with a tiny stone from the earring, if not too elaborate. Doorplates are not necessary but can be made from copper sheeting or plastic acetate cut to ½″ × 1″ and painted to match the knobs. Door hinges are again cut from small safety pins and painted black, or you can use pieces of straight pins. Glue everything in place.

MISCELLANEOUS

To make bed bolt covers and keyholes, use the metal prongs sold for attaching rhinestones. Paint them gold and press into the wood's surface.

PART III

Building Dollhouse Interiors

CHAPTER 10 *Walls, Floors, Ceilings*

The walls, floor, and ceiling of a room play a large part in determining the tone or mood of that room, for unlike furniture and accessories, they offer broad expanses of color, texture, and sometimes pattern.

WALLS

There are several ways to treat walls, each one of which can yield vastly different results. The most obvious treatment is paint. But you can also stain, paper, stencil, or marbleize walls; apply fabric to walls; put a mural on them; or put up panels. Each of these methods can be used alone or in combination.

Before attempting any wall treatment on unfinished wood, you must sand the walls until smooth with a sanding block (a block of wood wrapped with sandpaper) or electric sander, working in the direction of the grain of the wood. Use medium-grade sandpaper. If you are working on a dollhouse wall which has been previously decorated, remove existing wallpaper and sand the walls; and if there is old paint on the walls, it's a good idea to sand over that. However, if the dollhouse is an antique and there is original wallpaper or paint beneath the surface that's worth preserving, you have to chip off the surface paper or paint with your thumbnail; do not sand or use paint remover when you get down to the original wall treatment.

PAINT

Before painting an unfinished wall, brush on a wood stabilizer or sealer to seal wood pores and make them less obvious; let dry thoroughly.

Now apply two coats of flat wall paint, letting paint dry between coats. For big areas, it's more economical to use paints left over from painting a real house. For small areas, such as below a chair rail, use flat model paint purchased at a craft or hobby store. Model paints come in pale and bright colors and in flat and glossy finishes.

Paint details like moldings, chair rails, and baseboards with a semi-gloss finish.

STAIN

If you do not use the Minwax brand of stain, you must first apply a wood stabilizer or sealer. We prefer the Minwax stains because a sealer is mixed in with the stain. Brush on the stain, allowing the area to dry horizontally, if possible. Leave the stain on for five minutes, then wipe area dry and rub with paper toweling to prevent streaking. Wait 30 minutes, then apply a coat of half shellac and half denatured alcohol. Wait ten minutes, then rub lightly with steel wool; always use 0000 steel wool, nothing coarser. Wipe away any grit from the steel wool with a paper towel. Shellac again and wait ten minutes, then steel wool again lightly and wipe off grit.

Apply a coat of eggshell finish or satin finish varnish to stained wall. Avoid a spray varnish as it tends to run if you're the least bit heavy-handed with the can's aerosol nozzle. *Most important to remember:* Always work in a well-ventilated area, but do not work outdoors because tiny bits of dust and debris in the air will become imbedded in the finish.

These simple staining directions work also for floors and ceiling beams.

WALLPAPER

First, cut the paper to fit on the walls, taking care to match the pattern and to join the seams in an inconspicuous place, such as the corners of the room. With a 1"-wide brush, apply a commercial wheat paste for wallpaper on the back of the paper, smoothing it all the way out to the edges. Gently fold the wallpaper in half (do *not* crease) with pasted sides together and let it sit for a few minutes; this allows the paper to become more pliable, making it easier to fit and apply. Apply paper to the walls and, if necessary, trim with an X-acto knife. Use a clean damp rag to push out any air bubbles and smooth the surface, and with another rag, clean off any paste on the surface. The wallpaper will look streaked while it is drying, but when dry, it will look fine.

The choice of wallpaper for a dollhouse will depend, in part, on economics. Most real wallpaper is fairly expensive, though you can find bargains at sales and elsewhere. You might ask around among friends for leftover lengths of paper. Some stores will give away wallpaper samples from an outdated sample book, which is usually enough to paper above the chair rail of a dollhouse room. Be sure to select a paper with a tiny pattern, for if the pattern is too large, it will ruin the appearance of a miniature room.

Of course, you don't have to use real wallpaper. Gift wrap paper works just as well, and is available in a wide array of diminutive patterns and colors; some of it is flocked. You should back gift wrap paper with plain white shelf paper, and apply it to walls with rubber cement instead of wallpaper paste.

Another good material for walls is the lovely end paper from the insides of old books, but this tends to be expensive and hard to find.

We frown on the self-adhering plastic wall coverings except for two designs: a dark green velour, which works well on Victorian walls; and an imitation wood pattern in a parquet design that, when properly antiqued and shellacked, can be used for floors.

Murals

This interesting wall treatment should be reasonably neutral in color and depict a rather stylized subject relating to the house or the period. A mural should be placed only in an important area, such as on a very large wall above a chair rail. Cut your print to size and attach to the wall with white resin glue applied sparingly.

Fabric

A heavy fabric, such as brocade or cotton, can be applied to walls of a dollhouse with interesting results. Cut the fabric to fit. Then brush on the walls a thin coat of white resin glue, being careful to use glue sparingly or it will soak through the fabric. Let the glue dry until just tacky and apply fabric, turning under any raw edges or trimming them so they don't ravel.

Stenciling

This wall treatment is much easier to fake than to actually do. Simply choose a wallpaper with a tiny pattern that looks like a stencil design, such as the paper in the Colonial bedroom. You could use a larger pattern if you cut the design into small bands or strips to go below a chair rail or along the ceiling, as in the Colonial dining room.

If you are determined to create your own stencil design for either walls or floor, study a book of Pennsylvania Dutch motifs to get ideas for stencil designs to adapt and scale down to miniature size. Using carbon paper, repeat your design on stencil paper as many times as you need to cover the area to be stenciled. Cut out the repeated design with an X-acto knife, making sure to put in a new blade and to cut on an old board.

We suggest that beginners stencil a rug on a floor for their first stenciling project because the floor is much more accessible than walls. A stencil design on walls is most easily applied before the room is assembled; however, you can apply it to fake walls and then glue these over real walls. In any case, before you begin stenciling, put a base coat of flat paint on the walls, or a coat of semi-gloss on a floor; let dry, then secure your stencil to walls or floor with masking tape.

A stenciling job calls for several jars of acrylic or water-base paint in assorted colors. Begin stenciling at the middle of the surface and work your way out toward the edges. From time to time, clean off the stencil with a damp rag and dry it with a paper towel before continuing. *Most important:* Paint with an almost dry brush, for if you load the brush with paint, you'll be sure to smear. If you do smear paint, touch up the smear and incorporate it into the design with a tiny artist's brush.

When the stencil design has been applied and the paint is dry, give walls a spray coat of acrylic sealer, or paint a polyurethane varnish on a floor.

Marbleizing

This treatment, which can be applied to walls or a floor, is fairly tricky and shouldn't be tackled by an amateur without practicing on a scrap piece of wood. The first step in marbleizing is to paint the surface with a base coat of semi-gloss in white, black, gray, or pinky beige; let it dry for only a few minutes. Then paint in the veins of marble with a contrasting color of paint (for example, gray on white; white on black; dark red, brown, or any other pleasing combination on beige). For this step, use a tiny, very dry artist's brush, or a bird's feather. After the veins are painted in, smear the veining just slightly and feather it out with the tip of your little finger.

An acceptable substitute for marbleizing by hand is to use marble-patterned Formica, some of which is difficult to tell from the real thing. Of course you'll have to locate a company that makes kitchen counter tops or the like and ask for their scraps of Formica. Unless you have a hack saw or electric saw, pay the company a small amount of money to cut the Formica for you. Formica is impractical for areas that require tricky cutting, such as a fireplace, so use it strictly on floors, walls, and furniture tops.

In a fairly small area, it is all right to use self-adhering plastic covering in a marble pattern.

PANELS

A most elegant-looking dollhouse room is one with paneled walls. There are two types of wall panels. One is made of thin balsa sheets— either $\frac{1}{16}$″ or $\frac{3}{32}$″—cut to size with an X-acto knife. Our favorite size for a vertical panel above a chair rail is $2\frac{1}{2}$″ × $6\frac{3}{4}$″ (see page 51 for an actual panel); we often use this same panel to run horizontally under a chair rail interspersed with shorter panels of the same height. If painting the panel, seal it with wood stabilizer or sealer before gluing to wall; paint after gluing. If staining panel, do not stain until after gluing. Be sure the wood grain runs in the direction of the length of the panel. Hold panel in place with masking tape while glue dries.

The other type of panel is more difficult to make, but worth the effort. It consists of $\frac{1}{16}$″ balsa strips cut into four sections resembling a picture frame—that is, two short and two long strips. Follow procedures for previous panel vis-à-vis painting or staining. Glue to the wall as if you were making a picture frame (see directions for mitering) and hold in place with masking tape until glue dries.

With both types of wall panels, you must be careful to not use too much glue because if you get glue on panel or wall, a stain won't penetrate. If glue accumulates accidentally, sand it off with fine sandpaper. Of course if you're painting the walls, the paint will cover the glue.

You can add interest to paneled walls with embossed paper, but only if you have painted them—not stained them; see the Georgian hall, page 69, for this effect.

If you want a paneled room in your dollhouse, but it has already been painted or papered, or is made of pressboard instead of wood, take 6″-wide balsa sheets of $\frac{1}{8}$″ thickness and cut the necessary number of these sheets to ceiling height. Stain sheets in desired color. Then make a false wall by gluing together the sheets; this is called butting. Put masking tape on the back surface where the sheets are joined to help make seams nearly invisible, and dry under a suitable weight; remove tape. Apply wall paneling to false wall and glue entire unit to existing wall of the room.

FLOORS

Floors are not as inherently interesting as walls, but nevertheless there are numerous floor treatments, and the one you choose can do much to define the character of a period room.

WOOD

A wooden floor can be planks or pegged boards; it can be stained, painted, stenciled, or spatter-dashed. If you decide to stain, use a honey-colored pine in a Colonial room; a dark stain in a Georgian room; a light color, such as light oak, in a Victorian room.

For a planked floor, lay over the base floor thin strips of $\frac{3}{32}$″ balsa; strips can have the same width and length, or width and length can vary. Set strips in place with white resin glue, leaving very slight separations between the planks on the sides and at the ends. Stain planks in desired color.

If you want to peg the planks, take a very thin sheet of balsa and punch out little round circles with a paper punch; glue these in place at the ends of the planks. While this method is the most attractive, you can also draw small circles on the ends of the planks with India ink. After staining planks, antique them with burnt umber, and finish off with a coat of shellac.

A spatter-dashed floor looks especially nice in a Colonial room. If you can't spatter before the room is assembled, you must figure out a way to cover the walls and ceiling to protect from the paint. And if you've never spattered before, we recommend a practice session on scrap wood.

Sand your floor smooth and apply a wood stabilizer or sealer. Brush on a coat of flat paint, preferably in a dark color; if you use a light color, you may need two coats. Let base coat dry completely.

The paint to use for spattering should be flat model paint in assorted colors; we recommend light and dark gray, light green, and yellow, blue, red, white. Pour each color into a jar lid. Dip a haircomb with fairly large teeth into the paint; then, holding comb about 3" to 4" above the surface to be spattered, run the edge of an old, but clean, toothbrush over the comb's teeth. Apply the paints one color at a time and let each color dry completely before putting on the next. The dots of paint will vary in size, which is the look you want. If you get any blobs of paint on the surface, wipe off with turpentine and rework that spot in a few minutes. When all paint has been applied and is completely dry, cover with a coat of high gloss varnish.

You can also rub a toothbrush across a square piece of wire screening, which will produce a very fine spatter without as much character as the preceding method.

Marble or slate

Use Formica with a marble or small slate pattern for this floor treatment. Have it cut to fit the base floor, and glue in place with white resin glue; weight entire floor down with a suitable weight so Formica is firmly bonded to floor.

Brick

There are three ways to create a brick floor, all of which work for fireplaces, too. The first, and best, method is to make single bricks and glue them in place one by one. To begin, paint a sheet of fine grain sandpaper with a coat of brick-color red paint and let dry thoroughly (or if you're making yellow bricks, as for the fireplace in the Colonial bedroom, paint sandpaper gold). Carefully rule off the back side of the sandpaper into rectangles no larger than $\frac{1}{4}'' \times \frac{1}{2}''$; cut them apart and glue in place, making sure to stagger placement on alternating rows. Weight bricks down with a suitable weight until bonded to the floor.

The second method is to score the sandpaper's painted surface with a soft white lead pencil—again, staggering the bricks—and glue down the entire sheet after cutting to fit the floor; weight down with a suitable weight. The third method is to use brick-patterned paper, the kind intended for model trains; this doesn't look as authentic because the paper has no texture. If you use this paper, antique it slightly and shellac it after gluing in place.

CEILING

The easiest treatment for a ceiling is to paint it with two coats of flat white paint to resemble a plaster ceiling.

Medallions

For an ornamental ceiling medallion, such as in the Georgian dining room and bedroom, glue to the center of the ceiling two or three matching doilies stacked atop each other and apply two coats of flat white paint; use foil doilies because paint can disintegrate the paper kind.

Another type of medallion is found in the Victorian parlor, page 69. To make this you need a plastic top measuring $3\frac{1}{2}''$ in diameter with a $\frac{1}{4}''$ rim (such tops are on cans of nuts, hard candy, etc.). Paint the top with flat white paint and let dry. Cut a foil doily to fit plastic top and glue to outside surface; glue strip of embossed paper around the outside rim. Paint medallion with two coats of flat white paint. When dry, pierce a tiny hole in exact center of medallion. When ready to hang a chandelier, screw the hook at the end of the chandelier through this hole into the ceiling, which should hold the medallion firmly in place.

Beams

This most interesting of all ceiling treatments is suitable for any Colonial room. Buy a $\frac{3}{4}''$-sq. strip of soft wood—preferably pine—from the lumberyard and bang it with a hammer to give it an aged look. With a small saw, cut wood to proper length for the beams; in addition to ceiling beams, cut two support beams that will be placed along each wall at the ends of the ceiling beams, directly under them at a right angle. Apply burnt umber to age beams further,

then stain them with pine.

At this point you can either stain the ceiling the same color as the beams or apply a coat of flat white paint, which is more authentic. Glue beams to ceiling about 2″ apart. Apply a coat of high-gloss varnish to beams, and to the ceiling if it has been stained.

CHAPTER *11* *The Architectural Details*

In this chapter we present more architectural details from Colonial, Georgian, and Victorian periods, such as dados, windows, and fireplaces. For the first time you encounter specific projects for making these details; each project is designed similarly to later furniture and accessories projects.

Before proceeding, we want to differentiate between real and false architectural details. Wall, floor, and ceiling treatments in this book are real, in that they are made and operate as they do in real life. The doors, windows, and fireplaces in our dollhouses are false, because they cannot be worked as their real life counterparts; that is, windows are not set in the wall so you can see out of them, doors don't open and close, and fireplaces don't have deep openings, wide chimneys, and flues as they would if you could build a fire in them. Such false details are not only vastly easier to make; they also look exactly like real details. However, if you want to make windows and doors that work, you'll find the directions for doing so with the specific projects.

Many of the projects in this chapter are accompanied by specific measurements. These measurements are for a dollhouse room with dimensions of 12"W × 18"L × 12"H; so if your room has different dimensions, you'll have to adjust measurements accordingly.

MORE WALL TREATMENTS

In chapter 10 we dealt with major wall treatments; here we cover the refinements. Whether painted or stained, the following details can blend or contrast with the surrounding wall.

Planking, found in many Colonial homes, consists of interlocking wood planks or boards running vertically from floor to ceiling.

Wall *panels* were discussed briefly in chapter

10. These rectangular pieces of wood, which run above or below chair rail height, appear either sunken or raised in design.

Dados are that wood-paneled area of a wall below the chair rail, originally conceived to guard plaster walls from wear or damage; they are also a decorating device to lessen the height of a room. A dado's panels can vary in shape, such as a long horizontal panel alternating with a short horizontal panel. Clearly visible are the panels of the dado in the Georgian hall, page 69, although a dado usually contrasts with the rest of the wall, such as the painted dados in the Colonial and Georgian bedrooms and the stenciled dado in the Colonial dining room.

Wainscotting refers to wood paneling that runs vertically from the floor to more than half the height of the room, such as in the Victorian kitchen.

The *cornice*, a prerequisite in many period rooms, is a molding that appears where the wall joins the ceiling. Usually very wide and ornamental, a cornice should never be more than one-twelfth of a room's height.

A *chair rail* is a strip of wood running horizontally around a room at about window sill height. Designed to protect walls from damage caused by chairs being pushed back against them, chair rails appear alone on plaster walls or define the top of a dado.

Baseboards are pieces of wood that finish off the seam where the wall joins the floor.

In the following instructions you are told the kind of wood to use in making various wall details; and how to cut the wood, stain, and apply it. Be sure to use a stain appropriate to the period of your dollhouse, such as pine for a Colonial house, knotty pine or walnut for Georgian, and oak for Victorian.

PLANKING, PANELS, WAINSCOTS, diagram 1

Colonial planking: ¼" × 1" lumberyard pine firring. Cut planks to full height of wall.

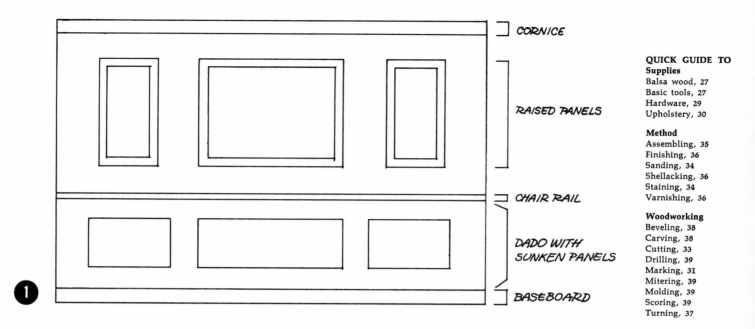

Georgian "sunken" panels: $\frac{1}{16}$" balsa sheet. Cut sheet into rectangles of desired design and size. Bevel edges of panels.

Georgian raised panels: $\frac{1}{16}$" sq. or $\frac{1}{8}$" sq. balsa strips. Cut strips and make rectangular frames of desired design and size. Miter corners.

Victorian wainscot: $\frac{1}{8}$" × $\frac{1}{4}$" balsa strips. Cut strips to about two-thirds the height of room.

Cornices, diagram 1

Colonial: $\frac{1}{8}$" × $\frac{1}{4}$"–1" balsa strips for plain molding, or $\frac{1}{2}$" × 1" lumberyard beaded molding.

Georgian: $\frac{1}{4}$"–$\frac{1}{2}$" × 1" lumberyard S-shaped or beaded molding.

Victorian: $\frac{1}{2}$" × 1" lumberyard S-shaped or concave molding. Cut all molding according to dimensions of room.

Chair rails, diagram 1

Colonial: $\frac{1}{8}$" × $\frac{1}{4}$" balsa strips for plain molding, or $\frac{1}{4}$" × $\frac{3}{8}$" lumberyard beaded molding.

Georgian: $\frac{1}{8}$" × $\frac{1}{4}$" balsa strips for plain molding, or $\frac{1}{4}$" × $\frac{1}{2}$" lumberyard beaded molding.

Victorian: $\frac{1}{4}$" × $\frac{1}{2}$" balsa strips for plain molding (rail is more likely to be part of wainscot or dado).

Cut all chair rails according to dimensions of room.

Baseboards, diagram 1

All periods: $\frac{1}{8}$" × $\frac{5}{8}$" balsa strips for plain molding. Cut according to dimensions of room.

If wood is to be painted, seal it first with a wood stabilizer or sealer. If staining wood, follow the regular procedure. Glue wood to walls and hold in place with a suitable weight until dry; strips can be held in place with masking tape or spring-type clothespins. If you want, put a coat of shellac on Georgian panels, and a coat of high-gloss varnish on Victorian wainscotting; otherwise, these wall treatments need no more finish.

WINDOWS
Size: see diagrams 2, 3, 4, 5

Wood: pieces and kinds of wood are listed with each period window

Suggested finish: stain or paint

Basic tools and supplies, plus plastic acetate, scenic print (optional), paper punch for Victorian window

Colonial Diamond Pane Window

Pieces from $\frac{1}{8}$" × $\frac{1}{4}$" balsa strip
  A: two 4" pieces
  B: two 2$\frac{1}{2}$" pieces
  C: 2$\frac{1}{2}$" piece

Pieces from $\frac{1}{16}$" sq. balsa strip
  D: two 10" pieces
  E: two 10" pieces

COLONIAL DIAMOND PANE

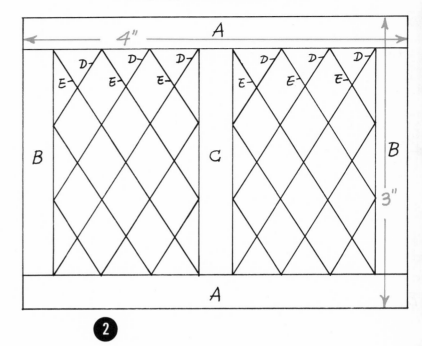

Colonial Twelve-pane Window

PIECES FROM ⅛″ × ¼″ BALSA STRIP
   A: two 3½″ pieces
   B: two 4¼″ pieces
   C: 3″ piece

PIECES FROM 1/16″ SQ. BALSA STRIP
   D: four 2″ pieces
   E: six 1″ pieces

Georgian Twelve-pane Window

PIECES FROM ½″-WIDE MOLDING
   A: 4″ piece
   B: two 10″ pieces

PIECE FROM ⅛″ × ¼″ BALSA STRIP
   C: 3″ piece

PIECES FROM 1/16″ SQ. BALSA STRIP
   D: four 2¾″ pieces
   E: six 1″ pieces
   F: two 2″ pieces
   G: two 2¼″ pieces

PIECE FROM ⅛″ BALSA SHEET
   H: 3″ × 3¾″ piece

PIECE FROM ½″-WIDE INLAY OR ⅛″ × ½″ BALSA STRIP
   I: 3″ piece

COLONIAL TWELVE PANE

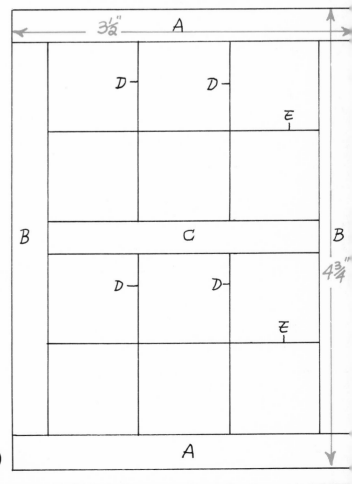

Victorian Window

PIECES FROM ⅛″ BALSA SHEET OR ⅛″ × ½″ BALSA STRIP
   A: two ½″ × 3½″ pieces
   B: two ½″ × 6⅜″ pieces

PIECES FROM ⅛″ SQ. BALSA STRIP
   C: 2½″ piece
   D: two ⅛″ × 3⅛″ pieces

PIECES FROM 1/16″ BALSA SHEET
   J: four circles ¼″ in diameter

CUTTING

1. Cut wood specified for your window, using single-edged razor blade to facilitate cutting of strips and cutting any balsa sheet on lengthwise grain.

2. For Georgian window, miter both ends of piece (A) and one end of each piece (B), at opposite angles. Miter ends of pieces (F) and (G) as though you were making a picture frame.

3. For Victorian window, cut ½″ from each end of pieces (A), then glue cut-off squares back in place. Use paper punch to cut pieces (J).

4 GEORGIAN

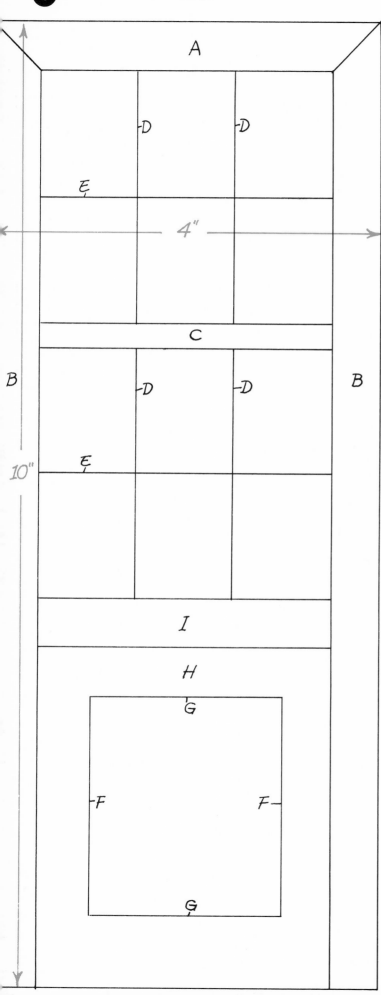

5 VICTORIAN

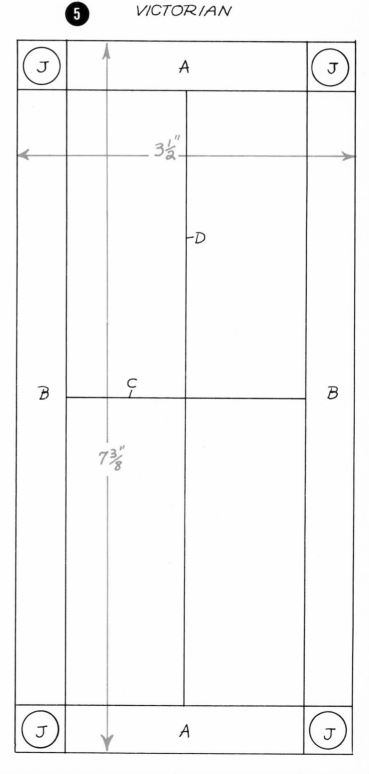

SANDING AND STAINING

1. Sand wood.

2. Stain wood *if* window is to be stained instead of painted. Colonial diamond pane is the only window that must be stained to be authentic.

ASSEMBLY, diagrams 2, 3, 4, 5

1. Glue window frame top and bottom pieces (A) to window frame sides (B) to form a perfect rectangle. For Georgian window, glue piece (H) between window frame sides (B) so bottom edge of (H) is flush with bottom edges of (B).

2. Center and glue crosspiece (C) between top and bottom edges of window frame. For Colonial diamond pane window, center (C) between window frame sides.

3. Space evenly and glue vertical glazing bars (D) between crosspiece (C) and top and bottom edges of window frame. Sand horizontal glazing bars (E) to fit between vertical bars (D) and frame sides (B); center and glue in place.

For Colonial diamond pane window, cut each 10″ piece (D) into five equal pieces and fit them diagonally, trimming if necessary, between crosspiece (C) and frame sides (B). Begin with longest diagonal piece and glue between upper left-hand corner and lower right-hand corner of each frame; space other pieces (D) evenly and parallel to each other and glue. Repeat procedure for each 10″ piece (E), only in opposite direction with (E) overlapping (D).

4. For Georgian window, glue piece (I) to top edge of piece (H). Glue pieces (F) and (G) to piece (H) to form rectangular panel.

5. For Victorian window, center and glue pieces (J) to corners of window frame.

FINISHING

1. Paint window in desired color unless it has been stained; if stained, apply one coat of shellac.

2. For window panes, cut plastic acetate to size of window frame; for Georgian window, cut 4″ × 7″ piece of acetate.

3. Cut out scenic print and glue to back of acetate. Garden magazines and seed catalogs are good sources for realistic scenes of trees, gardens, or something appropriate to your period. Remember that second-story windows would overlook mostly tree tops.

4. Put glue on back surface of window frame along inside edges and apply acetate; place under a suitable weight to dry.

5. Make draperies or curtains for window, if desired; see chapter 26.

6. Apply completed window to wall of room with glue or double-faced masking tape.

Variation: FIFTEEN- AND EIGHTEEN-PANE WINDOWS

For 15-pane (or six over nine pane) window, add 1″ to length of window frame sides (B) and 1″ to length of two lower vertical glazing bars (D), following diagram 3. Cut three more horizontal glazing bars (E) for additional row of three window panes.

For 18-pane (or nine over nine pane) window, add 2″ to length of window frame sides (B) and 1″ to length of four vertical glazing bars (D), following diagram 3. Cut six more horizontal glazing bars (E) for additional two rows of three window panes, one on each side of crosspiece (C).

Variation: SEE-THROUGH WINDOW

If you want a window you can actually see through, you must cut an opening in the dollhouse wall. To do this, drill four small holes about ½″ in from corners of proposed opening (window plus frame) and with a small saw, cut out opening to about ¼″ of proposed opening. The opening is deliberately ¼″ smaller than the window so the window frame, when glued in place, can cover up any imperfect cutting.

DOORS

SIZE: see diagrams 6, 7, 8

WOOD: pieces and kinds of wood are listed with each period door

SUGGESTED FINISH: stain or paint

BASIC TOOLS AND SUPPLIES, plus paper punch for Victorian door, assorted hardware (see chapter 11)

Colonial Door

PIECES FROM ⅛″ BALSA SHEET
A: 4″ × 7″ piece
B: ¼″ × 4″ piece
C: two ¼″ × 6¾″ pieces

PIECES FROM ¹⁄₁₆″ BALSA SHEET
 D: two 1″ × 1⅛″ pieces
 E: four 1″ × 1¾″ pieces
 F: ½″ × 2⅝″ piece

Georgian Door

PIECES FROM ⅛″ BALSA SHEET
 A: 4½″ × 8¾″ piece

PIECES FROM ¼″ × ¾″ GROOVED LUMBERYARD MOLDING
 B: 4½″ piece
 C: two 8″ pieces
 G: 6″ piece

PIECES FROM ¹⁄₁₆″ BALSA SHEET
 D: two 1″ × 1⅛″ pieces
 E: four 1″ × 1¾″ pieces
 F: ½″ × 2¼″ piece

Victorian Door

PIECES FROM ⅛″ BALSA SHEET
 A: 4″ × 7½″ piece
 B: ½″ × 4″ piece
 C: two ½″ × 7″ pieces

PIECES FROM ¹⁄₁₆″ BALSA SHEET
 D: four 1″ × 2⅞″ pieces
 H: two circles ¼″ in diameter

CUTTING

1. Cut wood specified for your door on lengthwise grain. Try to buy balsa strips instead of sheets for door frame pieces (B) and (C) on Colonial and Victorian doors; you'll save a lot of cutting time.

2. For Georgian door, miter both ends of piece (B) and one end of each piece (C) at opposite angles.

3. For Victorian door, cut ½″ from each end of piece (B), then glue cut-off squares back in place. Use paper punch to cut pieces (H).

SANDING AND STAINING

1. Sand wood.

2. For door panels (D), (E), and (F), bevel edges.

3. Stain wood *if* door is to be stained instead of painted.

ASSEMBLY, diagrams 6, 7, 8

1. Glue door frame sides (C) to side edges of door (A) so side edges of each piece are flush.

2. Glue door frame top (B) to top edge of door (A) so top edges of both pieces are flush.

3. For Georgian door, glue pediment (G) to top edge of door frame top (B) with mitered edges of both pieces lying at same angle.

4. Glue door panels (D), (E), and (F) to door (A), following diagrams for placement.

5. For Victorian door, center and glue pieces (H) to corners of door frame top (B).

6   *COLONIAL*

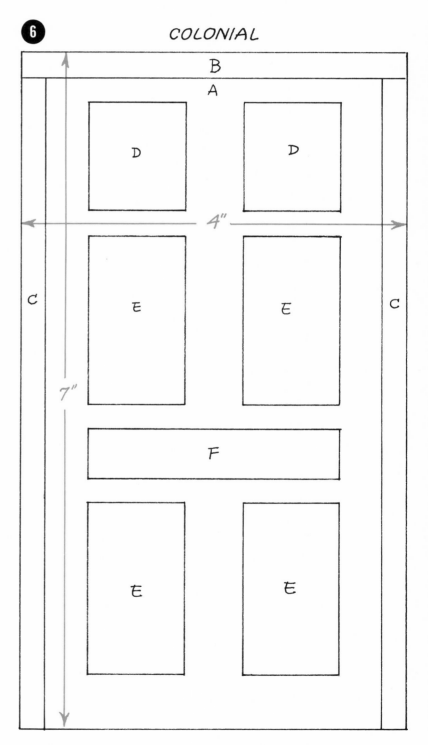

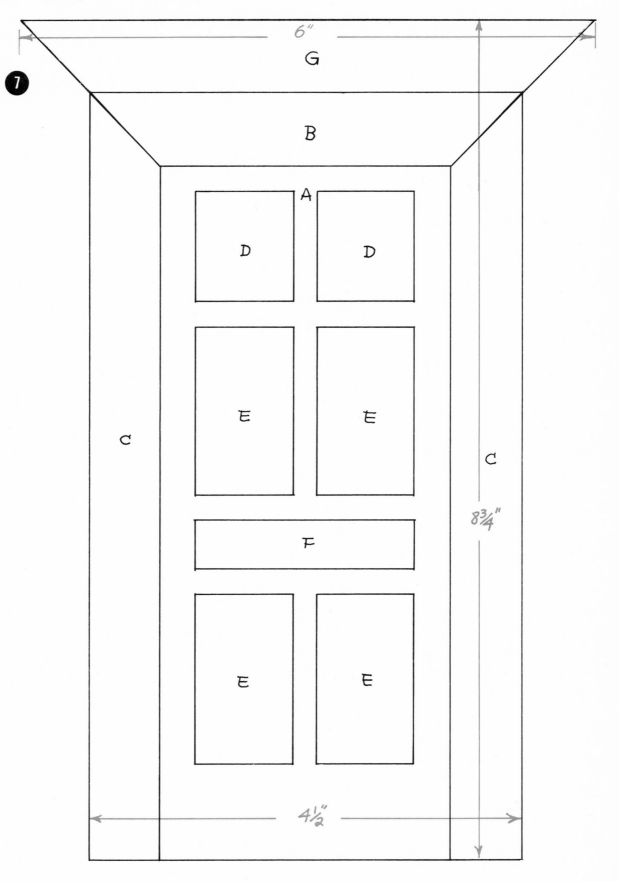

FINISHING

1. Paint door in desired color unless it has been stained; if stained, apply one coat of shellac.

2. Mount hinges, door knobs, and locks as directed in chapter 9.

3. Apply door to wall with glue or double-faced masking tape.

Variation: OPEN-AND-CLOSE DOOR

If you want a door that actually opens and closes, you must cut an opening in the dollhouse wall. To do this, drill four small holes about ¼" in from corners of proposed opening (door, excluding frame), and with a small saw, cut out opening. Hinge door in place according to directions on page 40.

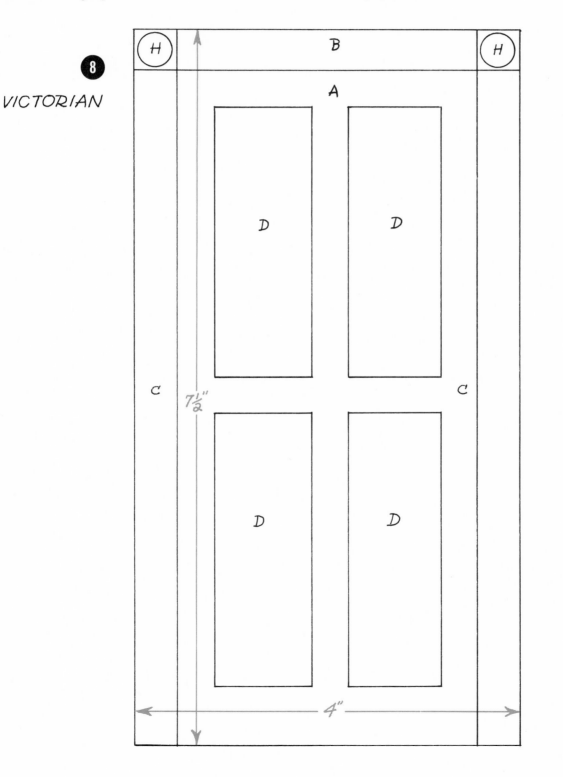

COLONIAL FIREPLACE
SIZE: 8″W × ¾″D × 5⅛″H

WOOD: ⅛″ balsa sheet, ¾″ sq. molding strip

SUGGESTED FINISH: brick-colored paint

BASIC TOOLS AND SUPPLIES, plus #220 sandpaper, flat or satin brick red paint, white drawing pencil, black enamel model paint, charcoal drawing stick, acrylic sealer

PIECES FROM ⅛″ BALSA SHEET
A: 4⅜″ × 7¾″ piece
B: two ¾″ × 4⅜″ pieces
C: two ¾″ × 4⅜″ pieces
D: two 1⅛″ × 4⅜″ pieces
E: 2″ × 8″ piece

PIECE FROM ¾″ SQ. MOLDING STRIP
F: 8″ piece

PIECES FROM #220 SANDPAPER
A: 4⅜″ × 7¾″ piece
B: two ¾″ × 4⅜″ pieces
C: two ¾″ × 4⅜″ pieces
D: two 1¼″ × 4⅜″ pieces
E: 2″ × 8″ piece

CUTTING
1. Cut wood pieces on lengthwise grain.
2. Before cutting sandpaper, paint one #220 sheet with brick red paint; when dry, cut out pieces (A), (B), (C), and (D). Paint approximately half a sheet of #220 sandpaper with black enamel model paint; when dry, cut out piece (E). If you can buy black sandpaper, you can skip the painting step for piece (E).

AGING AND STAINING
1. To give mantlepiece (F) a mellowed look, age the beams.
2. Stain mantlepiece (F).

ASSEMBLY, diagram 9
1. Glue sandpaper pieces (A), (B), (C), and (D) to wood pieces (A), (B), (C), and (D); sandpaper pieces (D) will extend ⅛″ beyond side edges of wood pieces (D). Place a suitable weight on pieces while drying.
2. With white drawing pencil (or white paint and tiny artist's brush), draw ¼″ × ¾″ bricks on each piece of red sandpaper, making sure each row of bricks continues at the same level on each piece.
3. Glue black sandpaper (E) to hearth (E) to resemble slate or stone.

4. Glue fireplace sides (B) to back (A) so back edges of (B) are flush with back surface of (A).
5. Glue front pieces (D) to sides (B), with ⅛″ sandpaper overlaps covering front edges of (B).
6. Glue sides (C) of fireplace opening on an angle between pieces (D) and back (A). For an accurate fit, the long edges of (C) should be trimmed on an angle.
7. Glue mantlepiece (F) to top edges of assembly from step 6 so back edge of (F) is flush with back surface of back (A).
8. Glue assembly from step 7 to hearth (E) so back edge of (E) is flush with back surface of back (A).

FINISHING
1. Shellac mantlepiece (F).
2. Paint black oven door in shape of a beehive on back (A); see broken line in diagram 9.
3. Blacken back (A) with charcoal drawing stick to resemble soot; spray with acrylic sealer.
4. Attach fireplace to wall with glue or double-faced masking tape.

GEORGIAN FIREPLACE
SIZE: 6″W × 1″D × 12″H

WOOD: ⅛″ balsa sheet, ⅝″ × ¾″ lumberyard S-shaped molding, ⅛″ × ½″ inlay (optional)

SUGGESTED FINISH: stain or paint

BASIC TOOLS AND SUPPLIES, plus flat black paint

PIECES FROM ⅛″ BALSA SHEET
A: 6″ × 11⅞″ piece
B: two 1″ × 11⅞″ pieces
C: 2¼″ × 6″ piece
D: 1″ × 6″ piece
E: ⅞″ × 5⅝″ piece
F: ¾″ × 5⅜″ piece
G: two 1⅛″ × 3¼″ pieces

PIECES FROM ⅝″ × ¾″ LUMBERYARD S-SHAPED MOLDING
H: 5″ piece
I: two 4½″ pieces

PIECES FROM ⅛″ × ½″ INLAY
J: 3½″ piece
K: two 3¾″ pieces

CUTTING
1. Cut wood on lengthwise grain.

9   *COLONIAL*

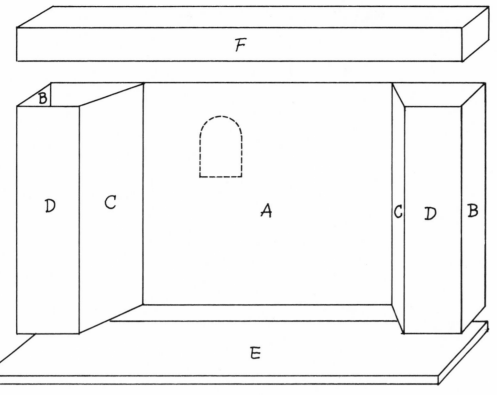

2. The height of fireplace front and side walls (A) and (B) is determined by height of room. Center and cut out rectangular opening 2½″ wide and 3¼″ high along bottom edge of wall (A).

3. Miter both ends of piece (H) and one end of each piece (I) at opposite angles.

Sanding and staining

1. Sand wood.

2. Stain wood *if* fireplace is to be stained instead of painted.

Assembly, diagram 10

1. Glue front wall (A) to side walls (B).

2. Glue top frame piece (H) to side frame pieces (I).

3. Center and glue assembly from step 2 to front of wall (A).

4. Center and glue together in correct order mantlepiece pieces (D), (E), and (F), making sure back edges are flush. Glue this assembly to top of frame (H), with front edge of (F) flush with front surface of (H).

5. If you have them, glue facing pieces (J) and (K) to wall (A) at fireplace opening. But if ½″-wide inlay strip for pieces (J) and (K) is unavailable, use black or white Formica in marbleized pattern; or eliminate facing pieces altogether and cover ½″-wide area around fireplace opening of wall (A) with black paint or black sandpaper.

6. Glue assembly from steps 1–5 to hearth (C) so back edges of side walls (B) are flush with back edge of (C).

7. Glue sides (G) of fireplace opening on an angle between pieces (K)—or whatever your facing material is—and wall (A). For an accurate fit, the long edges of (G) should be trimmed on an angle.

Finishing

1. Paint fireplace in desired color unless it has been stained. If stained, shellac.

2. Paint hearth (C) and sides (G) with flat black paint.

3. Glue fireplace to wall and paint wall inside fireplace opening black.

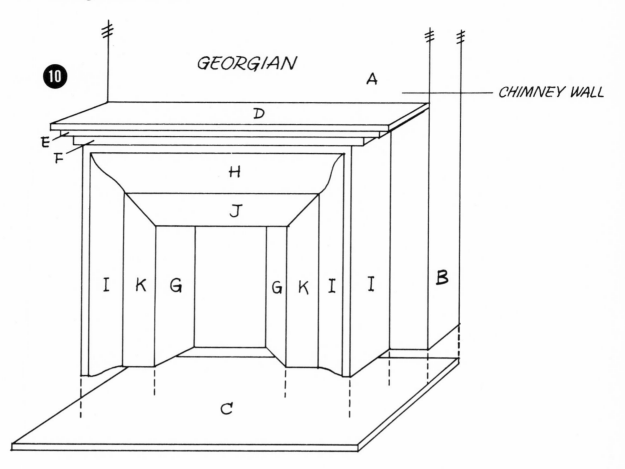

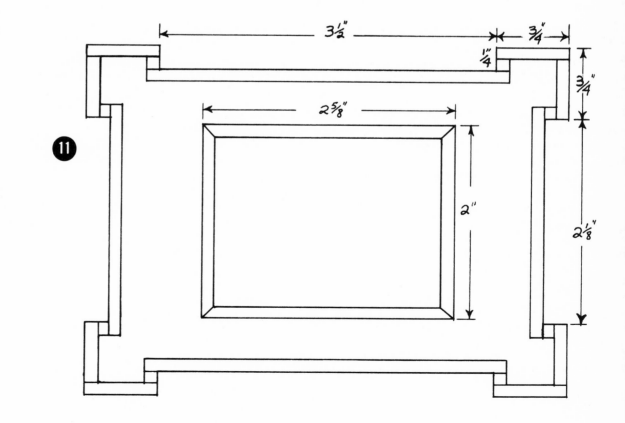

12 *OVERMANTEL*

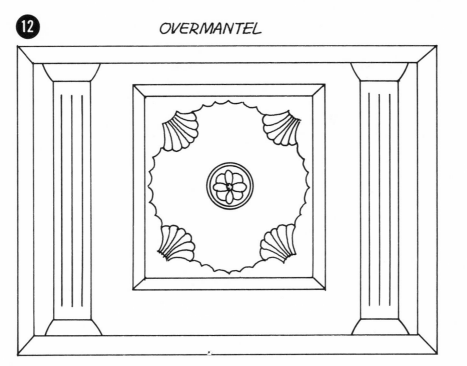

Variation: COLONIAL TILE FIREPLACE

A Colonial tile fireplace can be made with same mantelpiece pieces (D), (E), and (F), frame pieces (H) and (I), and hearth (C) shortened to $1\frac{1}{4}''$ depth. For false backing, cut $4\frac{7}{8}'' \times 5''$ piece from $\frac{1}{16}''$ balsa sheet and cover with medium grade sandpaper painted brick red or yellow. Draw bricks on sandpaper with white drawing pencil (or white paint and tiny artist's paintbrush). Glue together mantlepiece and frame and glue to brick backing.

For tile facing, you need 20 white or bluish-white $\frac{7}{16}''$-sq. ceramic tiles. Using the tiniest possible brush (two hairs in the brush would be perfect) and medium-blue enamel model paint, paint a Delft-like design on each tile. When dry, glue tiles to brick backing, with eight across top and six down each side. Cut $1\frac{1}{16}'' \times 3\frac{1}{2}''$ piece from $\frac{1}{8}''$ balsa sheet and glue to brick backing between top row of tiles and frame (H). Glue entire assembly to hearth (C). Paint or stain fireplace. If you wish, rub a charcoal drawing stick on brick backing to resemble soot.

Variation: GEORGIAN OVERMANTELS

A plain overmantel can be made with $\frac{1}{16}'' \times \frac{1}{8}''$ balsa strip. Follow diagram 11 for length of each piece and arrangement of design. Center and glue overmantel to fireplace wall (A).

For a more elaborate overmantel, cut frame for decorative panel from $\frac{1}{16}'' \times \frac{1}{8}''$ balsa strip, miter corners, and glue together to form a square. Simulate carving inside frame with embossed paper and decorative button; see diagram 12. Center and glue decorative panel to fireplace wall (A). Make flat columns out of corrugated balsa wood or scored $\frac{1}{16}''$ balsa sheet; make simple bases for ends of columns. Glue columns to wall (A) between sides of decorative panel and side edges of (A). Frame entire overmantel with $\frac{1}{16}'' \times \frac{1}{4}''$ balsa strips mitered at corners. Paint entire fireplace with two coats of satin enamel paint in desired color.

VICTORIAN FIREPLACE

SIZE: 5½″W × 1″D × 4½″H

WOOD: ⅛″ balsa sheet, 1/16″ balsa sheet

SUGGESTED FINISH: paint

BASIC TOOLS AND SUPPLIES, plus embossed paper, black enamel model paint, heavy picture wire, epoxy glue, small button with floral motif, paint for marbleizing

PIECES FROM ⅛″ BALSA SHEET
 A: 4⅜″ × 5″ piece
 B: two 1″ × 4⅜″ pieces
 C: 4⅜″ × 4¾″ piece (optional)
 D: 2¼″ × 5″ piece
 E: piece from pattern, diagram 13

PIECES FROM 1/16″ BALSA SHEET
 F: two pieces from pattern, diagram 14

CUTTING
 1. Cut wood on lengthwise grain.
 2. Note that only half the pattern for piece (E) is shown in diagram 14. Duplicate this in tracing for a solid piece measuring 5½″ in length.

SANDING
 1. Sand wood.

ASSEMBLY, diagram 15
 1. For fireplace front wall (A), draw an arched opening 3″ high and 3″ wide centered along bottom edge of (A), following same curve as in panel pieces (F). Glue embossed paper inside arch to resemble the cast iron enclosure for coal- and gas-burning fireplaces of the period; paint embossed paper and hearth (D) black.
 2. For molding, glue two rows of picture wire around cast iron enclosure with epoxy glue; place a suitable weight on this while drying.
 3. Glue panels (F) to wall (A) and dry under a suitable weight.
 4. Glue wall (A) to side walls (B).
 5. Glue optional back piece (C) to sides (B).
 6. Center and glue mantelpiece (E) to assembly from steps 4–5 so back edge of (E) is flush with back surface of (C).
 7. Glue entire assembly to hearth (D) so back edges of sides (B) are flush with back edge of (D).

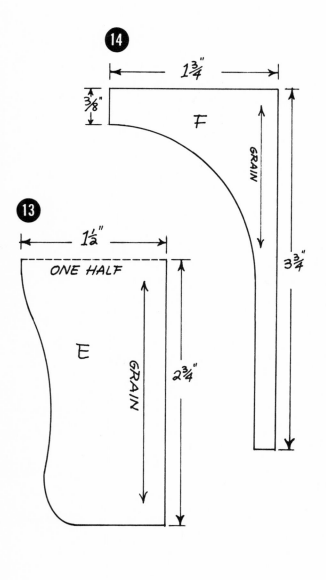

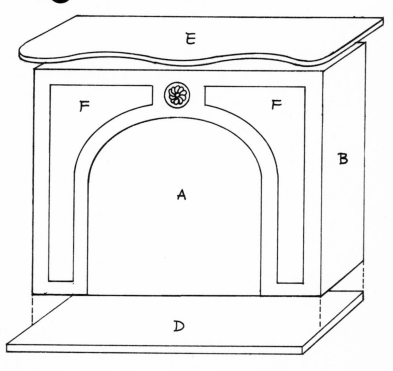

VICTORIAN

FINISHING

1. Glue button between panels (F).

2. Marbleize fireplace, including picture wire molding.

3. Glue fireplace to wall.

GEORGIAN STAIRCASE AND BALUSTRADE

WOOD: $\frac{3}{32}$″ balsa sheet, $\frac{1}{16}$″ balsa sheet, $\frac{3}{32}$″ sq. balsa strip, $\frac{1}{4}$″ dowel, $\frac{1}{8}$″ dowel, $\frac{1}{16}$″ × $\frac{1}{8}$″ balsa strip

SUGGESTED FINISH: mahogany stain and paint in desired color

BASIC TOOLS AND SUPPLIES, plus protractor, embossed paper (optional), half-inch straight pins, 4 flat buttons, 4 round beads, woodtone paint

PIECES FROM $\frac{3}{32}$″ BALSA SHEET

A: two pieces from pattern, diagram 16

B: $\frac{5}{8}$″ × $3\frac{1}{2}$″ pieces

C: $\frac{3}{4}$″ × $3\frac{1}{2}$″ pieces

D: $3\frac{1}{2}$″-wide piece

PIECES FROM $\frac{1}{16}$″ BALSA SHEET

E: $1\frac{3}{16}$″ × $3\frac{13}{16}$″ pieces

PIECE FROM $\frac{3}{32}$″ SQ. BALSA STRIP

F and G: 18′ piece

PIECES FROM $\frac{1}{4}$″ DOWEL

H: four $2\frac{1}{2}$″ pieces

PIECES FROM $\frac{1}{8}$″ DOWEL

I: two pieces to be cut later

PIECES FROM $\frac{1}{16}$″ × $\frac{1}{8}$″ STRIP

J: two pieces to be cut later

CUTTING

1. Cut wood on lengthwise grain.

2. Measure height of your dollhouse room from surface of first floor to surface of second floor. Determine how many $\frac{5}{8}$″-high steps are needed between the two floors, and add the correct number of steps to pattern for (A) when tracing onto paper. Because all steps *must* be on the same angle, use a protractor to make sure the bottom straight edge of (A) is 40°. If the pattern does not fit exactly between the two floors, make any adjustment on bottom step, *not* top step.

Cut two staircase sides (A) from your pattern. If you want to simulate carving on sides (A), cut and glue some embossed paper to right-angle corners of each step.

3. For risers (B) and steps (C), cut as many as you have steps.

4. For staircase bottom (D), cut a rectangle as long as measured staircase length.

5. For stair treads (E), cut as many as you have steps.

ASSEMBLING AND FINISHING STAIRCASE, diagram 16

1. Sand staircase pieces (A), (B), (C), and (D).

2. Glue each riser (B) to each step (C) to form right angle; the top edge of (B) is flush with top surface of (C).

3. Glue side edge of each riser-and-step assembly from step 1 to one staircase side (A), and glue bottom edge of each riser (B) to surface of preceding step (C) along back edge of (C); see dotted lines in diagram 1. Glue other staircase side (A) to other side edges of (B) and (C).

4. Glue staircase bottom (D) between sides (A) so bottom surface is flush with bottom edges of (A).

5. Paint staircase with two coats of flat paint.

ASSEMBLING AND FINISHING BALUSTRADE, diagram 16

1. Sand stair treads (E); round front and side edges by sanding gently the top and bottom surfaces until semi-circular (do not sand away corners). Stain treads (E). Shellac (E) and varnish tops.

2. Paint the 18′ piece of balsa strip for posts (F) and (G) to match staircase. Trace pattern for (F) and (G) onto paper, making sure you follow the diagonal dotted line in the diagram for the top edges of the posts; because the angle on top edges of (F) and (G) *must* be the same 40° angle as staircase sides, use a protractor.

Place painted balsa strip on pattern for post (F) and cut along dotted line for top edge of (F) and along stair tread (E) for bottom edge of (F); repeat for rest of posts (F), of which you will need two for each stair tread minus the top tread. Repeat entire procedure for posts (G).

3. Mark each stair tread (E) with four pencil dots, placing two dots $\frac{3}{16}$″ from front edge and $\frac{1}{16}$″ from side edges, and two dots $\frac{1}{4}$″ from back edge and $\frac{1}{16}$″ from side edges. Glue two posts (F) to two front dots of (E) and two posts (G) to two back dots, with these exceptions: Bottom tread (E) has (G) posts only, and

top tread (E) has no posts. Make sure angle of posts' top edges face forward. Reinforce each post with half-inch straight pins, following directions for reinforced gluing.

4. Glue each tread-and-post assembly from step 3 to steps (C) so treads overlap front and side edges of (C) $\frac{1}{16}$".

5. Sand newel posts (H) and glue a button and bead to top of each. Stain or paint posts (H); if staining, paint buttons and beads with woodtone paint to match stain. Glue two posts (H) to front corners of bottom stair tread (E) and two posts (H) to front corners of top tread (E).

6. Cut two pieces (I) from $\frac{1}{8}$" dowel and two pieces (J) from $\frac{1}{16}$" × $\frac{1}{8}$" balsa strip to fit between top and bottom posts (H), but make all pieces about $\frac{1}{2}$" longer than the distance between the posts. Sand (I) and (J) pieces, then stain or paint them. Glue each piece (I) to the $\frac{1}{8}$" surface of each piece (J) to form two railings.

Trace onto paper pattern where a railing meets a post (H) at the vertical dotted line; place one railing on pattern along (I) and cut end along dotted line. Fit railing between posts (H) and mark other end where it will be cut; turn railing upside down, place it on pattern along (I), place the cutting mark along dotted line, and cut. Repeat procedure for other railing.

7. Glue railings between top and bottom newel posts.

8. Glue posts (F) and (G) to underside of railings, gluing one post at a time and holding with hands until glue is firmly set.

9. Position staircase in room and attach with glue or double-faced masking tape.

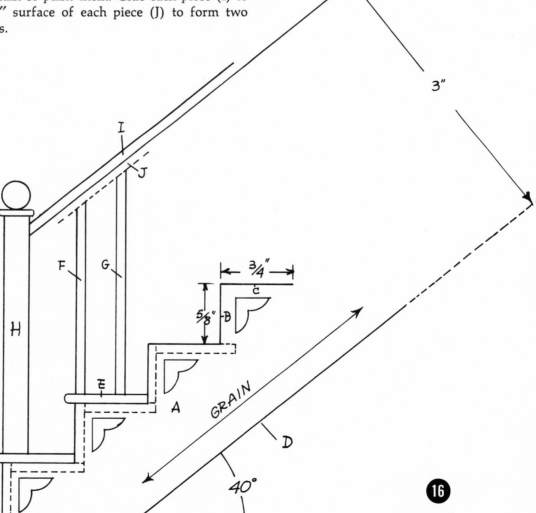

The following pages
show color close-ups of miniature rooms
for Colonial, Georgian and Victorian dollhouses.
Everything in them is true to scale,
one inch to the foot,
which is why they look so real.

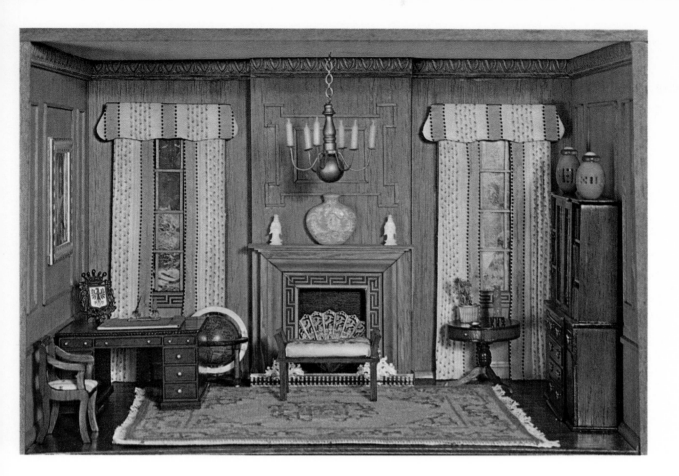

PART IV   *Furniture Projects*

CHAPTER 12

Three Model Dollhouses

This chapter is the heart of our book, for here you see the three model dollhouses on which the entire book is based, with their rooms designed and decorated according to the styles and tastes of Colonial, Georgian, and Victorian times. You have already learned how to fashion the walls, windows, doors, ceilings, floors, and fireplaces in these rooms. In the book's remaining chapters, we tell you how to make every piece of furniture and accessory in the rooms.

Of course, you do not have to copy these rooms; nor do you have to make each piece of furniture or accessory for the same room or the same purpose as we did. For example, you may prefer more elegant furniture in the Colonial keeping room, such as the dining room table and rush-bottomed chairs which we have placed in the Colonial dining room (most small Colonial homes did not have separate dining rooms, anyway).

If you wish, you can make minor structural changes in a piece of furniture, and you can stain it a different color than the one we suggest. For instance, the mahogany highboy in the Colonial living room could have a flat top and apron (bottom edge) instead of the intricately carved one we've put on it, and it could be stained cherry instead of mahogany. We've given you not only patterns, but also variations, and you can invent variations of your own.

The point is: We don't want you to feel bound by the limitations of the book. We want you to learn from it, and use what you can. But we hope the book will inspire new and different decorating ideas.

Each furniture and accessory project in the following chapters is labeled so you can tell to which room in the model dollhouse it belongs; thus, you can study the finished project while in the throes of making it. For example, as you work on the console table, you can see it in the color photograph of our Victorian dining room.

Finally, each of our dollhouse rooms measures 18"L × 12"W × 12"H.

COLONIAL LIVING ROOM

Usually called drawing room or parlor, this room reflects the relative prosperity of the inhabitants because of its wallpaper, ornate bolection molding, elegant dado, silk draperies, and Oriental rug. The most interesting piece of furniture is the magnificent Chippendale highboy, which in real life might have been two separate pieces of furniture placed one atop the other; the bottom part was called a lowboy. You can follow directions for the bottom only, and create a lowboy in addition to the highboy for your dollhouse. The Chippendale sofa has eight straight legs with stretcher supports, although you can give it only six legs.

COLONIAL DINING ROOM

The braided rug over the spatter-dashed floor is not truly necessary in this inviting room, though it does add interest. Curtains are cotton homespun. The ladderback, or slat back, chairs could have hooked chair pads on them for additional comfort and design.

COLONIAL BEDROOM

The windows in this room are treated with valences of embroidered organdy to match the curtains; dust ruffle on bed and bolster pillow are of the same fabric, which could also be cotton. The smaller rug is braided and the larger one is hooked. Yellow brick lines the interior of the fireplace opening. The blanket chest has a Hitchcock-type stencil design, but it could have a Pennsylvania Dutch motif, or simply be painted or stained. The cherry chest could be made larger, and the rockers on the Windsor rocking chair could be left off to become a Windsor side chair.

COLONIAL KEEPING ROOM

Beamed ceiling, pegged floors, diamond-shaped window panes, large fireplace—the features often associated with Colonial architecture are all in this friendly room. If working with larger dimensions than our room, you can include a simple cot or trundle bed, and perhaps a cupboard or dresser. You can also build a smaller version of the trestle table to serve as an additional table. The chandelier could be put in a dining room; if you decide to leave it out of the keeping room, we suggest you hang another pair of sconces. The earliest examples of the deacon's bench were made of stained wood, but we exercised artistic license and made a Pennsylvania Dutch version of the bench, using tulips for motif; other popular motifs were birds, hearts, and hex signs.

GEORGIAN HALL

The first thing you see in this great front hall is the staircase, called a flying staircase be-

cause it has no under support. The floor is brown and black marble partially covered with Oriental scatter rugs. The mural is framed by paneled walls embellished with fruit motifs.

GEORGIAN LIBRARY

This library manifests the elegance and luxury of the Georgian style. Note the abundance of rich knotty pine paneling. The graceful windows are framed by draperies and cornices of heavy silk in a Chinese Chippendale design. The Sheraton drum table could have an octagonal top, in which case it would be called a rent table because rent from tenants on the property would be stored here.

GEORGIAN DINING ROOM

The walls here are covered with pale beige silk moiré. Depending on the size of the room,

Georgian Rooms

Victorian Rooms

the two-pedestal dining table could have three pedestals and be called a banquet table. The Hepplewhite card or gaming table is used as a serving piece until a game of whist is anticipated, when it is moved into the hall and opened up.

GEORGIAN BEDROOM

Green and gold silk damask covers the walls and bed in this bedroom fit for royalty. Gold antique satin draperies match bed curtains, canopy, and dust ruffle. The open fretwork shelf hanging above the dressing table contains a collection of rare seashells, but could display a miniature collection of practically anything belonging to the woman of the house.

VICTORIAN LIVING ROOM

From the Florentine wallpaper to the velvet Axminster rug, this living room (or parlor) is Victoriana at its best. Silk brocade draperies, topped by gilt cornices, are enhanced by lace undercurtains. A late Victorian living room could have shelves built in over the fireplace for books and bric-a-brac instead of a gilt framed mirror. Other accessories you might find in a Victorian living room are a bronze statue, a sporting trophy, a stuffed bird, some souvenirs, Berlin needlework, and lots of framed family photographs.

VICTORIAN DINING ROOM

Although not as ornate as the living room, this Victorian dining room is still relatively formal, yet it generates a feeling of comfort. Wallpaper is flocked; draperies are silk, again with lace undercurtains. The room's dark woodwork was popular until mid-19th century. The massive oak, pedestal-type table could have a round, oval, or rectangular top.

VICTORIAN BEDROOM

Decorated in the fashionable colors of lavender and cream, this room is quite lovely for the second floor of a Victorian home. It has definitely been "recently redecorated." Brass bed and door hardware are among the new and stylish acquisitions. Draperies are satin over fabric shades edged in lace.

VICTORIAN KITCHEN

A cast-iron stove, icebox, and linoleum floor are signs of an up-to-date, late Victorian kitchen. The dry sink, too, with its tin liner and running water from nickel faucets, is a recent model. The wainscot of dark oak panels is topped by marbleized wallpaper.

BASSINETTE
(*Victorian bedroom*)

SIZE: $1\frac{1}{2}''$W × $3\frac{1}{2}''$L × $5\frac{1}{2}''$H

BASIC TOOLS AND SUPPLIES, plus $5\frac{3}{4}''$-high twisted wire brass cup and saucer easel, $1\frac{3}{4}''$ × $2\frac{1}{2}''$ metal change purse, or plastic or paper party favor basket, $\frac{3}{8}''$-thick piece of foam rubber, fabric scrap, $2\frac{1}{4}''$-wide lace edging, 5″ to 6″-wide lace edging, 2″ piece of tiny floral trim, #28 wire, $5\frac{1}{4}''$ piece of small gold chain.

CUTTING

1. Cut $\frac{3}{4}''$ off brass easel (A) at broken line; see diagram 1.
2. Trim basket (B) to depth of $\frac{3}{4}''$. If you can't find party favor basket, make one with same dimensions out of $\frac{3}{32}''$ balsa sheet.
3. Cut foam rubber mattress (C) to fit inside basket (B).
4. Cut fabric scrap to cover mattress (C), allowing enough to tuck in at sides and turn back $\frac{1}{2}''$ hem along broken line; see diagram 1.
5. Cut 13″ piece of the narrower lace edging; cut 6″ piece of the wider lace edging.

ASSEMBLY, diagram 1

1. Glue chain (D) to basket (B) at bottom corners.
2. Attach head corners of basket to easel (A) with #28 wire twisted and cut very close. Hook chain from other end over easel and bend back cut end of easel to form a curve until basket chain is locked in place.

FINISHING

1. Turn 13″ lace edging under $\frac{1}{4}''$ and glue to basket (B) to make softly gathered skirt; begin and end at back of basket.
2. Pinch 6″ lace edging in middle to form $\frac{1}{2}''$ pouf, and place at top of brass easel; glue at top to secure and on sides to form pull-back side curtains.
3. Glue floral trim around pouf at top and on sides where curtains are pulled back.

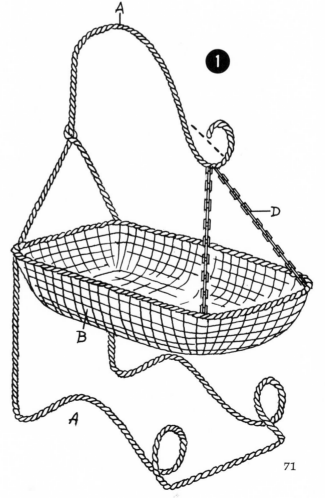

BRASS BED
(*Victorian bedroom*)

SIZE: 4¼"W × 7"L × 5"H

WOOD: ⅛" balsa sheet

BASIC TOOLS AND SUPPLIES, plus 4 aluminum knitting needles (single point, #5, 10"), 4 aluminum knitting needles (double point, #3, 7"), flat metal file, 3 decorative rings, gold or brass paint, liquid solder

PIECE FROM ⅛" BALSA SHEET
   A: 4" × 7" piece

PIECES FROM SINGLE POINT KNITTING NEEDLES
   B: from one needle—4½" piece with head, 4" piece without head and point
   C: from one needle—4½" piece with head, 4" piece without head and point
   D: from one needle—3¾" piece with head, 3¼" piece with point
   E: from one needle—3¾" piece with head, 3¼" piece with point

PIECES FROM DOUBLE POINT KNITTING NEEDLES
   F: from one needle—two 3¼" pieces with point
   G: from one needle—two 3¼" pieces with point
   H: from one needle—two 2⅜" pieces with point, 2¼" piece without point
   I: from one needle—two 2⅜" pieces with point, 2¼" piece without point

CUTTING
   1. Cut wood on lengthwise grain.
   2. Measure and saw each piece of needle as accurately as possible.

SANDING
   1. Sand bed base (A) and round the 4" sides.
   2. Line up the six 3¼" bed posts (D), (F), (G), and (E) and, using flat metal file, file flat ends until posts are equal in length; repeat for the four 2⅜" bed posts (H) and (I), and the two 2¼" posts (H) and (I).

ASSEMBLING HEADBOARD, diagram 1
   1. Draw a line across one 4" end of base (A) ⅛" from edge. Mark six dots on line, with first and sixth dots ¾" from 7" sides of (A) and four remaining dots evenly spaced ½" apart between first and sixth dots.
   2. With round metal file, drill six tiny holes on marked dots and put small amount of glue in each hole. Fit pointed ends of posts (D) and (E) into first and sixth holes ⅛" into base (A); fit pointed ends of posts (F) and (G) into second through fourth holes in same manner.
   3. Mark 4" horizontal bed post (B) with six dots as you did on base (A). With a toothpick, put small amount of liquid solder on dots and on flat top ends of vertical posts from step 2; wait five minutes, then reapply liquid solder to same dots. Match up vertical posts with dots on horizontal post (B), making sure vertical posts are evenly spaced, and glue together; let liquid solder dry one hour.

ASSEMBLING FOOTBOARD, diagram 1
   1. Draw a line across other end of base (A) ⅛" from edge. Mark six dots on line as you did for headboard.
   2. With round metal file, drill only four tiny holes on second, third, fourth, and fifth marked dots and put small amount of glue in each hole. Fit pointed ends of 2⅜" posts (H) and (I) into holes ⅛" into base (A). Put small amount of glue on remaining marked dots and glue flat ends of 2¼" posts (H) and (I) to dots.
   3. Mark 4" horizontal post (C) with six dots as you did on base (A). Put small amount of liquid solder on dots and on flat top ends of vertical posts from step 2; wait five minutes, then reapply liquid solder to same dots. Match up vertical posts with dots on horizontal post (C), making sure vertical posts are evenly spaced, and glue together; let liquid solder dry one hour.

ASSEMBLING CORNER POSTS, diagram 1
   1. When glue begins to set on headboard and footboard, prop assembly on deck of cards or

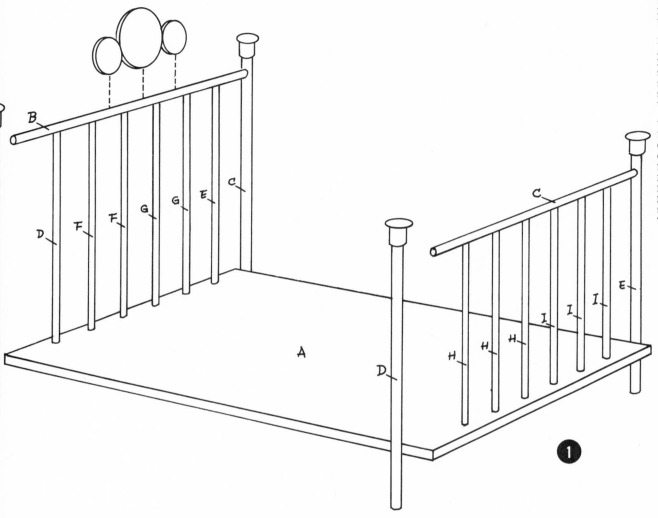

some ¾"-high object, with four corners of base (A) an equal distance from floor. Put small amount of liquid solder on ends of horizontal post (B) and on headposts (B) and (C) ¼" from top ends of (B) and (C); wait five minutes, then reapply liquid solder to same spots and glue headposts (B) and (C) to horizontal post (B). Glue headposts (B) and (C) to sides of base (A) at ends of marked line on (A). Use white resin glue for wood and metal.

2. Put small amount of liquid solder on ends of horizontal post (C) and on footposts (D) and (E) ¼" from top ends of (D) and (E); wait five minutes, then reapply liquid solder to same spots and glue footposts (D) and (E) to horizontal post (C). Glue footposts (D) and (E) to sides of base (A) at ends of marked line on (A). Change glue.

3. The decorative rings on horizontal post (B) can be any pleasing combination of metal buttons, dimestore finger rings, brass curtain rings, or a small pin or locket. Center rings on (B) and glue them with liquid solder, applied twice. Prop rings until glue begins to set.

4. Let entire assembly dry for 24 to 72 hours.

FINISHING

1. Cover up any signs of liquid solder with gold or brass paint. Paint short ends of base (A) with gold or brass paint for a distance of about ½"; paint sides of (A), too, if bedspread does not cover.

2. Spray entire bed with gold or brass paint, unless you were able to purchase brass-colored knitting needles.

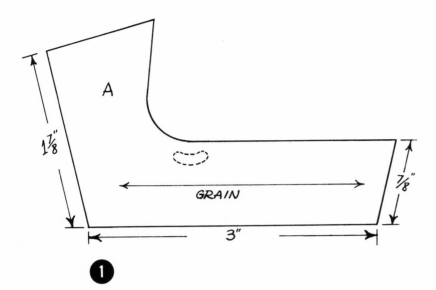

1

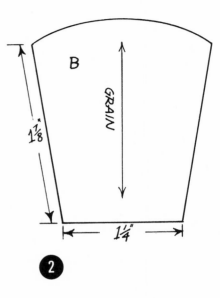

2

HOODED CRADLE
(Colonial bedroom)

Size: $2\frac{7}{8}''$W $\times$ $3\frac{1}{2}''$L $\times$ $3''$H

Wood: $\frac{3}{32}''$ balsa sheet, $\frac{1}{16}''$ balsa sheet

Suggested finish: maple

Basic tools and supplies, plus elastic band

Pieces from $\frac{3}{32}''$ balsa sheet
  A: two pieces from pattern (solid outline only), diagram 1
  B: piece from pattern, diagram 2
  C: piece from pattern, diagram 3
  D: $1\frac{1}{2}''$ × $3\frac{1}{16}''$ piece
  E: two pieces from pattern, diagram 4

Pieces from $\frac{1}{16}''$ balsa sheet
  F: piece from pattern, diagram 5
  G: piece from pattern, diagram 6

Cutting
  1. Cut wood on lengthwise grain except for cradle hood (G), which is cut on crosswise grain.
  2. With round metal file, drill tiny, kidney-shaped openings in cradle sides (A); see broken line in diagram 1 for placement of these openings, which are the cradle's hand grips.

Sanding and staining
  1. Sand wood.
  2. Round long curved edge of sides (A), and top curved edge of foot (C).
  3. Stain wood.

Assembly, diagram 7
  1. Glue sides (A) to side edges of head (B) and foot (C).
  2. Center and glue assembly from step 1 to bottom (D); the edges of (D) should extend slightly all the way around.
  3. Glue visor (F) between top corners of inside surface of sides (A).
  4. Glue hood (G) to top edges of sides (A), back (B), and visor (F), making sure back and side edges of hood are flush with outside surfaces of back and sides of cradle; the hood will overlap visor by $\frac{1}{4}''$ at the front. The hood will bend easily because it was cut on crosswise grain, and is thin. When glue begins to set, hold hood in place with elastic band until glue is completely dry.
  5. Glue rockers (E) to bottom surface of (D), with top straight edges centered and placed $\frac{1}{4}''$ in from head and foot.

Finishing
  Shellac, then varnish.

Variation: OPEN CRADLE

Do not cut visor (F) and hood (G). Cut back piece (B) $\frac{5}{8}''$ shorter at top and round this edge. Cut sides (A) $\frac{5}{8}''$ shorter at top slanted edge and make parallel to bottom edge. Round this new top edge.

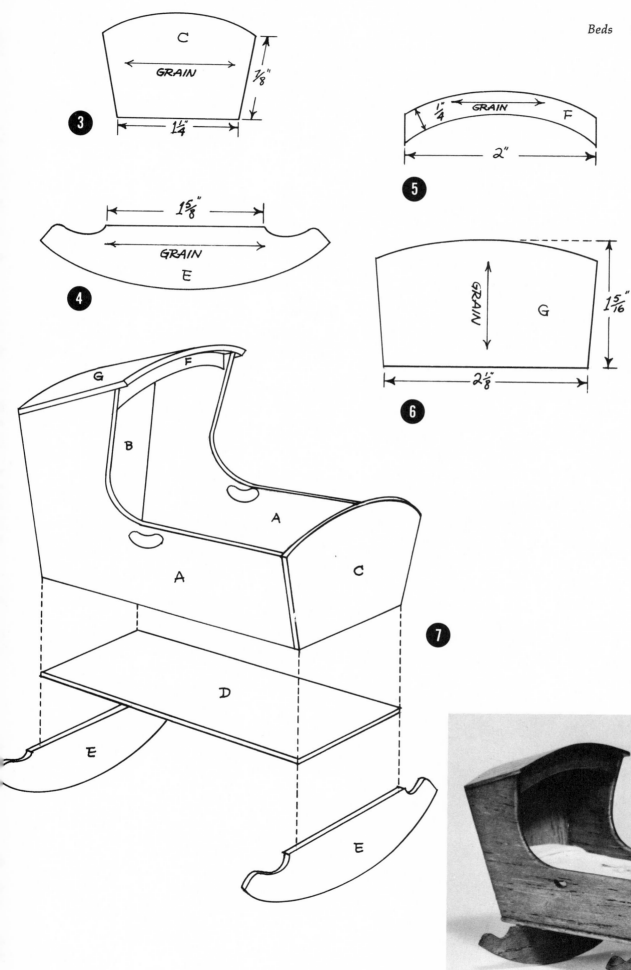

3 C — GRAIN — $1\frac{1}{4}''$ — $\frac{7}{8}''$

5 $\frac{1}{4}''$ — GRAIN — F — 2"

4 $1\frac{5}{8}''$ — GRAIN — E

6 GRAIN — G — $1\frac{5}{16}''$ — $2\frac{1}{8}''$

7 G F B A A C D E E

QUICK GUIDE TO
Supplies
Balsa wood, 27
Basic tools, 27
Staining, 34
Hardware, 29
Upholstery, 30

Method
Assembling, 35
Finishing, 36
Sanding, 34
Shellacking, 36
Varnishing, 36

Woodworking
Beveling, 38
Carving, 38
Cutting, 33
Drilling, 39
Marking, 31
Mitering, 39
Molding, 39
Scoring, 39
Turning, 37

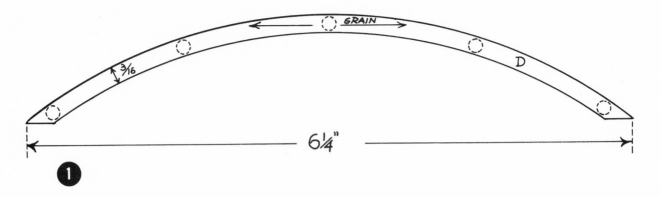

CURVED TESTER BED
(Colonial bedroom)

Size: 4⅝″W × 6¼″L × 6¼″H

Wood: ⅛″ balsa sheet, ⅛″ dowel, ¼″ sq. balsa strip, 4 artist's wooden brush handles (each 4″– 5″ long and ¼″ thick at widest circumference)

Suggested finish: maple stain or woodtone paint

Basic tools and supplies, plus nose pliers, 4 prongs (for holding rhinestones—optional), gold paint, 24 half-inch straight pins, heavy thread or string, 4 round beads, 4 oval beads

Pieces from ⅛″ balsa sheet
A: piece from pattern, diagram 1
B: two ½″ × 5¾″ pieces
C: ½″ × 4⅛″ piece
D: two pieces from pattern (solid outline only), diagram 1

Pieces from ⅛″ dowel
E: five 4¼″ pieces

Pieces from ¼″ sq. balsa strip
F: four 2″ pieces

Pieces from artist's brush handles
G: four 3⅛″ pieces

Cutting
1. Saw wood on lengthwise grain.
2. Try to buy cheap, short artist's brushes with unpainted handles. Remove metal from handles with nose pliers and discard brush. Measure 3⅛″ from thicker, bottom ends of handles and saw.

Sanding and staining
1. Sand wood.
2. Turn top and bottom corners of each post (F).
3. Sand away words from unpainted brush handles, if any. If handles are painted, you will spray them later with woodtone paint; don't try to remove paint.
4. Stain wood.

Assembly, diagram 2
1. Reinforce thicker ends of posts (G) with straight pins, and glue to posts (F).

2. Glue headboard (A) between two post assemblies from step 1 with bottom edge of (A) 1⅜" from floor.

3. Center and glue foot rail (C) between other two post assemblies from step 1 with bottom edge of (C) 1⅜" from floor.

4. For rope pegs, paint half-inch straight pins with woodtone paint. Insert 12 pins ½" apart into top edge of each side rail (B).

5. Center and glue each rail (B) to posts (F) of assembly from step 2 with bottom edges of (B) 1⅜" from floor. Dry in perpendicular position, propping if necessary. Repeat procedure for rails (B) and posts (F) of assembly from step 3.

6. Glue dowels (E) between tester sides (D) where indicated by circles in diagram 1.

7. Glue tester assembly from step 6 to top ends of posts (G).

FINISHING

1. Tie one end of heavy thread to a rope peg and lace rails (B), lacing loosely so you don't bend rails; see diagram 2.

2. If bed has been stained, shellac; the bed is fragile, so one coat is sufficient. Use steel wool to smooth headboard only. Varnish.

3. If you have not stained the bed, paint with woodtone paint.

4. For optional bed bolt covers, paint prongs gold and press two into each post (F) at foot of bed, where indicated by circles in diagram 2.

5. Make four bedpost finials with round and oval beads and paint with woodtone paint. After fabric canopy is attached, insert finials with straight pins through ends of testers (D) to tops of posts (G); see diagram 2.

Variation: CANOPY BED WITH SLATS

If you want bed slats instead of rope pegs and rope, cut three slats as directed for straight tester bed.

Variation: SINGLE CANOPY BED

To make a single-width curved tester bed, cut foot rail (C) 3" long. Make a new pattern for headboard (A) by shortening middle section by ⅝" and removing ¼" from each side edge. Adjust horizontal dowels (E) to fit new bed width. Cut rest of pieces the same.

STRAIGHT TESTER BED
(*Georgian bedroom*)

SIZE: 4⅝"W × 6¼"L × 7½"H

WOOD: ⅛" balsa sheet, 1/16" × ¼" balsa strip, ¼" sq. balsa strip, 4 artist's wooden brush handles (each 5"–6" long and ¼" thick at widest circumference)

SUGGESTED FINISH: mahogany stain or woodtone paint

BASIC TOOLS AND SUPPLIES, plus nose pliers, 4 prongs (for holding rhinestones—optional), gold paint

PIECES FROM ⅛" BALSA SHEET
A: piece from pattern, diagram 1
B: two ½" × 5¾" pieces
C: ½" × 4⅛" piece
D: three ⅜" × 4⅜" pieces

PIECES FROM 1/16" × ¼" BALSA STRIP
E: two 5¾" pieces
F: two 4⅝" pieces

PIECES FROM ¼" SQ. BALSA STRIP
G: four 2⅛" pieces

PIECES FROM ARTIST'S BRUSH HANDLES
H: four 5⅜" pieces

CUTTING

1. Cut wood on lengthwise grain.

2. Try to buy cheap, short artist's brushes with unpainted wooden handles. Remove metal from handles with nose pliers and discard brush. Measure 5⅜" from thicker, rounded ends of handles and cut.

SANDING AND STAINING

1. Sand wood.

2. Turn top and bottom corners of each post (G).

3. Sand away words from unpainted brush handles, if any. If handles are painted, you will spray them later with woodtone paint; don't try to remove paint.

4. Stain wood.

ASSEMBLY, diagram 2

1. Reinforce thicker ends of posts (H) with straight pins, and glue to posts (G).

2. Glue headboard (A) between two post assemblies from step 1 with bottom edge of (A) 1⅜″ from floor.

3. Center and glue foot rail (C) between other two post assemblies from step 1 with bottom edge of (C) 1⅜″ from floor.

4. Center and glue each side rail (B) to posts (G) of assembly from step 2 with bottom edges of (B) 1⅜″ from floor. Dry in perpendicular position, propping if necessary. Repeat procedure for rails (B) and posts (G) of assembly from step 3.

5. Glue together tester pieces (E) and (F) to form tester frame measuring 4⅝″ × 6¼″. Glue tester frame to top ends of posts (H).

6. Glue slats (D) between rails (B) at bottom edge of each rail, spacing slats evenly.

FINISHING

1. If bed has been stained, shellac. The bed is fragile, so one coat is sufficient. Use steel wool to smooth headboard only, then varnish.

2. If you have not stained the bed, paint with woodtone paint.

3. For optional bed bolt covers, paint prongs gold and press two into each post (G) where indicated by circles in diagram 2.

Variation: LOW POST BED

For low post bed, cut posts (G) at head of bed 3¼″ long and posts (G) at foot of bed 2½″ long. Eliminate posts (H) and tester pieces (E) and (F). Cut rest of pieces the same. Glue top edge of headboard (A) flush with top edges of head posts (G); bottom edges of (A) and foot rail (C) are 1¼″ from floor.

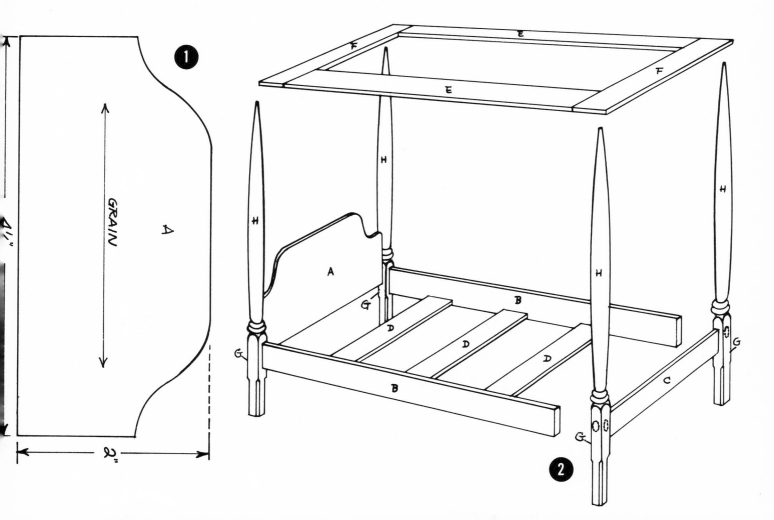

CHAPTER *14* *Benches*

DRESSING TABLE BENCH
(*Georgian bedroom*)

SIZE: 1¼"W × 1⅞"L × 1½"H

WOOD: ⅛" × ¼" balsa strip, ⅛" sq. balsa strip

SUGGESTED FINISH: mahogany

BASIC TOOLS AND SUPPLIES, plus 1¾" × 2⅜" fabric, 1¼" × 1⅞" cotton padding, 1¼" × 1⅞" cardboard

PIECES FROM ⅛" × ¼" BALSA STRIP
  A: two 1⅝" pieces
  B: two 1" pieces

PIECES FROM ⅛" SQ. BALSA STRIP
  C: four 1⅜" pieces

CUTTING
  Cut wood on lengthwise grain.

SANDING AND STAINING
  1. Sand wood.
  2. Stain wood.

ASSEMBLY, diagram 1
  1. Glue each of sides (A) between a pair of legs (C), with top edges and front surfaces of all pieces flush.
  2. Glue sides (B) between each of the two assemblies from step 1, with top edges and outside surfaces of all pieces flush.

FINISHING
  1. Shellac; one coat is sufficient. Smooth with steel wool very carefully.
  2. Varnish.
  3. Cut a piece of fabric following outline of bench seat, but add ¼" seam allowance on all four sides. Cut one or two pieces of cotton padding and a cardboard base, also following outline of bench seat. Place fabric right side down on your work surface, then padding on top of fabric and cardboard on top of padding. Glue fabric side seams, then front and back seams, to cardboard and glue cushion in place.

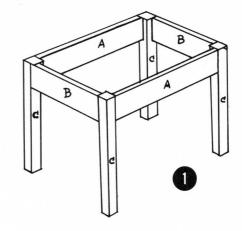

SHAKER BENCH
(*Colonial keeping room*)

SIZE: 1"W × 5"L × 1½"H

WOOD: ⅛" balsa sheet

SUGGESTED FINISH: pine

BASIC TOOLS AND SUPPLIES

PIECES FROM ⅛" BALSA SHEET
  A: 1" × 5" piece
  B: two pieces from pattern (solid outline only), diagram 1
  C: ⅜" × 4⅞" piece

HIGH STOOL
(*Victorian kitchen*)

Size: ⅞″W × 2″H

Wood: 3/16″ balsa sheet, 3/16″ dowel, ⅛″ dowel

Suggested finish: oak

Basic tools and supplies, plus compass

Piece from 3/16″ balsa sheet
   A: circle ⅞″ in diameter

Pieces from 3/16″ dowel
   B: four 1⅞″ pieces

Pieces from ⅛″ dowel
   C: four ½″ pieces

Cutting
Cut tops of legs on angle of about 10°, making sure angle is the same for each leg.

Sanding and staining
1. Sand wood.
2. Round top edge of seat (A).
3. Round bottom edge of legs (B).
4. Stain wood.

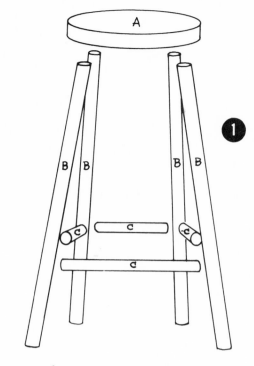

Assembly, diagram 1
1. Glue two legs (B) to bottom of seat (A), directly opposite each other and 1/16″ in from edge of seat; slant legs outward in same direction as seat's grain of wood. Repeat for other two legs.
2. Glue a rung (C) between two legs (B) 15/16″ from floor; repeat for other three rungs.

Finishing
Shellac, then varnish.

QUICK GUIDE TO
Supplies
Balsa wood, 27
Basic tools, 27
Hardware, 29
Upholstery, 30

Method
Assembling, 35
Finishing, 36
Sanding, 34
Shellacking, 36
Staining, 34
Varnishing, 36

Woodworking
Beveling, 38
Carving, 38
Cutting, 33
Drilling, 39
Marking, 31
Mitering, 39
Molding, 39
Scoring, 39
Turning, 37

Cutting
1. Cut wood on lengthwise grain.
2. See directions for cutting decorative edges on legs (B). Cut out ⅛″ × ¼″ rectangles from legs; see broken line, diagram 1.
3. Cut away rectangles measuring ⅛″ (vertical edge) × 3/16″ (horizontal edge) from top corners of stretcher (C).

Sanding and staining
Sand wood, then stain.

Assembly, diagram 2
1. Insert stretcher (C) through cut-out rectangles in legs (B), gluing ⅛″ cut-out edges of stretcher, if necessary.
2. Center and glue assembly from step 1 to underside of bench top (A). When glue begins to set, place suitable weight on top.

Finishing
Shellac, then varnish.

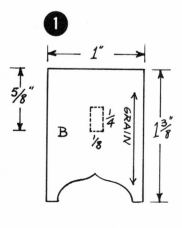

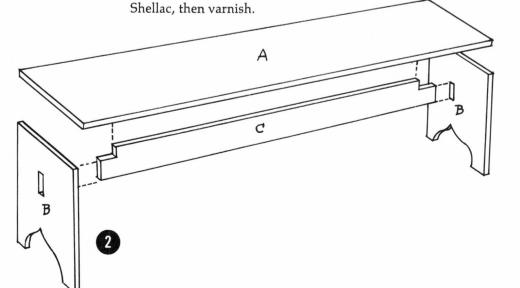

FIRESIDE BENCH
(*Georgian library*)

SIZE: 1¾"W × 3⅜"L × 2⅛"H

WOOD: ⅛" balsa sheet, 1/16" balsa sheet, 1/16" × ⅛" balsa strip

SUGGESTED FINISH: mahogany

BASIC TOOLS AND SUPPLIES, plus 2" × 3½" fine mesh nylon net in neutral shade

PIECES FROM ⅛" BALSA SHEET
 A: four pieces from pattern, diagram 1
 B: two 3/16" × 1⅜" pieces

PIECES FROM 1/16" BALSA SHEET
 C: two 3/16" × 1⅜" pieces
 D: two 3/16" × 1⅜" pieces
 E: two 9/16" × 1⅜" pieces

PIECES FROM 1/16" × ⅛" BALSA STRIP
 F: four 2¾" pieces
 G: four 1⅜" pieces
 H: two 3⅜" pieces
 I: two 1⅝" pieces

CUTTING
1. Cut wood on lengthwise grain.
2. Cut nylon net to measure 2" × 3½".

SANDING AND STAINING
1. Sand wood, making sure legs (A) are identical in length and shape.
2. Stain wood.

ASSEMBLY, diagram 3
1. Make two rectangular frames from two pieces (F) and two pieces (G) by gluing 1/16" sides of pieces (F) to the 1/16" side edges (G); each frame is 1⅝" × 2¾".
2. Glue nylon net between two frames from step 1, pulling it taut and making sure frames are lined up evenly. When glue dries, trim away excess fabric.

3. Glue legs (A) on their ⅛" side edges, with curved part turning outward, to ends of pieces (F) 1¼" from floor. Glue two legs to one side first and let dry, then glue two legs to other side; some propping may be necessary.
4. Glue ⅛" long side edge of one piece (B) to side edge of piece (G) between legs (A), with outside edge of (B) and outside edge of legs (A) flush and measuring 1⅝" in total width. Repeat for other pieces (B).
5. Glue ⅛" surface of one molding (I) to ⅛" outside edge of piece (B) and two legs (A). Repeat for other molding (I).
6. Glue ⅛" surface of one molding (H) to ⅛" long edge of seat frame, pair of legs (A), and moldings (I). Repeat for other molding (H). Check that enclosed legs are straight and touch the floor evenly. Make sure that the seat is level.
7. Make sure pieces (E) fit perfectly between top curves of legs (A). Sand sides of pieces (E), if necessary, so legs (A) are perfectly parallel to each other. Glue each piece (C) to 1⅜" edge of each piece (E), and glue each piece (D) to other 1⅜" edge of each piece (E), so that 1/16" edges of (C) and (D) are flush with surface of (E); see diagram 2. Let dry completely because these assemblies are slightly curved when glued in place.
8. Glue short edges of one assembly from step 7 and attach between legs (A) so piece (D) is ⅛" up from bench seat and surfaces of assembly (E—C) are flush with inside and top edges of (A). Hold piece (E) in place with hands and bend slightly while glue is setting to conform to top curve of legs. Repeat procedure for other assembly from step 7.

FINISHING
1. Shellac, then varnish.
2. You may need to darken nylon net to make it more visible. Oak stain is the color of caning, but you can use a darker stain or paint.

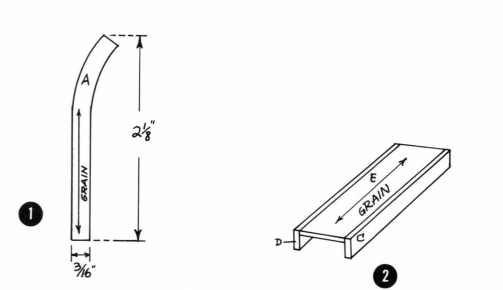

1

2

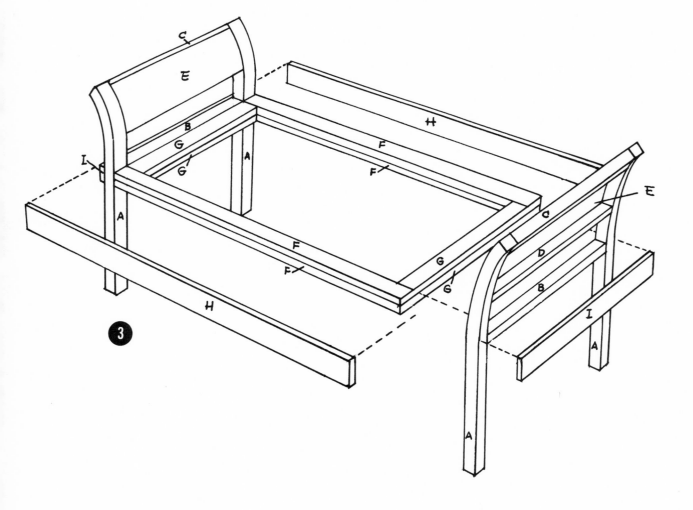

3

CHAPTER *15* *Bookcases*

SECRETARY BOOKCASE
(Georgian hall)

SIZE: 3½"W × 1"D × 4½"H

WOOD: ⅛" balsa sheet, ³⁄₃₂" balsa sheet, ¹⁄₃₂" balsa sheet, ¹⁄₁₆" quarter-round basswood strip

SUGGESTED FINISH: mahogany

BASIC TOOLS AND SUPPLIES, plus ³⁄₁₆" × 6" embossed paper strip, round bead, oblong bead, woodtone paint

PIECES FROM ⅛" BALSA SHEET
   A: piece from pattern, diagram 1
   B: 1" × 3½" piece
   C: 1" × 3½" piece

PIECES FROM ³⁄₃₂" BALSA SHEET
   D: two 1³⁄₁₆" × 3¼" pieces
   E: two 1¹¹⁄₁₆" × 3¼" pieces
   F: 3³⁄₁₆" × 3⁷⁄₁₆" piece
   G: ³⁄₁₆" × 3⅜" piece
   H: two ³⁄₁₆" × 1³⁄₁₆" pieces

PIECES FROM ¹⁄₃₂" BALSA SHEET
   I: two 1¼" × 2¾" pieces

·PIECE FROM ¹⁄₁₆" QUARTER-ROUND WOOD STRIP
   J: 4½" piece

CUTTING
   1. Cut wood on lengthwise grain.
   2. Piece (J) is cut later. If you can't find quarter-round basswood for (J), use ¹⁄₁₆" × ⅛" balsa strip.
   3. For pediment (A), cut a curved line.

SANDING AND STAINING
   1. Sand wood.
   2. Bevel front and side edges of top (B) and bottom (C).
   3. Bevel all four edges of door panels (I).
   4. Stain wood.

ASSEMBLY, diagram 2
   1. Center and glue door panels (I) to doors (E), and place suitable weight on top.

2. Glue sides (D) to side edges of back piece (F) so back edges of (D) and back surface of (F) are flush; (F) should be taller than (D) at the top by ³⁄₁₆".

3. Glue assembly from step 2 to bottom (C), with beveled edge of (C) right side up and back edge flush with surface of back (F).

4. Glue one door panel assembly from step 1 to front edge of a side (D) so side edge of panel (E) is flush with outside surface of (D); repeat for other door panel assembly. Do not glue door panel assemblies together.

5. Paint embossed paper strip with woodtone paint. When dry, cut paper to fit pieces (G) and (H), and glue to (G) and (H) to resemble fretwork. Glue bottom and a side edge of (H) to top edge of side (D) and back piece (F); repeat for other piece (H). Glue bottom edge of (G) to top edges of doors (E) and side edges of (H).

6. Glue bookcase top (B) so back edge is flush with outside surface of back (F) and beveled edges are on bottom.

7. Cut molding (J) in half and place one piece along one slanted edge of pediment (A) so the two flat surfaces of (J) are flush with both surface and top slanted edge of (A). Cut each end of (J) on a slant to match slant of pediment; see detail in diagram 2. Repeat procedure for other half of molding (J) and other slanted edge of pediment (A).

8. Glue bottom edge of pediment (A) to

bookcase top (B) $\frac{1}{16}''$ from front edge of (B) and extending $\frac{1}{8}''$ on each side of (B).

FINISHING

1. Shellac, then varnish.

2. For carved finial, paint beads and head of straight pin with woodtone paint and insert between broken pediment; see diagram 2.

This bookcase is designed to be placed on top of the slant top desk.

Variation: SECRETARY BOOKCASE WITH OPEN DOORS

To turn this piece of furniture into a display unit for books and ornaments, do not glue piece (G) to doors (E), make the doors open out by following directions under hardware for straight pin hinges; insert pins through pieces (C) and (G) into doors (E). Trim doors so they fit flush with front edge of sides (D). Make two $\frac{3}{4}'' \times$ $3\frac{3}{8}''$ shelves and glue inside so they're level and spaced evenly. For door handles, paint two small beads and two pinheads with woodtone paint and glue to doors near center.

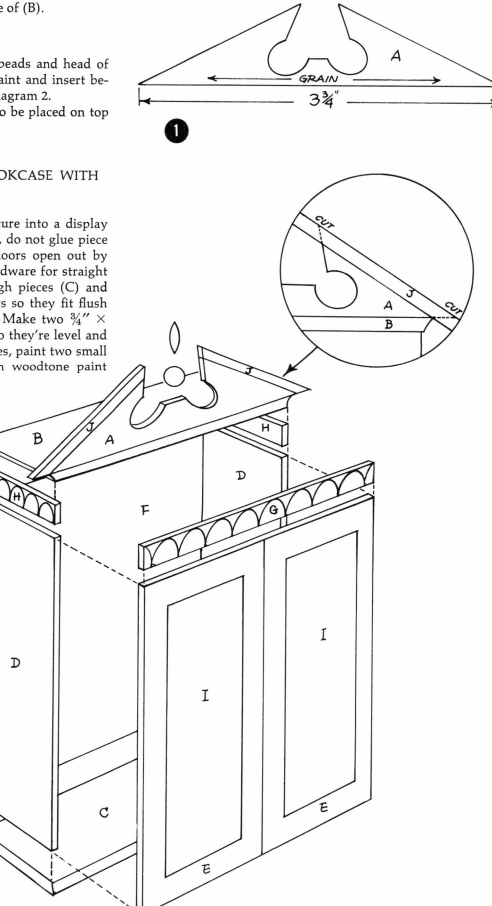

BREAKFRONT
(*Georgian library*)

Size: 6″W × 1½″D × 7″H

Wood: ⅛″ balsa sheet, ³⁄₃₂″ balsa sheet, ¹⁄₃₂″ balsa sheet, ¹⁄₁₆″ × ¼″ balsa strip

Suggested finish: mahogany

Basic tools and supplies, plus 10 sewing loops, gold paint, 2 pairs of pliers, ⅛″-wide brown charting tape, acetate

Pieces from ⅛″ balsa sheet
- A: piece from pattern (solid outline only), diagram 1
- B: piece from pattern (solid outline only), diagram 1
- C: piece from pattern (solid outline only), diagram 1
- D: 3″ × 3″ piece

Pieces from ³⁄₃₂″ balsa sheet
- E: 3⅝″ × 5⁷⁄₁₆″ piece
- F: two 1⅛″ × 3⅝″ pieces
- G: two 1″ × 5⁷⁄₁₆″ pieces
- H: 3″ × 5⁹⁄₁₆″ piece
- I: two 1³⁄₁₆″ × 3″ pieces
- J: two 1½″ × 3″ pieces
- K: six 1″ × 1³⁄₁₆″ pieces

Pieces from ¹⁄₃₂″ balsa sheet
- L: four ⁹⁄₁₆″ × 2¾″ pieces
- M: two ⁹⁄₁₆″ × 1⅛″ pieces
- N: two 1⅛″ × 1¹⁵⁄₁₆″ pieces

Pieces from ¹⁄₁₆″ × ¼″ balsa strip
- O: four 3⅝″ pieces
- P: four 1″ pieces

Cutting
1. Cut wood on lengthwise grain except for pieces (E), (H), and (J), which are cut on crosswise grain.
2. For top (A), cut away ⅛″ along back edge as indicated by broken line in diagram 1.

Sanding and staining
1. Sand wood.
2. Bevel front and side edges of top (A) and bottom (C); but do not bevel ⅛″ sides of the projection on these pieces.
3. Bevel four edges of drawers (L) and (M).
4. Cut off four corners of door panels (N) in a straight line, making sure you cut equal amount from each corner; see detail in diagram 2. Curve cut corners with dowel sandpaper file and bevel all straight and curved edges on panels (N).
5. Stain wood.

Assembling top shelf section, diagram 2
1. Glue surface of sides (F) at long edges to side edges of back piece (E).
2. Divide inside of back piece (E) into three

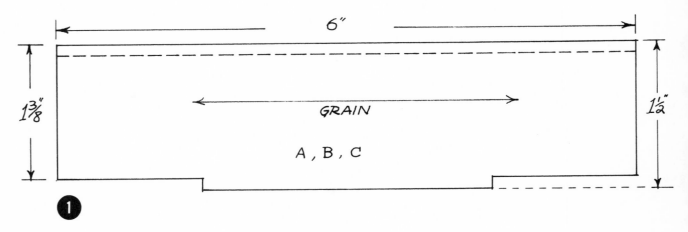

6″

1³⁄₈″

1½″

GRAIN

A, B, C

1

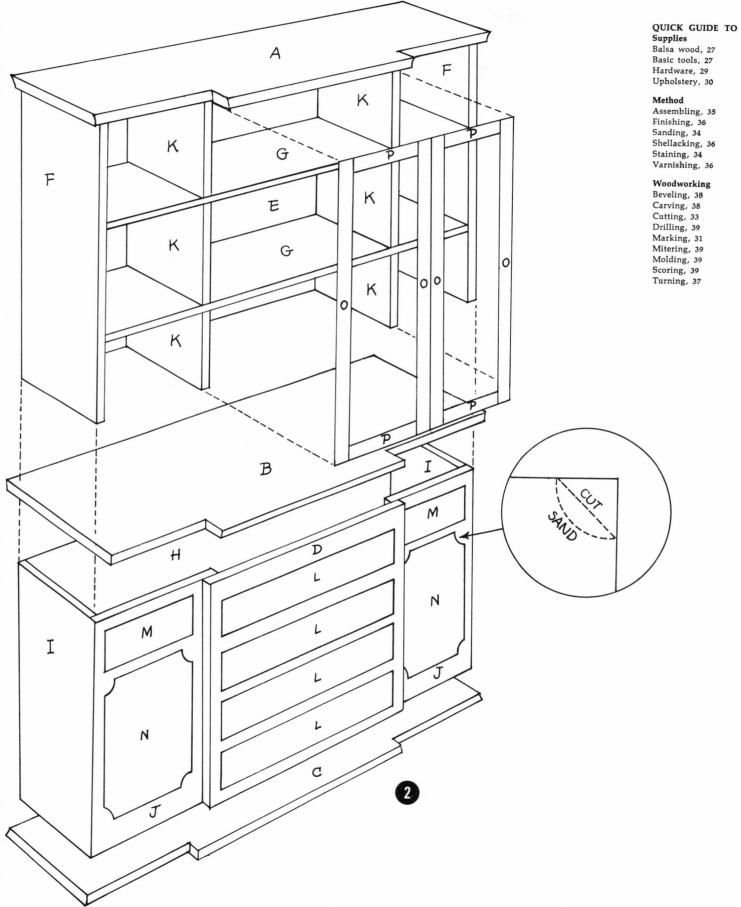

equal parts vertically by putting pencil dots 1 3/16″ apart; repeat for side pieces (F). Glue shelves (G) along pencil dots, making sure they are level and evenly spaced, and perfectly perpendicular to back (E).

3. Center and glue top piece (A) to top edges of assembly from step 1, with beveled edges of (A) on bottom and back edge flush with back surface of back (E).

4. Divider pieces (K) create the three-inch center of top shelf section indicated by 1/8″ projection of piece (A). Sand two dividers along one-inch edges to fit between top piece (A) and top shelf (G); apply glue to dividers along one-inch edges and insert with dividers measuring exactly three inches apart, from their outside surfaces. Repeat procedure for other four dividers (K).

5. For center section doors, cut a 3″ × 3 5/8″ piece of acetate. Make six panes for each door by putting charting tape on acetate horizontally at same level as shelves (G), 1 3/16″ apart, and vertically 3/4″ in from side edges of acetate. (If you can't buy charting tape, use 1/32″ × 1/8″ stained balsa wood strips and glue in place; or paint on panes by hand with fast-drying woodtone paint, using masking tape as guide for making straight lines.)

6. Glue two pieces (O) at longer side edges of acetate; glue other two pieces (O) at center of acetate parallel to longer side edges.

7. Glue pieces (P) between pieces (O) at shorter side edges of acetate to form two doors. Place suitable weight on top of doors.

Assembling bottom drawer and cabinet section, diagram 2

1. Glue drawers (L) to front center piece (D), with grain of wood (D) running lengthwise as does grain of wood of drawers; leave 1/8″ between drawers, 1/8″ between drawers and side edges of piece (D), and 3/16″ between top and bottom edges of (D). Place suitable weight on top of drawers.

2. Glue drawers (M) to front side pieces (J), leaving 3/16″ between drawers (M) and top edges of pieces (J), 1/8″ between drawers and outside edges of (J), and 1/4″ between drawers and inside edges of (J). Center and glue door panels (N) between drawers (M) and bottom edges of (J), aligning sides of (N) with sides of (M). Place suitable weight on drawers and door panels.

3. Glue assembly from step 1 to assemblies from step 2, with inside side edges of pieces (J) 1/8″ in and behind side edges of piece (D); assembly is 3″ × 5 3/4″.

4. Glue assembly from step 3 to front edges of side pieces (I).

5. With beveled surface of bottom (C) right side up, glue assembly from step 4 to it so (C) extends 1/8″ on sides, 1/16″ on front, and the back edge is flush with back edges of (I).

6. Put glue on bottom and side edges of back piece (H) and glue to assembly from step 5; the back surface of (H) should be flush with back edges of (I).

7. Center and glue middle piece (B) to assembly from step 6 so back edge of (B) is flush with back piece (H) and (B) extends 1/8″ on sides and 1/16″ on front. Place suitable weight on top of bottom drawer and cabinet section.

8. Center and glue top shelf section to bottom drawer and cabinet section with back pieces of both sections flush. Place suitable weight on top of breakfront.

Finishing

1. Shellac, using one coat of shellac where surface is difficult to steel wool. Shellac wood frames of center section doors separately.

2. Varnish. (Varnish wood frames of center section doors separately.)

3. Fill shelves (G) with books or small objets d'art, such as vases and compotes made from beads and plates made from buttons. Put glue on top and bottom edges of center section door assembly and on side edges of dividers (K); glue doors in place.

4. Make drawer handles out of sewing loops and attach. The two handles on each drawer (L) are placed 1/2″ from sides and centered between top and bottom; the handle on each drawer (M) is centered.

Variation: OPEN BREAKFRONT

A less formal breakfront or china cabinet can be made by eliminating shelf dividers (K) and door pieces (O), (P), and acetate.

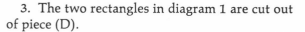

CHAPTER *16* *Chairs*

BALLOON BACK CHAIR
(Victorian dining room)

SIZE: 1⅝″W × 1½″D × 3⅛″H

WOOD: ³⁄₁₆″ balsa sheet, ⅛″ balsa sheet, ³⁄₃₂″ balsa sheet, ³⁄₁₆″ sq. balsa strip

SUGGESTED FINISH: walnut

BASIC TOOLS AND SUPPLIES, plus 4″ diameter coffee can, wide elastic bands or masking tape, 2 half-inch straight pins, woodtone paint, ³⁄₁₆″-thick cotton padding, 3″ sq. of fabric, soutache braid, dye or felt tip pen.

PIECE FROM ³⁄₁₆″ balsa sheet
   A: piece from pattern (solid outline only), diagram 1

PIECES FROM ⅛″ BALSA SHEET
   B: piece from pattern (solid outline only), diagram 2
   C: two pieces from pattern, diagram 3

PIECE FROM ³⁄₃₂″ BALSA SHEET
   D: piece from pattern (solid outline only), diagram 1

PIECES FROM ³⁄₁₆″ SQ. BALSA STRIP
   E: two 1⁷⁄₁₆″ pieces

PIECES FROM COTTON PADDING
   A: two pieces from pattern (solid outline only), diagram 1

PIECES FROM FABRIC
   A: piece from pattern (dotted outline only), diagram 1
   B: piece from pattern (dotted outline only), diagram 2

CUTTING WOOD
   1. Cut wood on lengthwise grain. Cut a curved line, which applies to all pieces except (E).
   2. Base (D) may be made from 2 pieces of ³⁄₃₂″ balsa sheet glued together to obtain required ³⁄₁₆″ thickness.

   3. The two rectangles in diagram 1 are cut out of piece (D).

CUTTING COTTON PADDING AND FABRIC
   1. Cut the four pieces, cutting fabric crosswise.

SANDING AND STAINING
   1. Sand wood.
   2. Round curved edges of chair back (B) slightly. Soak (B) in warm water for five minutes, then bend carefully around coffee can with grain running vertically and secure in place with elastic bands or masking tape; don't let elastic bands indent the soft, wet wood. Dry at room temperature or in low oven for ten minutes. When dry, cut out along broken line in diagram 2 and sand edges.
   3. Stain wood, except piece (A).

ASSEMBLY, diagram 4
   1. Carefully cut out two ⅛″ × ¼″ rectangles from base (D), as indicated by broken lines in diagram 1. Glue legs (C) into these cut-outs, with top edges of (C) flush with top surface of (D).
   2. Glue legs (E) at each corner of back edge of base (D), with top edges of (E) flush with top surface of (D). Reinforce each leg (E) with straight pins, pushing pin from back surface of (E) into back edge of (D). Paint pinhead with woodtone paint to match stain. Make sure all legs touch the floor and the base is level.
   3. Glue bottom edges of chair back (B) to top edges of legs (E). When glue begins to set, tilt back (B) at a slight angle. Back (B) will not be secure until upholstered seat frame is glued in place.

FINISHING
   1. Shellac, then varnish.
   2. For seat (A), place fabric (A) right side down on work surface and place cotton padding (A) on fabric. Put glue on front, side, and back edges of seat (A) and place it on cotton padding. Glue fabric to edges of (A) as follows: Gather

fabric at four corners (do not fold) and hold in place with straight pins while glue dries; when dry, trim excess fabric from edges of seat along bottom surface of (A). Glue upholstered seat assembly to platform (D) and back (B). Dye

and glue soutache braid to raw edges of fabric along front, side, and back edges of (D).

3. Glue fabric (B) to back (B) as indicated by dotted line in diagram 2. Cover raw edges with soutache braid following outline of fabric.

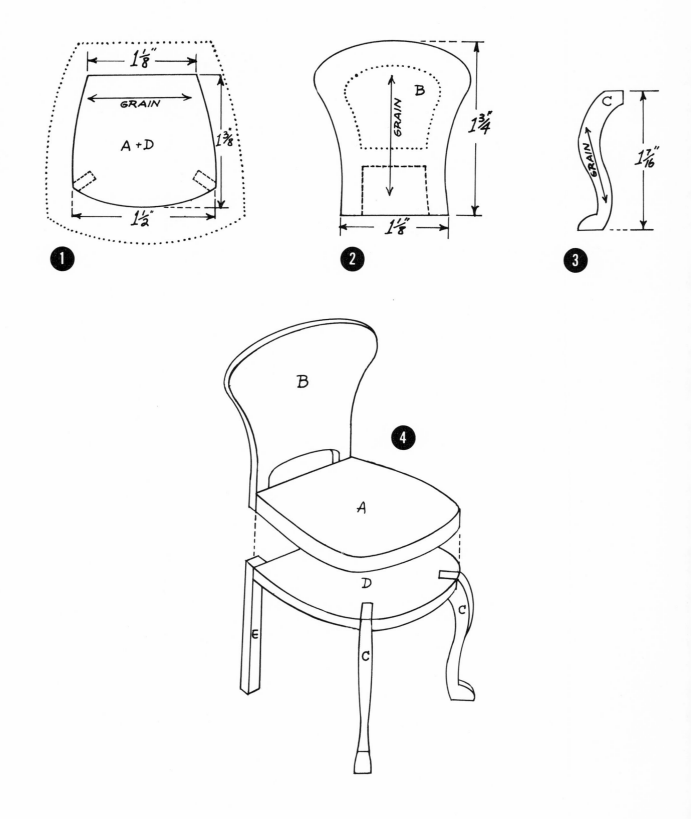

BELTER PARLOR CHAIR
(Victorian living room)

SIZE: 2⅛″W × 1⅞″D × 4¼″H

WOOD: ³⁄₁₆″ balsa sheet, ⅛″ balsa sheet

SUGGESTED FINISH: walnut

BASIC TOOLS AND SUPPLIES, plus small frozen orange juice can, wide elastic bands or masking tape, embossed paper picture frame, woodtone paint, oaktag cardboard, ³⁄₁₆″-thick cotton padding, ⅛ yard fabric, soutache braid, dye or felt tip pen, embroidery floss

PIECE FROM ³⁄₁₆″ BALSA SHEET
   A: piece from pattern (solid outline only), diagram 1

PIECES FROM ⅛″ BALSA SHEET
   B: two pieces from pattern (solid outline only), diagram 2
   C: piece from pattern (solid outline only), diagram 3
   D: two pieces from pattern, diagram 4
   E: two pieces from pattern, diagram 5

PIECE FROM OAKTAG CARDBOARD
   C: piece from pattern (dotted curved outline to solid sloped outline), diagram 3

PIECES FROM COTTON PADDING
   B: two pieces from pattern (solid curved outline plus dotted outline), diagram 2
   C: two pieces from pattern (dotted curved outline to solid sloped outline), diagram 3

PIECES FROM FABRIC
   A: piece from pattern (solid curved outline plus dotted outline), diagram 1
   C: piece from pattern (dotted outline only), diagram 3
   C: piece from pattern (solid outline only), diagram 3

CUTTING WOOD
1. Cut wood on lengthwise grain except for piece (C), which is cut on crosswise grain.
2. Base (A) may be made from two pieces of ³⁄₃₂″ balsa sheet glued together to obtain ³⁄₁₆″ thickness.
3. The four rectangles on piece (A) are cut out later.
4. Glue together two ⅛″ pieces (B) to form chair seat ¼″ thick; or you may cut one piece for seat (B) out of ¼″ balsa sheet.
5. For legs (D) and (E), cut a curved line.

CUTTING OAKTAG, COTTON PADDING, AND FABRIC
Cut the eight pieces, cutting fabric crosswise.

SANDING AND STAINING
1. Sand wood.
2. Round curved edges of chair back (C) slightly. Soak (C) in warm water for five minutes, then bend carefully around frozen orange juice can with grain running vertically and secure in place with elastic bands or masking tape; don't let elastic bands indent the soft, wet wood. Dry at room temperature or in low oven for ten minutes.
3. Stain wood.

ASSEMBLING AND FINISHING CHAIR BASE, diagram 6
1. Carefully cut out four ⅛″ × ³⁄₁₆″ rectangles from base (A), as indicated by broken lines in diagram 1. Glue legs (D) into cut-outs on straight edge of (A), with top edges of (D) flush with top surface of (A), and the long, ⅛″ edges of (D) curving out at top and in near bottom. Glue legs (E) into cut-outs on curved edge of (A) in the same manner; the long, ⅛″ edges of (E) curve out.
2. Shellac assembly from step 1, then smooth legs with steel wool very carefully.
3. Varnish assembly from step 1.

FINISHING CHAIR BACK
1. Shellac all surfaces of chair back (C), then varnish all surfaces of chair back (C).
2. Cut three corners of the embossed paper picture frame so they fit together nicely around top curved edge of chair back (C), and trim if necessary. Place one embossed paper corner at top of curved edge and two corners on each side of curved edge; glue in place, using a few

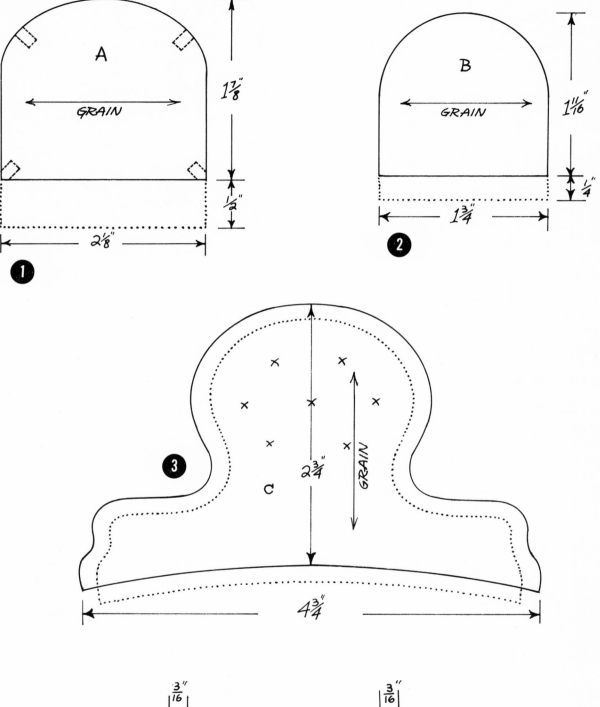

A

GRAIN

$1\frac{7}{8}"$

$\frac{1}{2}"$

$2\frac{1}{8}"$

1

B

GRAIN

$1\frac{11}{16}"$

$\frac{1}{4}"$

$1\frac{3}{4}"$

2

3

C

GRAIN

$2\frac{3}{4}"$

$4\frac{3}{4}"$

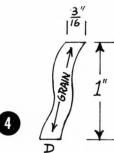

$\frac{3}{16}"$

GRAIN

$1"$

4

D

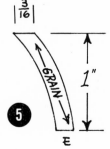

$\frac{3}{16}"$

GRAIN

$1"$

5

E

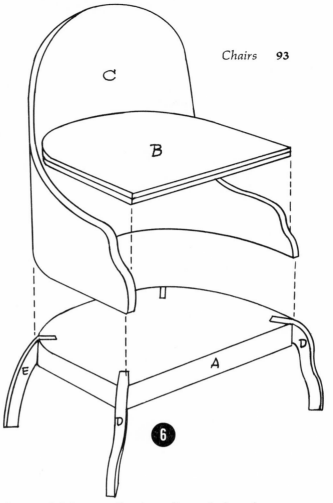

straight pins to hold paper until glue begins to set. Paint embossed paper with woodtone paint to match stain.

3. Glue fabric (C) that was cut from dotted line pattern as follows: Put small amount of glue along curved edge of fabric (not sloping bottom edge) and glue to outside of chair back (C), beginning ³⁄₁₆″ down from top curved edge; smooth out fabric over curved arms as much as possible without breaking arms. Put glue along molded bottom edge of chair back (C) and turn ³⁄₁₆″ of fabric (C) under bottom edge of chair back and glue; be sure fabric is smooth and taut.

4. Dye soutache braid to match fabric. Glue braid to raw edges of fabric from step 4, following contour of curved edge; turn braid ends under bottom edge of chair back and glue.

Assembling and finishing chair, diagram 6

1. Glue chair base assembly to chair back assembly: Bottom edge of (C) is glued to curved edge of (A), and outside surface of (C) is flush with curved edge of (A). This may require some refitting and re-gluing.

2. For carving on base (A), glue 2″ piece of embossed paper picture frame to straight edge of (A) between legs (D); paint embossed paper with woodtone paint to match stain.

3. Fit oaktag (C) to inside surface of chair back (C) so a ³⁄₁₆″ curved edge of back (C) shows evenly; you may have to trim oaktag. With oaktag on work surface, put small amount of glue along sloped bottom edge of oaktag and place two pieces of cotton padding (C) on top. Put small amount of glue along wrong side of sloped bottom edge of fabric (C)—cut from solid line pattern—and put fabric on top of padding right side up. You may have to secure these bottom edges further with needle and thread. Turn assembly over so oaktag is on top. Put glue along curved edge of oaktag and glue the ³⁄₁₆″ curved edge of fabric to back of oaktag. To facilitate gluing, make tiny cuttings on edges of seam allowance, especially at narrow curved portions of oaktag. Glue fabric as smoothly and tautly as possible because when oaktag assembly is put in place, it will be curved.

4. Mark fabric (C) with straight pins for placement of French embroidery knots made to resemble the buttons used on heavily tufted furniture. Embroidery floss should match fabric. To make one French knot: Knot one end of embroidery floss and stitch from oaktag back to front of fabric, pulling needle and thread completely through; wind floss around tip of needle twice and return needle from fabric front to oaktag back as near as possible to the same hole. Repeat procedure for rest of French knots.

5. Glue entire oaktag assembly to inside surface of chair back (C), making sure a ³⁄₁₆″ curved edge of (C) shows evenly.

6. Place both pieces of cotton padding (B) on top surface of chair seat (B) so padding overlaps straight front edge. Place fabric (A) right side up on top of padding so curved edge of fabric overlaps ³⁄₁₆″ along curved edge of padding and straight edge of fabric overlaps ½″ along straight edge of seat. Glue fabric to bottom surface of seat ¼″ from straight front edge; glue curved edge of fabric to curved edge of seat, making sure fabric is smooth and taut; turn in and fold fabric at two corners and glue to side edges of seat. Glue seat assembly to top surface of base (A) and to bottom edge of chair back assembly so seat fits snugly.

Variation: OVAL PARLOR CHAIR

A typical Victorian parlor chair may be made with the same directions by eliminating embossed paper carving.

LADDERBACK CHAIR
(Colonial dining room)

SIZE: $1\frac{1}{2}$"W × $1\frac{3}{8}$"D × $3\frac{3}{8}$"H

WOOD: $\frac{3}{32}$" balsa sheet, $\frac{1}{16}$" corrugated balsa, $\frac{3}{16}$" dowel, $\frac{1}{8}$" dowel, $\frac{1}{16}$" × $\frac{1}{4}$" balsa strip

SUGGESTED FINISH: maple

BASIC TOOLS AND SUPPLIES

PIECE FROM $\frac{3}{32}$" BALSA SHEET
 A: piece from pattern (solid outline only), diagram 1

PIECE FROM $\frac{1}{16}$" CORRUGATED BALSA
 B: piece from pattern (solid outline only), diagram 1

PIECES FROM $\frac{3}{16}$" DOWEL
 C: two $3\frac{3}{8}$" pieces
 D: two $1\frac{5}{8}$" pieces

PIECES FROM $\frac{1}{8}$" DOWEL
 E: three $1\frac{1}{8}$" pieces
 F: four 1" pieces

PIECES FROM $\frac{1}{16}$" × $\frac{1}{4}$" BALSA STRIP
 G: three $1\frac{1}{8}$" pieces

CUTTING
 1. Cut wood on lengthwise grain except for piece (B), which is cut on crosswise grain.
 2. Cut chair seat bottom (A) on lengthwise grain as directed so grain of seat runs from side to side.
 3. For chair seat top (B), buy corrugated balsa wood with the narrowest possible ridges so it will resemble a woven rush seat. Cut corrugated balsa on crosswise grain so grain of seat runs from front to back; cut pieces indicated by broken lines later. If you can't find corrugated balsa wood, use $\frac{1}{8}$" balsa sheet for entire seat (A and B), and score the wood.

SANDING AND STAINING
 1. Sand wood, except for seat (B).
 2. For back legs (C), slant top edges of dowels at about a 45° angle with emery board file, curving slanted edge slightly; see detail in diagram 4.
 3. Round top edges of front legs (D).
 4. For each chair slat (G), cut off in a straight line an equal amount from each corner of the top edge; curve these lines with dowel sand-

paper file. Sand two or more pieces at the same time.
 5. Stain wood, except chair seat (A) and (B).

ASSEMBLY, diagram 4
 1. To make "woven rush" seat, turn corrugated piece (B) over to smooth side; mark into four parts, following broken lines in diagram 1, and cut along these lines. The ridges of the two four-sided pieces run from front edge of chair seat to back; save these pieces. The ridges of the two triangular pieces also run from front to back. Use these two pieces as second patterns for two new triangular pieces the same size but with ridges running from side edge to side edge of chair seat; discard first two triangular patterns. The four pieces of chair seat (B), with ridges running in opposite directions, must fit together perfectly; glue pieces to chair seat bottom (A) and place suitable weight on top.
 2. Trim away any excess corrugated wood overlapping seat bottom (A). Round four side edges of chair seat assembly. Sand carefully so you don't destroy straight edges while rounding them, though it's all right if corner edges of corrugated wood break a little while being sanded.
 3. Following diagram 2, make cardboard pattern guide to help you glue chair slats (G) levelly, evenly spaced, and centered on round inside surface of each back leg (C). Glue slats to back legs, with slanted tops of legs facing forward. You may have to re-glue two or three times until pieces stick together properly.
 4. Glue two of the three $1\frac{1}{8}$" chair rungs (E) to front legs (D) in the same manner as you did for the slats in step 3 by making a cardboard pattern guide from diagram 3.
 5. Cut away a $\frac{1}{16}$"-square area from each back corner of chair seat assembly (A and B); cut away a $\frac{1}{8}$"-square area from each front corner of chair seat. With $\frac{1}{8}$" dowel sandpaper

file, round cut-away areas until both back and front edges of chair seat measure 1⅛″ and both side edges measure ¹⁵⁄₁₆″. The front edge of the seat is ⅛″ wider than the back edge, so you will sand away more from front corners than from back corners to get both edges to measure 1⅛″.

6. Using guide from diagram 2, glue back of chair seat to back legs; the chair legs should fit perfectly into rounded back corners of chair seat.

7. Using guide from diagram 3 in step 4, glue front of chair seat to front legs; the chair legs should fit perfectly into rounded front corners of chair seat. Make sure chair seat is level.

8. Sand chair rungs (F) at ends until they fit snugly between front and back chair legs. Glue in place between front and back legs on a level with two front chair rungs (E).

9. Glue third chair rung (E) between two back legs at same level as bottom chair rungs (F).

Finishing

1. Shellac chair seat surfaces first; one coat of shellac is sufficient. Because chair is fragile and has few flat surfaces, do not use steel wool or sand after shellacking.

2. Varnish.

Variation: LADDERBACK ROCKING CHAIR

Make front legs (D) 2″ long, and do not round top edges. Make two 1¼″ armrests from ¹⁄₁₆″ × ³⁄₁₆″ balsa strip, and round front edges. Fit and glue back edges of armrests to back legs (C) and glue front edges of armrests to top edges of front legs (D). Make sure armrests are level. Make two rockers from rocker pattern, diagram 2. Glue ladderback chair to rockers following directions for Windsor rocking chair.

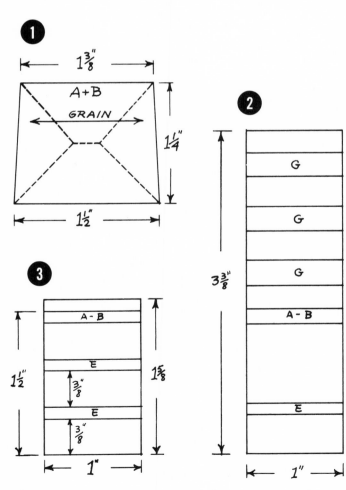

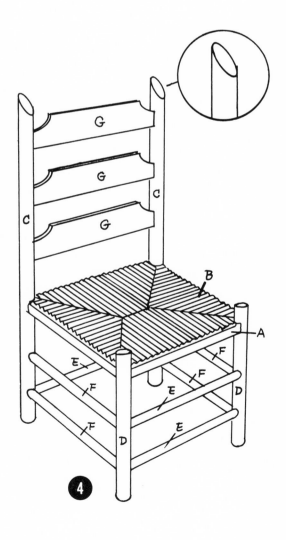

SHERATON ARM CHAIR
(Georgian library and dining room)

SIZE: 1¾"W × 1⅝"D × 2⅞"H

WOOD: ⅛" balsa sheet, ⅛" × ¼" balsa strip

SUGGESTED FINISH: mahogany

BASIC TOOLS AND SUPPLIES, plus ¼" × ½" embossed paper strip, woodtone paint, 1⅝" × 2" fabric, cotton padding, cardboard frame

PIECES FROM ⅛" BALSA SHEET
    A: two pieces from pattern, diagram 1
    B: piece from pattern, diagram 2
    C: two pieces from pattern, diagram 3
    D: two pieces from pattern, diagram 4

PIECES FROM ⅛" × ¼" BALSA STRIP
    E: 1¼" piece
    F: 1¼" piece

CUTTING

1. Piece (A) is very likely to break during cutting. Use a new #11 blade in the X-acto knife and a new single-edged razor blade. Follow directions on page 33 for cutting a curved line, and cut in this order to prevent breakage:
    (1) inside edge of back leg, inside edge of front leg, bottom edge of chair seat;
    (2) outside edge of front leg;
    (3) top edge of chair seat, inside edge of chair back;
    (4) outside edge of chair back, outside edge of back leg.

If you are making several chairs at the same time, secure legs of cardboard pattern for piece (A) with a toothpick; see diagram 1.

2. Cut rest of wood on lengthwise grain.

SANDING AND STAINING

1. Sand wood. For chair sides (A), see directions for sanding two or more pieces together at the same time.

2. Stain wood. Pay particular attention to ⅛" edges of sides (A); if necessary, use turpentine to lighten these edges.

ASSEMBLY, diagram 5

1. Glue chair seat (B) between chair sides (A) 1¼" from floor, with front and back edges of seat flush with outside edges of legs. Be sure all legs touch the floor and chair seat is level.

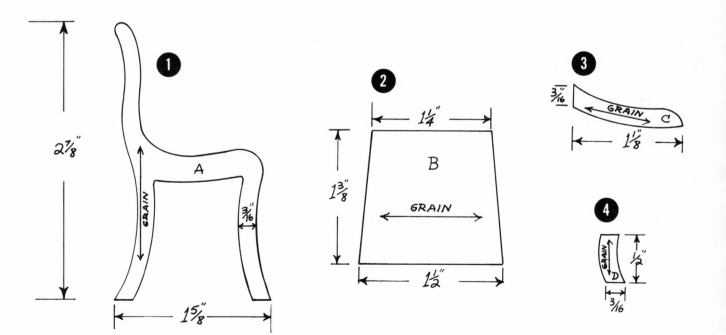

2. Glue chair slat (E) between chair sides (A), with top edge of (E) flush with top of sides (A) and back surface of (E) flush with back edges of (A).

3. Glue chair slat (F) between chair sides (A) so bottom edge of (F) is ⅝″ from seat (B).

4. Glue armrests (C) to arm supports (D) so arm pieces form one long, continuous curve.

5. Sand short edges of arm pieces from step 4 with dowel sandpaper file and check the fit before gluing to chair sides (A). Glue pieces (C) to front edges of sides (A) ⅜″ from top of (A), and pieces (D) to seat edge at front curve.

FINISHING

1. Shellac; one coat is sufficient.

2. Varnish.

3. For carving on chair slat (F), paint embossed paper with woodtone paint to match stain; when dry, center paper and glue to slat.

4. For chair cushion, cut a piece of fabric following outline of chair seat, but add a ¼″ seam allowance on all four sides. Cut one or two pieces of cotton padding and a cardboard base, also following outline of chair seat. Place fabric right side down on work surface, then cotton padding on top of fabric, and cardboard base on top of padding. Glue fabric side seams to cardboard base first, then glue front and back seams. Glue cushion to chair seat (B).

Variation: SHERATON SIDE CHAIR
(*Georgian dining room*)

For dining room chairs or for an occasional chair, eliminate arm pieces (C) and (D), and cut chair seat (B) so front edge measures 1⅜″ and back edge 1⅛″.

Variation: DUNCAN PHYFE CHAIR

A Duncan Phyfe chair differs from a Sheraton chair in style and placement of top slat (E). For slat (E), cut a ¼″ × 1¾″ piece on the crosswise grain of a ⅛″ balsa sheet; this piece must be cut on the crosswise grain because you will bend it later. Cut away 3/16″ from top edges of chair sides (A) and make level. Center and glue (E) to top edges of sides (A), *not* between them. While glue is setting, hold (E) in place with your hands, and at the same time, bend (E) slightly to conform to curve of (A); release when glue holds.

5

WINDSOR ROCKING CHAIR
(Colonial bedroom)

SIZE: 1⅝″W × 2¼″D × 3″H

WOOD: ⅛″ balsa sheet, ¹⁄₁₆″ × ¼″ balsa strip, ³⁄₁₆″ dowel, ⅛″ dowel, round wooden tooth-picks

SUGGESTED FINISH: cherry

BASIC TOOLS AND SUPPLIES, plus drinking glass or tin can about 3″ in diameter, wide elastic band or masking tape

PIECES FROM ⅛″ BALSA SHEET
  A: piece from pattern, diagram 1
  B: two pieces from pattern, diagram 2

PIECE FROM ¹⁄₁₆″ × ¼″ BALSA SHEET
  C: piece from pattern, diagram 3

PIECES FROM ³⁄₁₆″ DOWEL
  D: four 1⅛″ pieces

PIECES FROM ⅛″ DOWEL
  E: two 1″ pieces
  F: 1⅛″ piece

PIECES FROM TOOTHPICKS
  G: three 1⁷⁄₁₆″ pieces
  H: two 1½″ pieces
  I: two 1⁹⁄₁₆″ pieces

CUTTING
  1. Cut wood on lengthwise grain. The grain of piece (A) runs from front to rear.
  2. For chair back rail (C), see directions for cutting a curved line.
  3. Cut away tops of chair legs (D) on an angle of about 20°, making sure the amount cut away is the same on all four legs.

SANDING AND STAINING
  1. Sand wood.
  2. Soak chair back rail (C) in warm water for five minutes, then bend carefully around drinking glass or tin can with grain running horizontally and secure in place with elastic band or masking tape. Dry at room temperature or in low oven for ten minutes.
  3. Round bottoms of legs (D).
  4. Stain wood.

ASSEMBLY, diagram 4
  1. Place glue on pointed end of one chair slat (G) and insert ¹⁄₁₆″ into molded straight bottom edge of back rail (C) at center. Repeat procedure for other two slats (G), spacing each ⅛″ from center slat. Repeat procedure for two slats (H), spacing ⅛″ from slats (G). Repeat procedure for two slats (I), spacing ⅛″ from slats (H). Make sure all slats dry firmly.
  2. Make a pencil mark ¹⁄₁₆″ in from back edge of chair seat (A) at the center. Make six

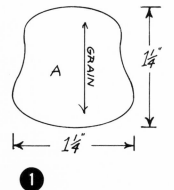

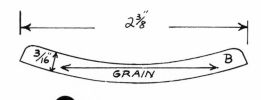

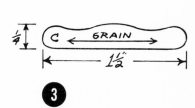

more pencil marks, ⅛″ apart, three to the left of center mark and three to the right, following contour of back edge of (A). Glue slats from step 1 to pencil marks; the slats are graduated so they will slope automatically at the correct angle. Hold chair back assembly in place with hands until glue begins to set.

3. Glue chair legs (D) to underside of corners of seat (A) with each leg facing outward. Make sure legs are lined up evenly from front to back and from side to side.

4. Glue chair rungs (E) between front and back chair legs slightly up from bottom. A little sanding will be necessary for an accurate fit.

5. Glue stretcher (F) between chair rungs (E) at the center.

6. Glue rockers (B) to front and back legs (D) so each rocker extends ¼″ from front leg and ⅝″ from back leg.

FINISHING

1. Shellac chair legs, rungs, and stretcher only once. Smooth with steel wool very carefully.

2. Varnish.

Variation: WINDSOR CHAIR

For a Windsor chair with no rockers, cut front legs (D) 1¼″ long.

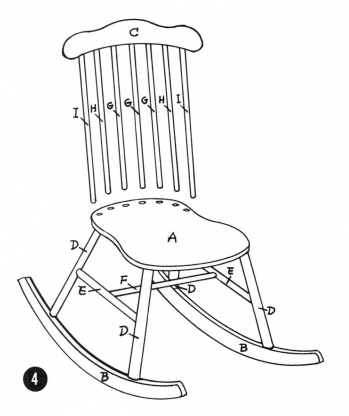

WING CHAIR
(Colonial living room and Georgian bedroom)

SIZE: 3″W × 2⅛″D × 4″H

WOOD: ³⁄₃₂″ balsa sheet, ³⁄₁₆″ balsa sheet, ³⁄₁₆″ sq. balsa strip, ⅛″ sq. balsa strip

SUGGESTED FINISH: mahogany

BASIC TOOLS AND SUPPLIES, plus ³⁄₁₆″-thick cotton padding, ⅛ yard fabric, soutache braid, dye or felt tip pen, cardboard

PIECES FROM ³⁄₃₂″ BALSA SHEET
    A: piece from pattern, diagram 1
    B: piece from pattern (solid outline only), diagram 2
    C: two pieces from pattern (solid outline only), diagram 3

PIECES FROM ³⁄₁₆″ BALSA SHEET
    D: two pieces from pattern (solid outline only), diagram 4

PIECES FROM ³⁄₁₆″ SQ. BALSA STRIP
    E: two ¾″ pieces
    F: two ⅞″ pieces
    G: two ¹⁵⁄₁₆″ pieces

PIECES FROM ⅛″ SQ. BALSA STRIP
    H: two 1⅝″ pieces
    I: 2⅛″ piece

PIECES FROM COTTON PADDING
    B: piece from pattern (solid outline only), diagram 2
    C: two pieces from pattern (solid outline only), diagram 3
    D: two pieces from pattern (solid outline only), diagram 4

PIECES FROM FABRIC
    B: piece from pattern (dotted outline only), diagram 2
    C: piece from pattern (dotted outline only), top half diagram 3
    C: piece from pattern (dotted outline only), bottom half diagram 3
    C: piece from reverse side of pattern (dotted outline only), top half diagram 3
    C: piece from reverse side of pattern (dotted outline only), bottom half diagram 3
    D: piece from pattern (dotted outline only), diagram 4
    C–B–C: piece from pattern, diagram 5
    Cushion fabric: 2½″ × 3″ piece

CUTTING WOOD
1. Cut wood on lengthwise grain.
2. Instead of using two ³⁄₁₆″ pieces for chair seat (D), you may use any combination of thicknesses of wood you have on hand and cut the pieces you need to obtain the required ⅜″ thickness.
3. Cut away top and bottom edges of back legs (G) on an angle of about 20°; see detail in diagram 6. Make sure the slanted top and bottom edges are exactly parallel.
4. For stretchers (H) and (I), you may want to cut one 6″ strip and later cut the three pieces exactly to size.

CUTTING COTTON PADDING AND FABRIC
1. Cut pieces of cotton padding, using same cardboard patterns as for marking wood pieces (B), (C), and (D).
2. Cut fabric crosswise. Because chair wings (C) face each other, be sure to reverse top and bottom patterns on the same side of the fabric when cutting.

SANDING AND STAINING
1. Do not sand or stain wood pieces (B), (C), (D), and (E) because they will be covered with fabric.
2. Sand rest of wood, then stain.

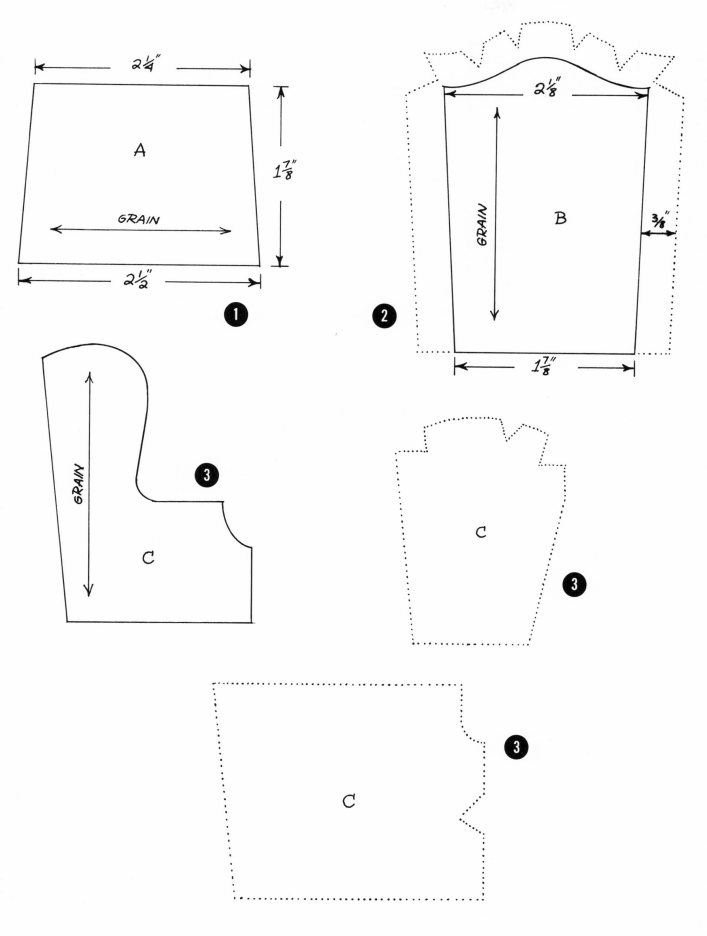

ASSEMBLING CHAIR BASE, diagram 6

1. Glue front legs (F) to bottom of chair base (A) at each corner along front edge. Reinforce legs wtih straight pins from top surface of (A); see directions for reinforced gluing. Repeat procedure for back legs (G), gluing them along back edge of (A).

2. If you haven't already cut stretchers (H), measure exact distance between front and back legs (F and G) and cut stretchers to fit. Slant one end of each stretcher to fit properly against back legs. Glue stretchers in place about midway between floor and base (A).

3. Measure exact distance between stretchers (H) and cut stretcher (I) to fit between them; center and glue (I) between stretchers (H).

ASSEMBLING UPHOLSTERED PART OF CHAIR, diagram 6

1. Glue together chair seat pieces (D) to form one piece. After drying, put glue on top and bottom surfaces of (D) but not on the 2⅛″ front edge. Glue fabric (D) to chair seat (D), tucking ⅜″ fabric extensions to each side edge.

2. Place chair back (B) on work surface and secure cotton padding (B) to it with a few dots of glue. Place fabric (B) right side facing up on top of padding, with bottom edge of fabric flush with bottom edges of padding and chair back; hold these edges in place with glue or pins. Turn over assembly and glue ⅜″ fabric seams to back side of chair back, gluing straight side seams first and then curved, clipped top seam; trim seams if necessary to avoid extra thickness. Hold fabric in place with pins until glue is dry.

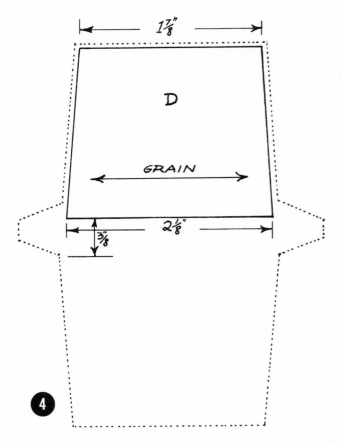

3. Center and glue fabric side of chair back (B) to back edge of chair seat (D) so bottom edge of (B) is flush with bottom surface of (D). Reinforce gluing with straight pins.

4. Glue armrest (E) to short straight top edge of chair wing (C) on outside surface of (C); the top edges of armrest and short straight edge of chair wing are flush. Repeat procedure for other chair wing and armrest.

5. Place one chair wing (C) on work surface

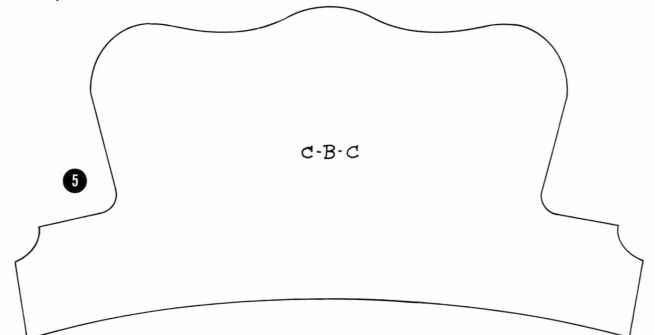

C-B-C

with armrest (E) facing down and cover with cotton padding (C); stretch padding over armrest and hold in place with dot of glue. Place bottom half wing fabric (C) right side up on top of bottom half of padding, with bottom edges flush; hold these edges in place with glue or pins. Turn assembly over to armrest side. Glue fabric seams to this side, gluing straight side seams first and then short, curved, clipped seam; trim seams if necessary to avoid extra thickness. Gluing fabric over armrest can be done smoothly if you tuck fabric over front edge of armrest first, holding it in place with glue or pins, and then draw fabric over top edge of armrest and glue seam to surface of wing

(C) along bottom edge of armrest. Hold seam in place with glue and pins until dry.

6. Turn over assembly from step 5 to fabric side. Fold under bottom edge seam of top half wing fabric (C) and cover top edge raw seam of bottom half wing fabric (C). Hold folded seam in place with a pin, if necessary, and turn entire assembly over again. Glue fabric seams to this side, gluing straight side seam first and then curved, clipped top and wing seams; trim seams if necessary to avoid extra thickness and hold in place with pins until glue is dry. Repeat steps 5 and 6 for other chair wing (C), padding (C), and top and bottom half wing fabric (C).

7. Glue fabric side of chair wings (C) to sides of chair seat (D) so bottom edges of (C) are flush with bottom surface of (D). Reinforce gluing with straight pins. Glue long straight back edges of (C) to side edges of chair back (B).

8. Fit right side of fabric (C–B–C) to outside surface of chair wings (C) and back (B). Place dots of glue as close to fabric edge as possible, an inch or so apart, and glue fabric along top, bottom, and side edges of chair back and wings to cover wood and raw seams.

9. Glue upholstered chair assembly to chair base assembly so four side edges from each are flush and matching in length.

Finishing

1. Shellac chair base assembly and varnish, but do not shellac or varnish side edges of base (A).

2. Dye soutache braid to match fabric as directed on page 30. Glue braid to raw seam edges of fabric (C–B–C), following contour of edges. Glue braid around base (A) to cover raw edges of fabric and side edges of (A).

3. Use solid outline pattern in diagram 4 to make cardboard base for chair cushion. Place cushion fabric right side down on work surface; place padding on top of fabric, and cardboard base on top of padding. Glue fabric side seams to cardboard base first, then glue front and back seams to base. Glue cushion to chair seat (D).

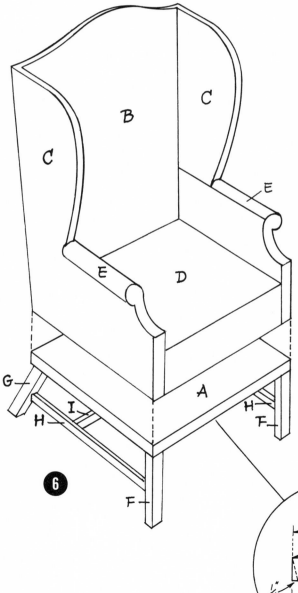

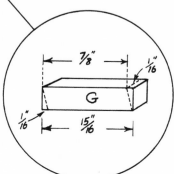

CHAPTER *17* *Chests*

BLANKET CHEST
(Colonial bedroom)

SIZE: 1⅜"W × 3⅞"L × 1⅞"H

WOOD: ³⁄₃₂" balsa sheet, ⅛" sq. balsa strip

SUGGESTED FINISH: paint

BASIC TOOLS AND SUPPLIES, plus pair of ⅝" decoupage hinges, paint, fruit or floral decal or suitable magazine picture, fruitwood glaze or burnt umber paint

PIECES FROM ³⁄₃₂" BALSA SHEET
  A: 1⅜" × 3⅞" piece
  B: two pieces from pattern, diagram 1
  C: two pieces from pattern, diagram 2
  D: 1⅛" × 3⁷⁄₁₆" piece

PIECES FROM ⅛" SQ. BALSA STRIP
  E: two 1⅜" pieces

CUTTING
  1. Cut wood on lengthwise grain except for pieces (C), which are cut on crosswise grain.
  2. For pieces (C), cut a decorative edge.

SANDING
  1. Sand wood.

2. Round bottom front corners on edge of each piece (E).

ASSEMBLY, diagram 3
  1. Glue chest front (B) and back (B) to side edges of chest sides (C).
  2. Glue bottom (D) ⅜" from floor.
  3. Glue the two pieces (E) to underside of chest top (A) along each side, with rounded corners of (E) at front edge of (A).
  4. Trim one side of decoupage hinges to ⅜" and insert hinges ¾" from each side of top (A) at back edge; see directions under Hardware for "blind" hinging. Fit (A) to assembly from steps 1 and 2 and secure in place by screwing hinges to back (B) from the outside. The top (A) will extend ¹⁄₁₆" beyond front (B).

FINISHING
  1. Paint chest in a color to harmonize with bedroom. Either oil base or latex paint can be used. If you use model paint, prime wood first with one or two coats of shellac to prevent wood from absorbing too much paint. Apply two coats of paint.
  2. When paint is thoroughly dry, apply a stencil-type design to chest, using fruit or floral

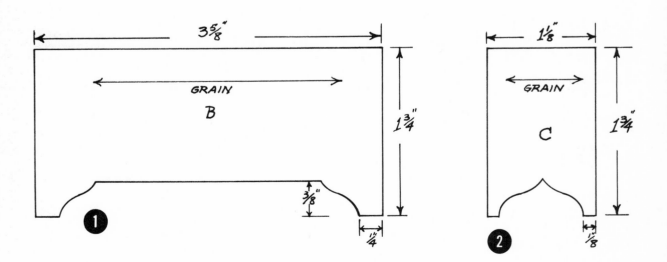

decal or suitable magazine picture; green and gold colors are best.

3. After paint has dried, liberally apply a prepared fruitwood glaze (available at hardware stores) or burnt umber paint (available at art supply stores). Then "dry brush" the glaze or paint with a bushy artist's brush; after a few brush strokes and a little practice, you will see the chest take on an antique appearance. If you want, you can shade areas of the chest darker or lighter than other areas with your brush.

4. Varnish.

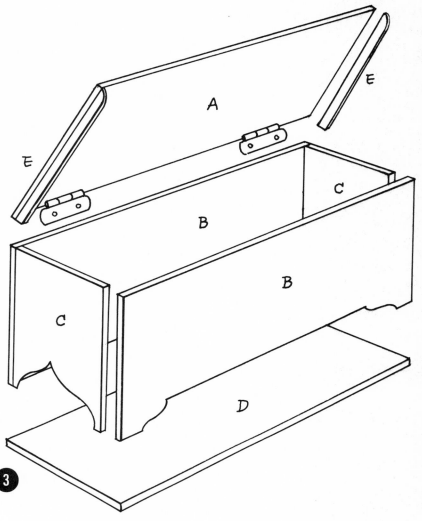

VICTORIAN BUREAU
(*Victorian bedroom*)

SIZE: $3\frac{5}{8}$"W × $1\frac{1}{2}$"D × 6"H

WOOD: $\frac{3}{32}$" balsa sheet, $\frac{1}{32}$" balsa sheet, $\frac{3}{16}$" sq. balsa strip, $\frac{1}{16}$" × $\frac{3}{32}$" balsa strip, $\frac{1}{16}$" × $\frac{3}{16}$" balsa strip, $\frac{1}{16}$" × $\frac{3}{8}$" balsa strip, $\frac{1}{4}$" sq. balsa strip (optional)

SUGGESTED FINISH: walnut

BASIC TOOLS AND SUPPLIES, plus $\frac{3}{16}$"-wide embossed paper strip, $\frac{1}{4}$"-wide embossed paper strip, two tiny round beads, woodtone paint, Formica with marble pattern, white model paint, $1\frac{1}{2}$" × $2\frac{3}{4}$" mirror

PIECES FROM $\frac{3}{32}''$ BALSA SHEET

A: piece from pattern, diagram 1
B: two $2\frac{3}{8}'' \times 3\frac{1}{8}''$ pieces
C: two $1\frac{1}{8}'' \times 2\frac{3}{8}''$ pieces
D: $1\frac{9}{16}'' \times 3\frac{5}{8}''$ piece
E: $1\frac{3}{16}'' \times 3\frac{1}{8}''$ piece

PIECES FROM $\frac{1}{32}''$ BALSA SHEET

F: two $\frac{3}{16}'' \times 1''$ pieces
G: four $\frac{3}{8}'' \times 1''$ pieces
H: piece from pattern (dotted outline only), diagram 2
I: two pieces from pattern (solid outline only), diagram 2

PIECES FROM $\frac{3}{16}''$ SQ. BALSA STRIP

J: four $2\frac{1}{2}''$ pieces

PIECES FROM $\frac{1}{16}'' \times \frac{3}{32}''$ BALSA STRIP

K: two $3\frac{1}{8}''$ pieces

PIECES FROM $\frac{1}{16}'' \times \frac{3}{16}''$ BALSA STRIP

L: $3\frac{1}{8}''$ piece
M: two $1\frac{1}{8}''$ pieces

PIECES FROM $\frac{1}{16}'' \times \frac{3}{8}''$ BALSA STRIP

N: $3\frac{1}{8}''$ piece
O: two $1\frac{1}{8}''$ pieces

PIECES FROM $\frac{1}{4}''$ SQ. BALSA STRIP (optional)

Top drawers: four $1''$ pieces

PIECES FROM FORMICA

D: $1\frac{9}{16}'' \times 3\frac{5}{8}''$ piece
Top drawers: two $\frac{1}{2}'' \times 1''$ pieces (optional)

CUTTING

1. Cut wood on lengthwise grain.
2. For piece (A), cut a curved line.
3. Saw Formica pieces slowly and carefully, then smooth edges with metal file.

SANDING AND STAINING

1. Sand wood.
2. Round inside edges of piece (A) and front and side edges of wood piece (D).
3. For Formica piece (D), slightly round front corners with metal file.
4. Stain wood.

ASSEMBLY, diagram 3

1. Glue piece (N) to bureau front (B) with bottom edges flush.
2. Glue one piece (K) to front (B) so top edge of (K) is $1''$ from bottom edge of (B).
3. Center and glue two drawer panels (G) to front (B) between pieces (N) and (K); one side of each panel (G) is flush with side edge of (B).
4. Glue one diamond-shaped panel (I) to front (B) so the four points of the diamond touch pieces (G), (N), and (K).
5. Glue second piece (K) to front (B) so bottom edge of (K) is $\frac{5}{8}''$ from top edge of first piece (K).
6. Center and glue two drawer panels (G) to front (B) between pieces (K); one side of each panel (G) is flush with side edge of (B).
7. Glue second diamond-shaped panel (I) to front (B) so the four points of the diamond touch pieces (G) and (K).
8. Glue piece (L) to front (B) with top edges of both pieces flush.
9. Center and glue two drawer panels (F) to front (B) between pieces (K) and (L); one side of each panel (F) is flush with side edge of (B).
10. Glue diamond-shaped panel (H) to front (B) so the four points of the diamond touch pieces (F), (L), and (K).
11. Glue a piece (M) to bureau side (C) so top edges of both pieces are flush. Glue a piece (O) to same side (C) so bottom edges of both pieces are flush. Repeat procedure for other side (C) and pieces (M) and (O).
12. Glue two legs (J) to each side of front (B) so back surface and top edge of each leg (J) is flush with back surface and top edge of (B).
13. Glue two other legs (J) to each side of bureau back (B) so front surface and top edge of each leg (J) is flush with front surface and top edge of back (B).
14. Glue one side (C) assembly between front (B) and back (B) assemblies so inside surfaces and top edges of legs (J) are flush with inside surface and top edge of side (C) assembly. Repeat procedure for other side (C).
15. Glue bureau top (D) to bureau back, front, and side assemblies; the back edge of (D) is flush with outside surface of back (B).
16. Glue bureau bottom (E) to bureau so underside of (E) is flush with bottom edges of back and front (B) and sides (C) assemblies. Place suitable weight on top of entire assembly.

FINISHING

1. Shellac. (Shellac mirror frame (A) separately.)
2. Varnish. (Varnish frame (A) separately.)
3. Make two drawer handles from the $\frac{1}{4}''$-wide embossed paper strip, and four handles

from the ³⁄₁₆″-wide strip to resemble wood carving, each measuring about ½″. Paint handles with woodtone paint to match stain and glue to drawer panels (F) and (G).

4. Paint edges of Formica pieces white. Glue Formica piece (D) to bureau top (D).

5. Glue mirror to back surface of mirror frame (A). Center and glue (A) along back edge of top (D) so back surface of mirror is flush with back edge of (D). It may be necessary to glue balsa sheet braces, with same thickness as the mirror, to back surface of (A) at the bottom edge.

6. For bureau top drawers (optional), glue together two ¼″ sq. balsa strips that are 1″ long; do likewise with two more identical strips. Stain, shellac, and varnish the two drawers. Glue drawers to top (D) and front surface of mirror frame (A) near bottom corners of (A). Glue ½″ × 1″ Formica top onto each drawer. For drawer knobs, paint heads of two half-inch straight pins with woodtone paint and insert in center of drawers.

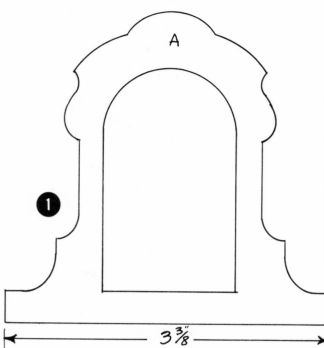

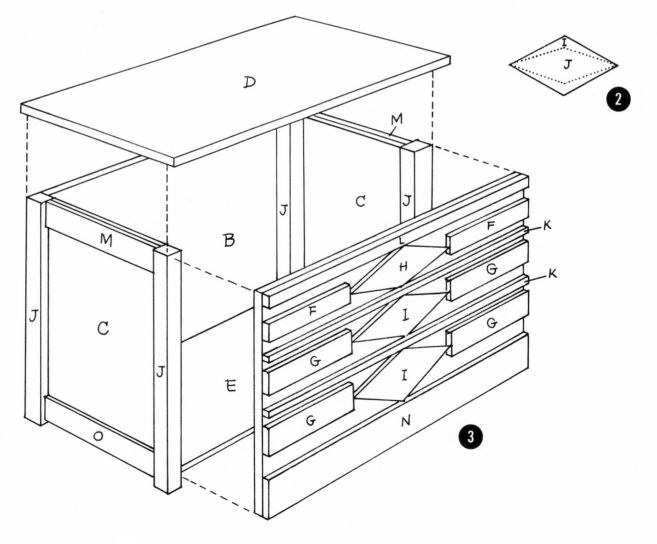

CHEST-ON-CHEST
(Colonial bedroom)

Size: $3\frac{1}{8}''$W × $1\frac{5}{8}''$D × $4\frac{1}{2}''$H

Wood: $\frac{1}{8}''$ balsa sheet, $\frac{3}{32}''$ balsa sheet, $\frac{1}{32}''$ balsa sheet

Suggested finish: pine

Basic tools and supplies, plus 12 sewing loops, gold paint, 2 pairs of pliers

Pieces from $\frac{1}{8}''$ balsa sheet
  A: three $1\frac{5}{8}'' \times 3\frac{1}{8}''$ pieces

Pieces from $\frac{3}{32}''$ balsa sheet
  B: $2\frac{1}{8}'' \times 3''$ piece
  C: two $1\frac{1}{2}'' \times 2\frac{1}{8}''$ pieces
  D: $2\frac{1}{8}'' \times 2\frac{13}{16}''$ piece
  E: $1\frac{3}{4}'' \times 2\frac{7}{8}''$ piece
  F: two $1\frac{7}{16}'' \times 1\frac{3}{4}''$ pieces
  G: $1\frac{3}{4}'' \times 2\frac{11}{16}''$ piece
  H: eight pieces from pattern (solid outline only), diagram 1

Pieces from $\frac{1}{32}''$ balsa sheet
  I: three $\frac{5}{8}'' \times 2\frac{3}{4}''$ pieces
  J: two $\frac{1}{2}'' \times 2\frac{5}{8}''$ pieces
  K: two $\frac{1}{2}'' \times 1\frac{1}{4}''$ pieces

Cutting
  1. Cut wood on lengthwise grain except for pieces (B) and (E), which are cut on crosswise grain.
  2. For legs (H), see directions for cutting a

curved line. Cut $\frac{1}{4}''$ off short side edge of four of legs (H); see broken line in diagram 1.

Sanding and staining
  1. Sand wood.
  2. For three pieces (A), bevel front and side edges.
  3. For drawers (I), (J), and (K), bevel all four edges.
  4. Stain wood.

Assembling bottom chest section, diagram 2
  1. Glue drawers (I) to chest front (B). Leave $\frac{1}{16}''$ space between drawers, between top drawer and top edge of (B), and between bottom drawer and bottom edge of (B). Leave $\frac{1}{8}''$ space between sides of drawers and side edges of (B). Place suitable weight on top of this assembly.
  2. Glue front edges of chest sides (C) to assembly from step 1.
  3. Glue side edges of chest back (D) to assembly from step 2. You may have to trim side edges of (D) so it forms a perfect right-angle rectangle when glued to sides (C).
  4. Center and glue assembly from steps 1–3 to chest bottom (A) so back edge of (A) is flush with outside surface of back (D).
  5. Center and glue chest middle piece (A) to assembly from steps 1–4 so back edge of (A) is flush with outside surface of back (D). Place suitable weight on top of the bottom chest section.

Assembly top chest section, diagram 2
  1. Glue drawers (K) $\frac{1}{16}''$ from top edge of chest front (E) and $\frac{1}{8}''$ from side edges of (E), leaving $\frac{3}{32}''$ space between drawers.
  2. Glue drawers (J) to front (E). Leaving $\frac{1}{16}''$ space between drawers (K) and top drawer (J) and between bottom drawer (J) and bottom edge of (E). Leave $\frac{1}{8}''$ space between sides of drawers (J) and side edges of (E). Place suitable weight on top of this assembly.
  3. Glue front edges of chest sides (F) to assembly from step 2.
  4. Glue side edges of chest back (G) to assembly from step 3. You may have to trim side edges of (G) so it forms a perfect right-angle rectangle when glued to sides (F).
  5. Center and glue chest top (A) to assembly from steps 1–4 so back edge of (A) is flush with outside surface of back (G).
  6. Center and glue top chest section to bottom chest section so outside surfaces of back pieces (G) and (D) and back edges of three

pieces (A) are flush. Place suitable weight on top of chest-on-chest assembly.

7. Apply glue to top long edges of two of the longer legs (H); glue to bottom of chest along front edge of (A), with short straight side edges of (H) flush with sides (C). Repeat procedure for other two longer legs (H), gluing along back edge of (A).

Apply glue to top long edges and short side edges of two of the shorter legs (H); glue to bottom of chest along side edges of (A) as well as to front legs so each short-long leg combination forms a perfect right angle. Repeat procedure for other two shorter legs (H), gluing to bottom of (A) and to longer back legs.

FINISHING

1. Shellac, then varnish.
2. Make drawer handles out of sewing loops and attach. Place handles ¼″ from sides of drawers (I) and (J), ³⁄₁₆″ from tops of drawers (I), and ⅛″ from tops of drawers (J). Center handles on drawers (K).

Variation: BACHELOR CHEST

The bottom chest alone is a very suitable piece for a dollhouse hallway or living room. Cut only two pieces (A) and all bottom chest pieces, including legs. Assemble chest following same procedure for bottom chest section. Many bachelor chests have an additional drawer handle on each side so they can be carried. Center and attach these handles ½″ from top edge of each side.

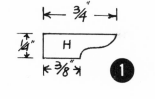

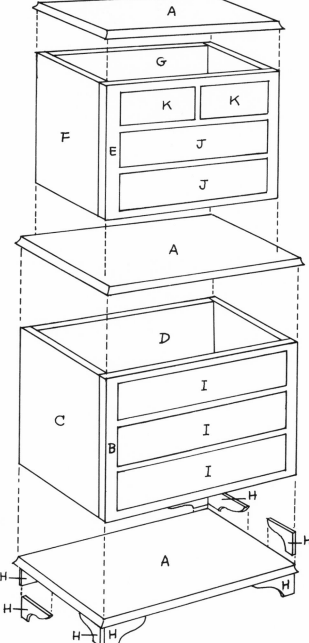

BOW FRONT DRESSER
(*Georgian bedroom*)

SIZE: 3¾"W × 1¾"D × 3"H

WOOD: ⅛" balsa sheet, ³⁄₃₂" balsa sheet, ¹⁄₁₆" balsa sheet, ¹⁄₃₂" balsa sheet, ³⁄₁₆" sq. balsa strip

SUGGESTED FINISH: mahogany

BASIC TOOLS AND SUPPLIES, plus 8" diameter cooking pot with straight sides, wide elastic bands or masking tape, 8 sewing loops, gold paint, 2 pairs of pliers

PIECE FROM ⅛" BALSA SHEET
 A: piece from pattern (solid outline only), diagram 1

PIECES FROM ³⁄₃₂" BALSA SHEET
 B: two 1" × 2⅝" pieces
 C: 2⅝" × 3⅛" piece
 D: piece from pattern (dotted outline only), diagram 1

PIECE FROM ¹⁄₁₆" BALSA SHEET
 E: piece from pattern, diagram 2

PIECES FROM ¹⁄₃₂" BALSA SHEET
 F: ⅜" × 3³⁄₁₆" piece
 G: two ½" × 3³⁄₁₆" pieces
 H: ⅝" × 3³⁄₁₆" piece

PIECES FROM ³⁄₁₆" SQ. BALSA STRIP
 I: four 2⅞" pieces

CUTTING
 1. Cut wood on lengthwise grain.
 2. For piece (E), cut a decorative edge.

SANDING AND STAINING
 1. Sand wood.
 2. Soak dresser front (E) in warm water for five minutes, then bend it lengthwise around cooking pot and secure in place with elastic bands or masking tape; don't let elastic bands indent the soft, wet wood. Dry at room temperature or in a low oven for ten minutes.
 3. For drawers (F), (G), and (H), bevel all four edges.
 4. Stain wood.

ASSEMBLY, diagram 3.
 1. Glue drawer (F) to front (E), leaving ⅛" space between top of (F) and top edge of (E); the side edges of (F) are flush with side edges of (E). Hold drawer in place with hands until glue begins to set.
 2. Glue drawers (G) to front (E). Leave ³⁄₃₂"

space between drawers (G) and between top drawer (G) and bottom edge of drawer (F); the side edges of (G) are flush with side edges of (E). Hold drawers in place with hands until glue begins to set.
 3. Glue drawer (H) to front (E), leaving ³⁄₃₂" space between top of (H) and bottom of drawer (G); the side edges of (H) are flush with side edges of (E). Hold drawer in place with hands until glue begins to set. Place entire dresser front assembly back on cooking pot mold and hold in place with elastic bands or masking tape until glue is dry.
 4. Glue dresser side (B) between two legs (I) with top edge and outside surface of (B) flush with top edge and outside side surface of each leg. Repeat procedure for other side (B) and two legs (I).
 5. Glue dresser back (C) between back legs (I) of each assembly from step 4, with top edges and back surfaces of all pieces flush.
 6. Center and glue dresser top (A) to assembly from step 5 so back edge of (A) is flush with back surface of back (C).
 7. Glue dresser bottom (D) to back (C) and to four legs (I) with underside of (D) flush with bottom edge of (C). The front edge of (D) must be glued to front legs on same level as (D) is glued to back legs. Also, the front corners of (D) should not be flush with front surfaces of front legs, but instead there should be a ¹⁄₁₆" space left for dresser front assembly; see detail in diagram 3.
 8. Remove dresser front (E) from cooking pot mold and check to see if it fits between front legs (I). If it doesn't curve accurately, you can

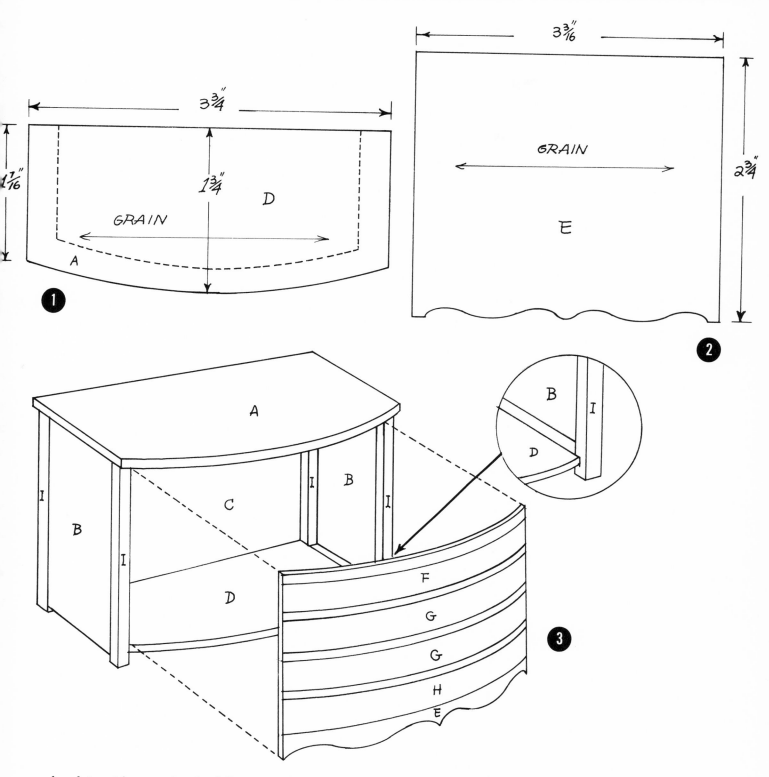

re-bend it with your hands following contour of curved edges of top (A) and bottom (D). Glue side edges of (E) between front legs; glue top edge of (E) to underside of (A) ⅛″ from curved edge of (A); glue curved edge of bottom (D) to hold decorative edge of (E) in place.

FINISHING

1. Shellac, then varnish.
2. Make drawer handles out of sewing loops and attach. Place drawer handles ½″ from side edges of drawers and centered between top and bottom edges of each drawer.

Variation: STRAIGHT FRONT DRESSER

The bow front dresser can be made with a straight front. Cut front (E) from ³⁄₃₂″ balsa sheet on lengthwise grain and trim off ¹⁄₃₂″ from each side edge. Cut drawers (F), (G), and (H) 3⅛″ long. Follow directions for making bow front dresser.

CHIPPENDALE HIGHBOY

SIZE: $3\frac{1}{2}$"W × $1\frac{7}{8}$"D × $7\frac{1}{4}$"H

WOOD: $\frac{1}{8}$" balsa sheet, $\frac{3}{32}$" balsa sheet, $\frac{1}{32}$" balsa sheet, $\frac{3}{16}$" × $\frac{3}{8}$" balsa strip, $\frac{3}{16}$" sq. balsa strip

SUGGESTED FINISH: mahogany

BASIC TOOLS AND SUPPLIES, plus 4" of $\frac{1}{8}$"-thick picture wire, 2 matching decorative buttons $\frac{3}{8}$" in diameter or 2 upholstery twist pins, 3 round beads, 3 oblong beads, $\frac{1}{2}$" scallop shell or scallop-shaped button or embossed paper in shell pattern, woodtone paint, 15 sewing loops, gold paint, 2 pairs of pliers

PIECES FROM $\frac{1}{8}$" BALSA SHEET
  A: $1\frac{11}{16}$" × $3\frac{1}{4}$" piece
  B: $1\frac{7}{8}$" × $3\frac{1}{4}$" piece

PIECES FROM $\frac{3}{32}$" BALSA SHEET
  C: two $1\frac{3}{8}$" × $1\frac{1}{2}$" pieces
  D: $1\frac{3}{8}$" × $2\frac{3}{4}$" piece
  E: piece from pattern, diagram 1
  F: two $1\frac{11}{16}$" × $3\frac{1}{4}$" pieces
  G: $2\frac{13}{16}$" × $3\frac{1}{4}$" piece
  H: piece from pattern, diagram 2

PIECES FROM $\frac{1}{32}$" BALSA SHEET
  I: three $\frac{3}{8}$" × $\frac{7}{8}$" pieces

  J: two $\frac{3}{8}$" × $2\frac{3}{4}$" pieces
  K: $\frac{1}{2}$" × $2\frac{3}{4}$" piece
  L: $\frac{9}{16}$" × $2\frac{3}{4}$" piece
  M: $\frac{5}{8}$" × $2\frac{3}{4}$" piece
  N: two $\frac{1}{2}$" × $\frac{7}{8}$" pieces
  O: $1\frac{1}{16}$" × $\frac{7}{8}$" piece

PIECES FROM $\frac{3}{16}$" × $\frac{3}{8}$" BALSA STRIP
  P: four pieces from pattern, diagram 3

PIECES FROM $\frac{3}{16}$" SQ. BALSA STRIP
  Finials: three $\frac{1}{2}$" pieces

CUTTING
  1. Cut wood on lengthwise grain except for piece (H), which is cut on crosswise grain.
  2. For pieces (E) and (H), see directions for cutting a curved line.
  3. For legs (P), see directions under wood turning for cutting cabriole legs.

SANDING AND STAINING
  1. Sand wood.
  2. For highboy top (A), bevel two side edges.
  3. For middle piece (B), bevel front and side edges.
  4. For drawers (I), (J), (K), (L), (M), (N), and (O), bevel all four edges.
  5. Stain wood.

ASSEMBLING BOTTOM SECTION, diagram 3
  1. Glue drawer (J) to front piece (E) $\frac{1}{8}$" from top edge of (E), with side edges of both pieces flush.
  2. Glue drawers (N) to front (E). Leave $\frac{1}{8}$" space between tops of drawers (N) and bottom of drawer (J); outside edges of drawers (N) are flush with side edges of (E).
  3. Center and glue drawer (O) to front (E) leaving $\frac{1}{8}$" space between top of (O) and bottom of drawer (J). Place suitable weight on top of front assembly.
  4. Glue a leg (P) to each side edge of assembly from step 3 so top edges and front surfaces of legs and front (E) are flush.
  5. Glue a leg (P) to each side edge of back piece (D) so top edges and back surfaces of all pieces are flush.
  6. Glue sides (C) between front and back legs (P) so top edges and outside surfaces of these pieces are flush. Make sure that a perfect right angle rectangle is formed measuring exactly $1\frac{3}{4}$" × $3\frac{1}{8}$".
  7. Glue middle piece (B) to top of bottom section assembly so back edge of (B) is flush with outside surface of back (D); the side edges of

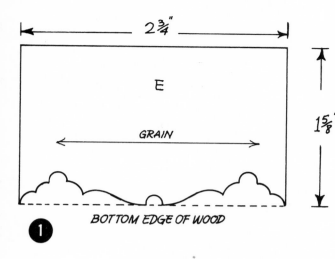

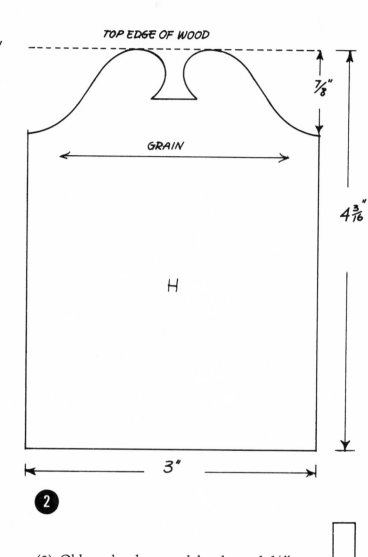

(B) should overlap the assembly less than ¹⁄₁₆″. Place suitable weight on top of bottom section.

Assembling top section, diagram 3

1. Arrange drawers (I), (J), (K), (L), and (M) on front piece (H) before gluing down. Leave 1″ space between tops of drawers (I) and topmost curved edge of (H), and ³⁄₃₂″ space between drawers (I). Leave ⅛″ space between tops and bottoms of all drawers, between sides of all drawers and sides of (H), and between drawer (M) and bottom edge of (H). Glue down drawers and place suitable weight on front (H).

2. Glue assembly from step 1 to front edges of sides (F).

3. Glue sides (F) to side edges of back piece (G). You may have to trim sides of (G) first to get right angle corners.

4. Glue top piece (A) to top edges of sides (F) behind front (H). Back edge of (A) is flush with outside surface of back (G), and beveled edges of (A) are upside down—in the opposite direction from beveled edges of middle piece (B).

5. Glue top section assembly to bottom section assembly, making sure to center carefully. The outside surfaces of backs (G) and (D) are flush.

Finishing

1. Shellac.

2. For carving on highboy, paint the following items with woodtone paint to match stain. When dry, glue them to highboy; see diagram 4.

(1) Thick picture wire; this becomes curved top edge of front (H).

(2) Two decorative buttons, preferably with floral motif, or heads of two twist pins; these go on top center of (H), almost as if a continuation of picture wire molding.

(3) Oblong beads, round beads, and ½″ pieces of ³⁄₁₆″ sq. balsa strip are held together with straight pins to form finials; these belong on top of highboy front corners and centered between the front corners.

(4) Scallop shell, ½″ in diameter, scallop-shaped button, or similarly shaped embossed paper design; center one of these on drawer (O), or you may use drawer handle here instead of shell.

3. Varnish highboy, including carving.

4. Make drawer handles out of sewing loops and attach. Center handles on drawers (I) and (N). On rest of drawers, place handles ½″ from sides and center between top and bottom edges.

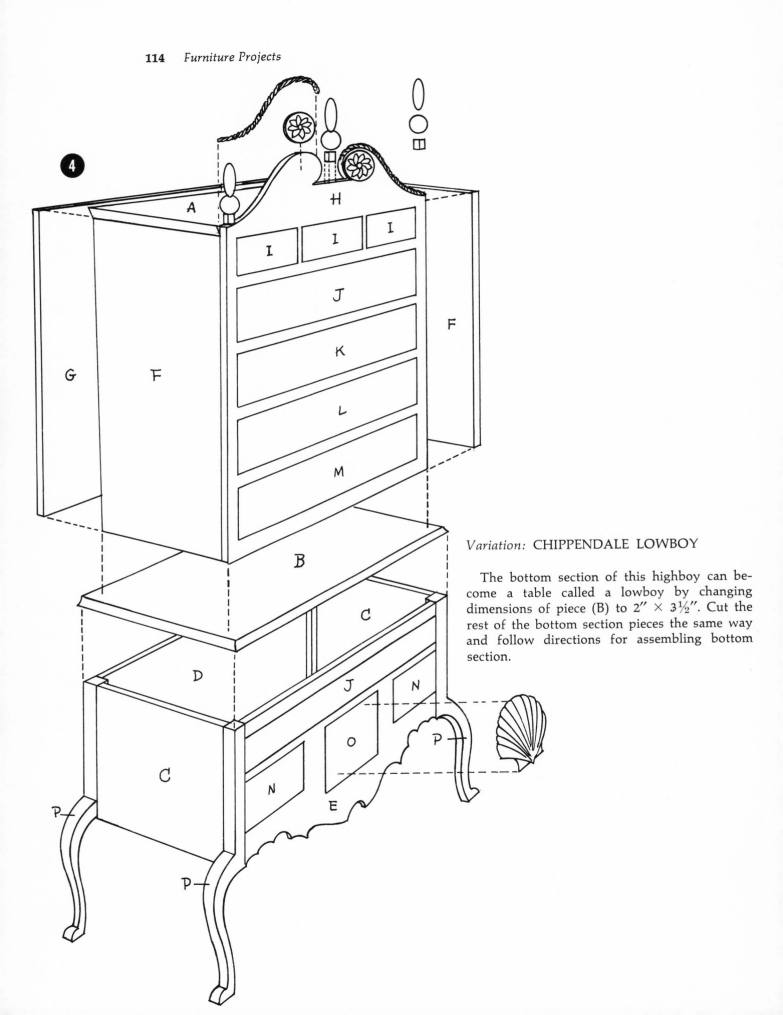

Variation: CHIPPENDALE LOWBOY

The bottom section of this highboy can become a table called a lowboy by changing dimensions of piece (B) to 2″ × 3½″. Cut the rest of the bottom section pieces the same way and follow directions for assembling bottom section.

CHAPTER *18* *Clocks*

GRANDFATHER CLOCK
(*Georgian hall*)

SIZE: $1\frac{1}{2}$"W × 1"D × $6\frac{3}{4}$"H

WOOD: $\frac{1}{8}$" balsa sheet, $\frac{1}{16}$" balsa sheet, $\frac{1}{32}$" balsa sheet, 2 round wooden toothpicks

SUGGESTED FINISH: mahogany

BASIC TOOLS AND SUPPLIES, plus picture of round clock face or actual wrist watch dial, acetate, wide silver embossed paper strip or picture frame, aluminum foil, 5 round beads, oblong bead, India ink (optional), woodtone paint, curved scissors

PIECES FROM $\frac{1}{8}$" BALSA SHEET
A: $1\frac{1}{16}$" × $1\frac{3}{8}$" piece
B: 1" × $1\frac{1}{4}$" piece
C: 1" × $1\frac{1}{4}$" piece
D: 1" × $1\frac{7}{16}$" piece

PIECES FROM $\frac{1}{16}$" BALSA SHEET
E: two $\frac{7}{8}$" × $1\frac{1}{2}$" pieces
F: $1\frac{1}{8}$" × $1\frac{1}{2}$" piece
G: $1\frac{1}{4}$" × $1\frac{1}{2}$" piece
H: two $1\frac{3}{16}$" × $2\frac{1}{2}$" pieces
I: $\frac{7}{8}$" × $2\frac{1}{2}$" piece
J: 1" × $2\frac{1}{2}$" piece
K: two $\frac{3}{4}$" × $1\frac{1}{2}$" pieces
L: $1\frac{1}{8}$" × $1\frac{1}{2}$" piece
M: piece from pattern, diagram 1
N: $\frac{3}{16}$" × $\frac{7}{8}$" piece
O: piece from pattern, diagram 2

PIECES FROM $\frac{1}{32}$" BALSA SHEET
P: piece from pattern, diagram 3
Q: 1" × $1\frac{1}{4}$" piece

PIECES FROM TOOTHPICKS
R: two $1\frac{1}{2}$" pieces

CUTTING
1. Cut wood on lengthwise grain except for piece (O), which is cut on crosswise grain.
2. For pieces (M), (O), and (P), cut a curved line.

3. For pieces (R), cut off both ends of toothpicks to obtain correct length.

SANDING AND STAINING
1. Sand wood.
2. For pieces (A), (B), (C), and (D), bevel front and side edges. After being beveled, piece (D) must measure 1" × $1\frac{7}{16}$" on bottom surface and $\frac{15}{16}$" × $1\frac{1}{4}$" on top surface.
3. For piece (P), bevel all four edges, including curved edge.
4. For piece (Q), cut off equal amount from each corner in a straight line; see detail in diagram 4. Curve these lines with a dowel sandpaper. Bevel all four straight and curved edges.
5. Stain wood.

ASSEMBLING BOTTOM SECTION, diagram 4
1. Place pieces (E), (F), and (G) onto bottom piece (A) to make sure of proper fit; cut and re-bevel (A) if necessary.
2. Center and glue door panel (Q) to front piece (G).
3. Glue front edges of sides (E) to front (G).

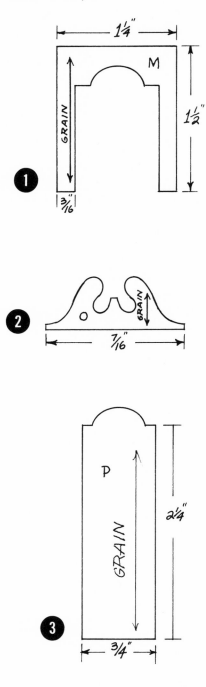

❶

❷

❸

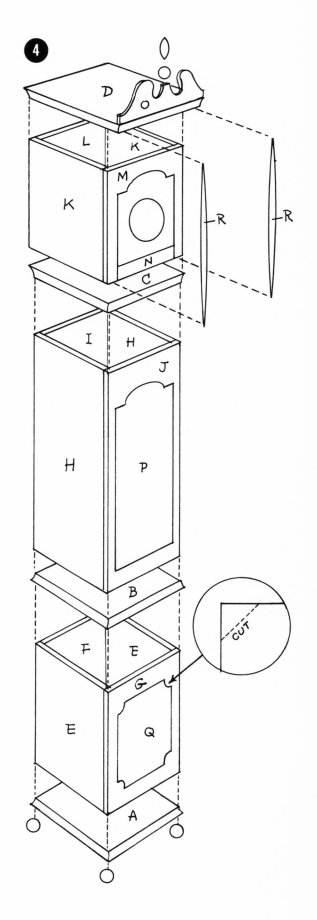

❹

4. Glue back piece (F) to assembly from step 3 so outside surface of (F) is flush with back edges of sides (E). Assembly must form a perfect rectangle.

5. Glue assembly from step 4 to bottom (A) so outside surface of back (F) is flush with straight back edge of (A).

Assembling middle section, diagram 4

1. Place pieces (H), (I), and (J) onto middle piece (B) to make sure of proper fit; cut and re-bevel piece (B) if necessary.

2. Center and glue door panel (P) to front piece (J).

3. Glue front edges of sides (H) to front (J).

4. Glue back piece (I) to assembly from step 3 so outside surface of (I) is flush with back edges of sides (H). Assembly must form a perfect rectangle.

5. Glue assembly from step 4 to piece (B) so outside surface of back (I) is flush with straight back edge of (B).

6. Center and glue middle piece (C) to assembly from step 5. Glue (C) upside down so beveled edges are on the bottom, and straight back edge of (C) is flush with outside surface of back (I).

7. Center and glue middle section assembly to bottom section so outside surfaces of backs (I) and (F) are flush. Both sections must stand perfectly perpendicular to the floor.

ASSEMBLING TOP SECTION, diagram 4

1. Glue piece (N) at bottom edge of front piece (M) to complete opening for the clock face.

2. Glue piece of acetate to back side of front (M) to cover opening.

3. Glue silver embossed paper strip to a piece of aluminum foil cut slightly larger than opening in front (M). If the embossed paper strip does not cover opening, cut it apart and glue to foil to form a pleasing pattern. The paper should resemble the metal engraving on clock faces of life-size grandfather clocks. You can "antique" the paper by painting black India ink on it and rubbing off with steel wool when dry. With curved manicure scissors, if you have them, cut a circle in center of embossed paper to fit picture of clock face or wrist watch dial, and glue embossed paper to picture or dial. Glue or tape entire clock face assembly to back side of front (M) to show through acetate.

4. Glue sides (K) to side edges of back piece (L).

5. Glue assembly from step 3 to front edges of sides (K). Assembly must form a perfect rectangle.

6. Center and glue top piece (D) to assembly from step 5. Glue (D) upside down so beveled edges are on the bottom, and straight back edge of (D) is flush with outside surface of back (L). The side edges along bottom surface of (D) should be flush with outside surface of sides (K), and front edge of (D) should overhang ⅛".

7. Glue bottom edge of pediment (O) to top

(D) so front surface of (O) is flush with beveled front edge of (D).

8. Center and glue top section assembly to middle and bottom section assemblies so outside surfaces of backs (L), (I), and (F) are flush. All three sections must stand perfectly perpendicular to the floor.

9. For columns (R), re-measure distance between bottom corner edges of top (D) and top corner edges of piece (C) and make any necessary adjustment to columns (R). Glue columns between corners of (D) and (C) so they stand ¹⁄₁₆" away from surface of (M).

FINISHING

1. Shellac, then varnish.

2. For finial carving, paint round bead, oblong bead, and straight pin with woodtone paint to match stain; insert assembly in middle of pediment (O).

3. For ball feet, paint four round beads with woodtone paint; pin beads to bottom surface of piece (A) at each corner.

SCHOOL CLOCK
(*Victorian kitchen*)

SIZE: 1"W × ³⁄₁₆"D × 1½"H

WOOD: ³⁄₃₂" balsa sheet

SUGGESTED FINISH: oak

BASIC TOOLS AND SUPPLIES, plus picture of round clock face or actual wrist watch dial—either one approximately ⅝" in diameter, watch crystal or acetate to cover clock face, small plastic curtain ring or round wire (optional), picture of pendulum (optional), rubber cement

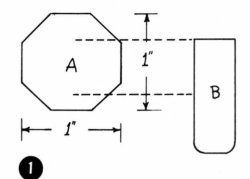

PIECES FROM ³⁄₃₂″ BALSA SHEET
  A: piece from pattern, diagram 1
  B. ½″ × 1⅜″ piece

CUTTING
  1. Cut wood on lengthwise grain.

SANDING AND STAINING
  1. Sand wood.
  2. After sanding side edges of piece (A) with straight emery board, round these sharp edges slightly on the front surface of (A) with finest grade sandpaper.
  3. For piece (B), round the bottom corners at the ends of the longer sides.
  4. Stain wood.

ASSEMBLY, diagram 2
  1. Center and glue to piece (A) either a picture of a clock face or a wrist watch dial; use rubber cement to glue picture. If a dial, cover with piece of acetate or the wrist watch's crystal, if the fit is correct. You can encircle the clock face with a piece of wire or a plastic curtain ring with the same diameter; either one should be painted gold.
  2. If you can find a picture of a pendulum, cut it to fit piece (B) and center and glue it to (B), using rubber cement.
  3. Glue piece (B) to back of piece (A) so the part of (B) that shows is ½″ long; the grain of the wood of (A) should run horizontally.

FINISHING
  1. Shellac, then varnish.

STEEPLE CLOCK
(Colonial living room)

SIZE: 1″W × ⅝″D × 1¾″H

WOOD: ³⁄₃₂″ balsa sheet, ³⁄₃₂″ sq. balsa strip, round wooden toothpick

SUGGESTED FINISH: maple

BASIC TOOLS AND SUPPLIES, plus pictures of a clock face and a scene (from mail order catalog or magazine), 1″ × 1¾″ acetate, rubber cement

PIECES FROM ³⁄₃₂″ BALSA SHEET
  A: ⅝″ × 1″ piece
  B: two pieces from pattern, diagram 1
  C: two ⁹⁄₁₆″ × 1″ pieces
  D: two ⁹⁄₁₆″ × 1³⁄₁₆″ pieces

PIECES FROM ³⁄₃₂″ SQ. BALSA STRIP
  E: two ³⁄₁₆″ pieces

PIECES FROM TOOTHPICK
  Clock spires: two ⅛″ pieces from each end

CUTTING
  1. Cut wood on lengthwise grain; cut toothpick pieces later.

SANDING AND STAINING
  1. Sand wood.
  2. Bevel top ⁹⁄₁₆″ edges of pieces (D) so they fit perfectly when forming clock roof; see directions for a straight bevel. Bevel bottom ⁹⁄₁₆″ edges of pieces (D) so they fit perfectly with top ⁹⁄₁₆″ edges of side pieces (C).
  3. Stain wood.

ASSEMBLY, diagram 2
  1. Center and glue picture of a clock face to clock front (B), and below clock face, glue picture of a scene; use rubber cement.
  2. Glue a long side of one side piece (C) to a side edge of front (B) so front edge of (C) is almost flush with front surface of (B) but actually projects ¹⁄₃₂″ from (B). Repeat for other side piece (C).
  3. Glue back piece (B) between sides (C) following procedure in step 2.
  4. Glue one roof piece (D) to slanted edge of front (B) and top edge of side (C); repeat for other piece (D). Glue together top ⁹⁄₁₆″ edges of each roof piece (D).
  5. Center and glue clock assembly to bottom piece (A) so outside surface of back (B) is flush with back edge of (A).

6. Cut piece of acetate to fit clock front (B) and glue only along the edges to sides (C) and roof (D).

7. For clock steeples, cut off ⅛″ from each end of toothpick and glue the tiny ⅛″ pieces to pieces (E). Cut away a ³⁄₃₂″ square from lower front corners of roof (D) and glue steeple assemblies into cut-out corners.

FINISHING

1. Shellac; one coat is sufficient.
2. Varnish.

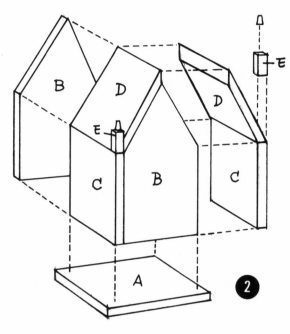

CHAPTER *19* *Cupboards*

ARMOIRE
(Victorian bedroom)

SIZE: 4¼"W × 1¾"D × 7⅛"H

WOOD: ³⁄₃₂" balsa sheet, ¹⁄₃₂" balsa sheet, ⅛" dowel

SUGGESTED FINISH: dark walnut

BASIC TOOLS AND SUPPLIES, plus 2 matching embossed paper oval picture frames, ³⁄₁₆"-wide embossed paper strip, 2 small round beads, woodtone paint

PIECES FROM ³⁄₃₂" BALSA SHEET
    A: three 1¹³⁄₁₆" × 4¼" pieces
    B: two 1¾" × 4" pieces
    C: two 1¾" × 1¾" pieces
    D: two 4" × 4⅛" pieces
    E: two 1¾" × 4" pieces
    F: piece from pattern, diagram 1
    G: two ⁵⁄₁₆" × 1¹¹⁄₁₆" pieces

PIECES FROM ¹⁄₃₂" BALSA SHEET
    H: two ⅝" × 4" pieces
    I: two ⅜" × 3½" pieces

PIECE FROM ⅛" DOWEL
    Closet rod: 4" piece

CUTTING
    1. Cut wood on lengthwise grain.
    2. For piece (F), cut a decorative edge.
    3. Cut one piece (D) in half lengthwise to form two rectangles, each 2" × 4⅛". Do not cut other piece (D).

SANDING AND STAINING
    1. Sand wood.
    2. For pieces (A), round front and side edges.
    3. For drawer panels (I), cut off an equal amount from each corner in a straight line. With a dowel sandpaper file, round each straight line and curve the side edges; see detail in diagram 2.
    4. Stain wood.

ASSEMBLY, diagram 2
    1. Glue drawers (H) to bottom front piece (B) so the top drawer is ³⁄₁₆" from top edge of (B) and the bottom drawer is ³⁄₁₆" from bottom edge of (B). The side edges of (H) are flush with side edges of (B).
    2. Center and glue drawer panels (I) to each drawer (H). Place suitable weight on top of bottom front piece assembly.
    3. Glue side pieces (C) to side edges of bottom back piece (B) with grain of sides (C) running vertically.
    4. Glue sides (C) to side edges of front (B).
    5. Center and glue assembly from steps 1–4 to bottom piece (A) so straight back edge of (A) is flush with outside surface of back (B). Place suitable weight on top of assembly.
    6. Glue side pieces (E) to side edges of top back piece (D).
    7. Center and glue assembly from step 6 to middle piece (A) so straight back edge of (A) is flush with outside surface of back (D).
    8. Center and glue top piece (A) to assembly from step 7 in same manner.
    9. The carvings on doors (D) are embossed paper picture frames. Make a pleasing arrangement of these on each door, glue down, and place suitable weight on doors. Do not paint paper until later. Fit doors between sides (E) and middle and top pieces (A), and hinge with straight pin hinges.
    10. Place glue along the three bottom edges of pieces (E) and (D). Center and glue top door assembly to bottom drawer assembly so outside surfaces of backs (D) and (B) are flush. Place suitable weight on top of entire assembly.
    11. Glue piece (F) to top of top piece (A) along front edge of (A).
    12. Glue pieces (G) to top piece (A) along side edges of (A), and glue a side edge of each piece (G) to back surface of piece (F).

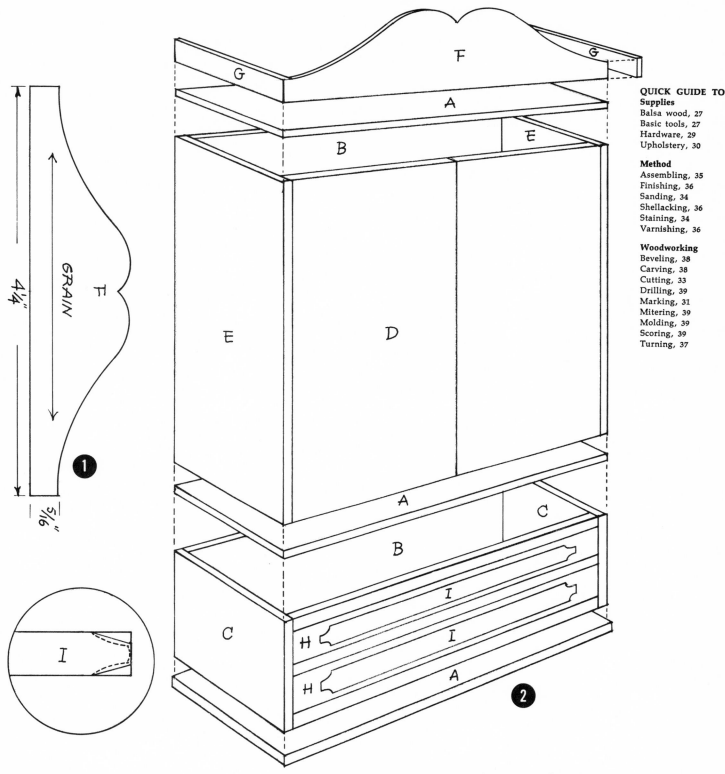

GRAIN

4¼″

5/16″

F

FINISHING

1. Shellac; use steel wool to smooth doors (D) very carefully.

2. Paint door carvings with woodtone paint to match stain after shellacking armoire and before varnishing it.

3. Varnish; open doors to varnish them and keep them open until varnish is dry.

4. For door knobs, paint beads and heads of two straight pins with woodtone paint; attach beads with pins to each door near the center and halfway between middle and top pieces (A).

5. Make two drawer handles to resemble wood carving from strip of embossed paper, each measuring about ½″. A small finial carving may also be made from embossed paper and attached to the top center edge of piece (F). Paint embossed paper with woodtone paint.

6. For closet rod, glue dowel to inside surfaces of sides (E) about ¾″ from top edges of (E).

VICTORIAN
CHINA CABINET
(Victorian dining room)

SIZE: $2\frac{3}{8}$"W × $1\frac{1}{4}$"D × $4\frac{5}{8}$"H

WOOD: $\frac{1}{8}$" balsa sheet, $\frac{3}{32}$" balsa sheet, $\frac{3}{16}$" sq. balsa strip, $\frac{1}{16}$" × $\frac{1}{8}$" balsa strip

SUGGESTED FINISH: walnut

BASIC TOOLS AND SUPPLIES, plus acetate, velvet (optional), $\frac{3}{16}$"-wide gold embossed paper strip, gold embossed paper picture frame, small round bead

PIECE FROM $\frac{1}{8}$" BALSA SHEET
    A: piece from pattern, diagram 1

PIECES FROM $\frac{3}{32}$" BALSA SHEET
    B: $1\frac{3}{4}$" × $2\frac{11}{16}$" piece
    C: $\frac{15}{16}$" × $1\frac{3}{4}$" piece
    D: $1\frac{1}{4}$" × $2\frac{1}{8}$" piece
    E: piece from pattern, diagram 2

PIECES FROM $\frac{3}{16}$" SQ. BALSA STRIP
    F: $1\frac{3}{4}$" piece
    G: two $\frac{7}{8}$" pieces
    H: four $4\frac{3}{8}$" pieces

PIECES FROM $\frac{1}{16}$" × $\frac{1}{8}$" BALSA STRIP
    I: four $1\frac{3}{4}$" pieces
    J: eight $\frac{7}{8}$" pieces
    K: twelve $2\frac{1}{4}$" pieces

PIECES FROM ACETATE
    Cabinet door: $1\frac{3}{4}$" × $2\frac{1}{2}$" piece
    Cabinet sides: two $\frac{7}{8}$" × $2\frac{1}{2}$" pieces

CUTTING
    1. Cut pieces (I), (J), and (K) first.
    2. Cut rest of wood on lengthwise grain.

SANDING AND STAINING
    1. Sand wood.
    2. For frames (I), (J), and (K), sand two or more pieces at the same time.
    3. Stain wood.

ASSEMBLING DOOR AND SIDES, diagram 3
    1. Glue a frame (I) to each short side of larger acetate piece so the edges of (I) and acetate are flush. Glue a frame (K) to each long side of acetate between frames (I) so edges of (K) and

acetate are flush; be sure to put small amount of glue on each end of frames (K) where glued to frames (I). You should have made a perfect rectangular frame. Place suitable weight on it. When dry, repeat procedure on reverse side of acetate with remaining frames (I) and four frames (K). Place suitable weight on top of entire assembly.

    2. For two cabinet sides, glue frames (J) and remaining frames (K) to the two smaller pieces of acetate, following procedure in step 1.

    3. Because you cannot easily get inside the china cabinet once it is assembled, shellac frames (I), (J), and (K) at this point. Also, shellac shelves (C) and (D), and back (B), if it is not going to be covered with velvet. It is not necessary to varnish the inside.

ASSEMBLING CHINA CABINET, diagram 3
    1. Glue piece (G) between two legs (H) so outside surface of (G) is flush with outside surfaces of (H) and top long edge of (G) is flush with top edges of (H). Repeat for other piece (G) and two legs (H).

    2. Glue one acetate-and-frame side assembly to piece ꞮG) and legs (H) so wood frame of assembly is flush with inside surfaces of (G) and (H); this will create a slightly receded side on outside of cabinet. Repeat for other acetate-and-frame side assembly and piece (G) and legs (H).

    3. Cut a piece of velvet the same size as back piece (B) and glue velvet to (B).

    4. Glue side edges of back (B) to back legs (H) so outside surfaces and top edges of all pieces are flush; velvet-covered surface of (B) is on the inside.

    5. Glue piece (F) between front legs (H) so front surface of (F) is flush with front surfaces of (H) and top long edge of (F) is flush with top edges of (H).

    6. Hinge top edge of acetate door-and-frame assembly to piece (F) with half-inch straight pin.

    7. Cut a $\frac{3}{16}$"-square piece from each corner of shelf (D) and place (D) between legs (H) to make sure it fits snugly; sand if necessary. Glue (D) to bottom edges of back (B) and frames (J), and to legs (H). Do not glue (D) to acetate door assembly.

    8. Hinge bottom edge of acetate door assembly to shelf (D) with half-inch straight pin.

    9. Glue shelf (C) inside the cabinet halfway between top and bottom edges of back (B);

back edge of (C) is glued to back (B) and the side edges of (C) are glued to frames (K), but not to the acetate.

10. Center and glue top (A) to top edges of back (B) and pieces (F) and (G).

11. Glue open shelf (E) to legs (H) ⅝″ from floor with curved edge of (E) in front. Place suitable weight on top of entire assembly.

FINISHING

1. Shellac outside of cabinet, excluding door and side frames and inside shelves.

2. Varnish outside of cabinet. Open door while varnish is drying to prevent it from sticking.

3. For brass gallery, cut two embossed paper strips to fit back and sides of cabinet and glue strips back to back. When dry, put glue along bottom edge of the reinforced strip and glue to top surface of cabinet top (A) ⅛″ in from back and side edges of (A).

4. Cut decorative ormolu work from embossed paper picture frame or strip and glue to piece (F) and to front surface of front legs (H) for a distance of about 1″.

5. For door handle, paint bead and head of straight pin gold; when dry, pin and glue bead to one outside frame (K) halfway between top and bottom edges. Decorate around handle with a little embossed paper ormolu work.

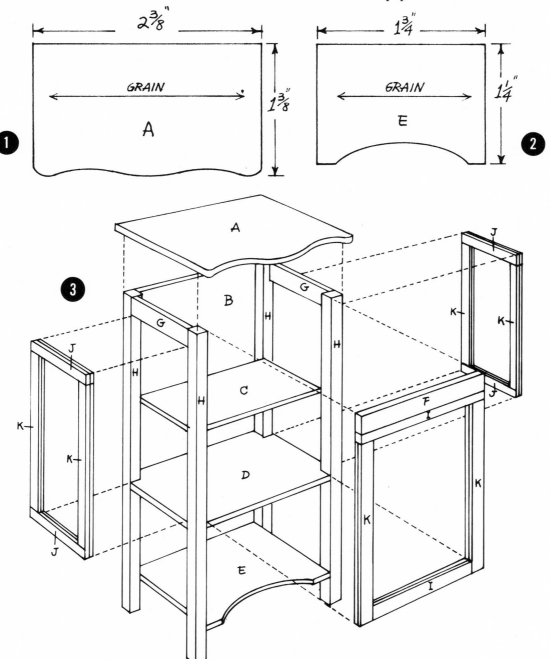

COMMODE
(Victorian bedroom)

SIZE: $2\frac{5}{8}$"W × $1\frac{1}{2}$"D × $3\frac{1}{4}$"H

WOOD: $\frac{3}{32}$" balsa sheet, $\frac{1}{32}$" balsa sheet, $\frac{3}{16}$" sq. balsa strip, $\frac{1}{16}$" sq. balsa strip, $\frac{1}{16}$" × $\frac{3}{16}$" balsa strip, $\frac{1}{16}$" × $\frac{1}{4}$" balsa strip

SUGGESTED FINISH: walnut

BASIC TOOLS AND SUPPLIES, plus $\frac{3}{16}$"-wide embossed paper strip, two small round beads, woodtone paint, Formica with marble pattern

PIECES FROM $\frac{3}{32}$" BALSA SHEET
A: piece from pattern, diagram 1
B: two $2\frac{1}{8}$" × $2\frac{1}{4}$" pieces
C: two $1\frac{1}{8}$" × $2\frac{1}{4}$" pieces
D: $1\frac{9}{16}$" × $2\frac{5}{8}$" piece
E: $1\frac{3}{16}$" × $2\frac{1}{8}$" piece

PIECES FROM $\frac{1}{32}$" BALSA SHEET
F: $\frac{3}{16}$" × $2\frac{1}{8}$" piece
G: two pieces from pattern, diagram 2

PIECES FROM $\frac{3}{16}$" SQ. BALSA STRIP
H: four $2\frac{3}{8}$" pieces

PIECES FROM $\frac{1}{16}$" SQ. BALSA STRIP
I: two $2\frac{1}{8}$" pieces

PIECES FROM $\frac{1}{16}$" × $\frac{3}{16}$" BALSA STRIP
J: four $1\frac{1}{16}$" pieces
K: six $1\frac{1}{8}$" pieces

PIECES FROM $\frac{1}{16}$" × $\frac{1}{4}$" BALSA STRIP
L: $2\frac{1}{8}$" piece
M: two $1\frac{1}{8}$" pieces

PIECES FROM FORMICA
A: piece from pattern, diagram 1
D: $1\frac{9}{16}$" × $2\frac{5}{8}$" piece

CUTTING
1. Cut wood on lengthwise grain.
2. Saw Formica pieces slowly and carefully, then smooth edges with metal file.

SANDING AND STAINING
1. Sand wood.
2. Round the curved top edge and short side edges of wood piece (A).
3. Round the front and side edges of wood piece (D).
4. For Formica piece (D), slightly round the front corners with metal file.
5. Stain wood.

ASSEMBLY, diagram 3
1. Glue piece (L) to commode front (B) so bottom edges of both pieces are flush.
2. Glue together short side edges of two pieces (J) and glue bottom edges of these pieces to top edge of (L).
3. Glue two pieces (K) to front (B) so long side edges of (K) are flush with side edges of (B) and short bottom edges of (K) are glued to top edges of pieces (J). Glue two other pieces (K) to (B) at the center, making sure to also glue pieces (K) together along long side edges.
4. Glue together short side edges of two other pieces (J) and glue bottom corner edges of each piece to top edges of four pieces (K).
5. Glue one piece (I) to front (B) and top edge of pieces (J) from step 4. Glue other piece (I) to (B) so top edges of both pieces are flush.
6. Center and glue drawer (F) to front (B) between pieces (I).
7. Glue diamond-shaped door panels (G) to front (B) so the four points of each diamond touch pieces (J) and (K).
8. Glue a piece (K) to surface of side (C) so top edges of both pieces are flush. Glue a piece (M) to same side (C) so bottom edges of both pieces are flush. Repeat procedure for other side (C) and other pieces (K) and (M).
9. Glue two legs (H) to each side of front (B) so back surface and top edge of each leg (H) are flush with back surface and top edge of (B).
10. Glue two legs (H) to each side of commode back (B) so outside surfaces and top edges of each leg (H) and back (B) are flush.
11. Glue one side (C) assembly between front (B) and back (B) assemblies so inside surfaces and top edges of legs (H) are flush with inside surface and top edge of side (C) assembly. Repeat procedure for other side (C) assembly.
12. Glue commode top (D) to commode back, front, and side assemblies; the back edge of (D) is flush with outside surface of back (B).
13. Glue commode bottom (E) to commode so underside of (E) is flush with bottom edges of back and front (B) and sides (C) assemblies. Place suitable weight on top of entire assembly.

FINISHING
1. Shellac; shellac piece (A) separately.
2. Varnish; varnish piece (A) separately.
3. Paint edges of Formica pieces white. Glue Formica piece (D) to commode top (D). Glue Formica piece (A) to commode back top (A),

and glue this assembly to (D) assembly so back surface of (A) is flush with back edge of (D).

4. Make two ½"-long drawer handles from embossed paper strip and paint with woodtone paint to match stain. Glue handles to drawer (F) ½" from side edges of (F).

5. For door knobs, paint beads and two pinheads with woodtone paint. Center beads on center pieces (K) and attach with pins.

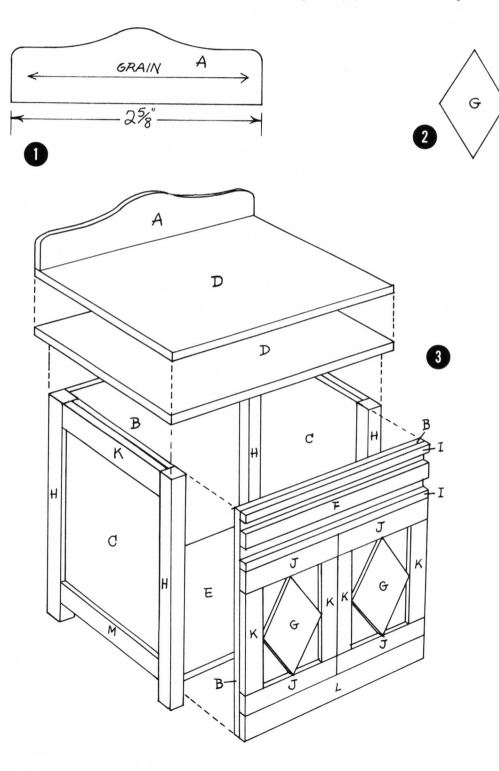

DRY SINK
(Victorian Kitchen)

SIZE: $3\frac{3}{4}''$W × $2''$D × $3\frac{1}{2}''$H

WOOD: $\frac{3}{32}''$ balsa sheet, $\frac{1}{16}''$ balsa sheet, $\frac{3}{32}''$ × $\frac{1}{4}''$ balsa strip, $\frac{1}{32}''$ scribed sheathing with scribes $\frac{3}{16}''$ apart

SUGGESTED FINISH: none

BASIC TOOLS AND SUPPLIES, plus 2 small round beads in white or gold, silver or pewter paint, 2 earring backs, half of a silver snap (optional)

PIECES FROM $\frac{3}{32}''$ BALSA SHEET
A: $3\frac{1}{2}''$ × $3\frac{1}{2}''$ piece
B: two $1\frac{7}{8}''$ × $3\frac{3}{4}''$ pieces
C: two $1\frac{3}{4}''$ × $2\frac{1}{8}''$ pieces
D: two $1\frac{9}{16}''$ × $1\frac{7}{8}''$ pieces
E: $\frac{3}{8}''$ × $2''$ piece
F: $\frac{1}{4}''$ × $\frac{1}{4}''$ piece

PIECES FROM $\frac{1}{16}''$ BALSA SHEET
G: $1\frac{1}{4}''$ × $2\frac{1}{4}''$ piece
H: two $\frac{1}{2}''$ × $2\frac{1}{4}''$ pieces
I: two $\frac{1}{2}''$ × $1\frac{1}{8}''$ pieces

PIECES FROM $\frac{3}{32}''$ × $\frac{1}{4}''$ BALSA STRIP
J: $3\frac{1}{2}''$ piece
K: $1\frac{7}{8}''$ piece
L: piece from pattern, diagram 1
M: two pieces from pattern, diagram 2

PIECES FROM $\frac{1}{32}''$ SCRIBED SHEATHING
D: two $1\frac{9}{16}''$ × $1\frac{7}{8}''$ pieces

CUTTING

1. Cut wood on lengthwise grain. See step 3 for possible exception for balsa sheet pieces (D).

2. For sink top (B), cut out a $1\frac{1}{8}''$ × $2\frac{1}{8}''$ rectangle from one of pieces (B); the long sides of the rectangular opening are $\frac{3}{8}''$ in from long sides of (B) and one short side of the opening is $\frac{3}{8}''$ in from one short side of (B).

3. If you are able to purchase scribed sheathing for doors (D), it is to be glued to balsa sheet doors (D), in which case cut balsa sheet doors (D) on crosswise grain. If you cannot purchase scribed sheathing, cut doors (D) on lengthwise grain as usual.

4. For shelf brackets (F), cut piece (F) in half diagonally.

5. For legs (L) and (M), cut a curved line.

SANDING AND STAINING

1. Sand wood.

2. Round the top corners of sink back (A). Grain of the wood of (A) should run horizontally.

3. Bevel front and side edges of top and bottom pieces (B) in a round bevel.

4. For shelf (E), round the corners of the front edge.

5. Although pine or oak are suitable finishes for a dry sink, the natural color of the balsa wood is the best choice for this piece of furniture.

ASSEMBLY, diagram 3

1. Glue balsa sheet doors (D) to scribed sheathing doors (D), with grain of balsa wood running in opposite direction from grain of sheathing to prevent warping. Place suitable weight on top doors.

2. Trim door divider (K) from $\frac{1}{4}''$ wide to $\frac{3}{16}''$ wide. Glue one $\frac{3}{16}''$ edge of (K) to bottom edge of door frame (J) exactly in the middle so the two pieces form a T. Following directions under hardware for straight pin hinging, hinge top edge of a door (D) to frame (J) $\frac{3}{32}''$ from end of (J); door (D) is flush with divider (K). Repeat procedure for other door (D).

3. Trim away a $\frac{3}{32}''$ × $\frac{1}{4}''$ rectangle from one top front corner of a side piece (C) so the $\frac{3}{32}''$ extension of frame (J) fits snugly into the cutting and front edge of (C) is flush with front surface of door (D). Repeat for other side piece (C). Glue the $\frac{3}{32}''$ extensions of frame (J) into cuttings of sides (C).

4. Center assembly from steps 1–3 on sink bottom (B). Glue bottom edges of sides (C) and divider (K) to (B) so straight back edge of (B) is flush with back edges of (C). Do not glue the bottom edges of doors (D) to (B), but hinge them together with straight pin hinge.

5. For the liner, glue a piece (I) between pieces (H) so a side edge of each piece (H) is flush with outside surface of (I); repeat for other piece (I). Glue bottom edges of this assembly to piece (G) so edges of (G) are flush with outside surfaces of the assembly. Glue top edges of the liner to underside of sink top (B) at the rectangular opening.

6. Center and glue sink top assembly from step 5 to top edges of sides (C) and door frame (J). Place suitable weight on top of entire assembly.

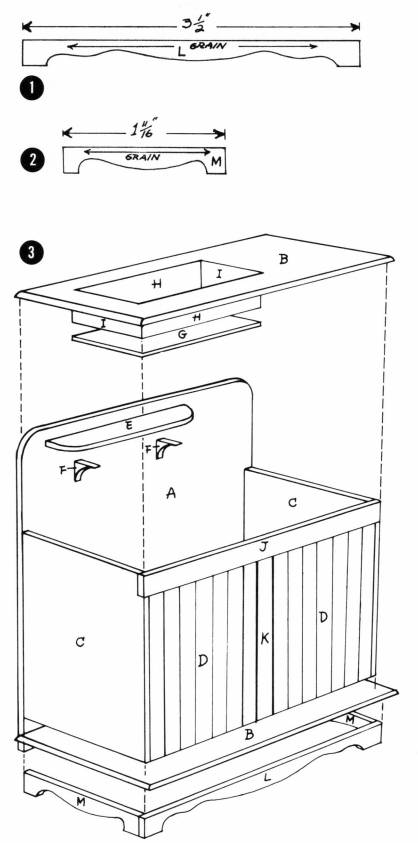

7. Glue assembly from step 6 to back piece (A) ¼″ from floor. The side edges of (A) are flush with outside surface of sides (C), and pieces (B) extend ⅛″ beyond each side edge of (A).

8. Glue leg (L) to underside of bottom (B) ⅛″ in from front edge of (B).

9. Glue leg (M) to underside of bottom (B) ⅛″ in from side edge of (B) with the outside surface of (M) flush with side edges of back (A) and leg (L); repeat for other leg (M).

10. Glue shelf (E) to back (A) ¼″ from top edge of (A) and centered over the sink.

11. Glue shelf brackets (F) to bottom surface of shelf (E) about ¼″ from side edges of (E). You may want to sand a curved line on the diagonal edge of each bracket before gluing in place.

FINISHING

1. Shellac, then varnish.

2. For door knobs, with a straight pin and a little glue attach a bead to each door (D) near door divider (K), halfway between top and bottom edges of doors.

3. Paint liner with silver or pewter paint to resemble metal. When dry, glue half of a silver snap to bottom of sink for a drain.

4. For sink faucets, cut the loop portions of two earring backs in half; the screw part of each back and half of the loop resemble a faucet. Glue faucets in place at back edge of sink.

HUTCH CUPBOARD
(*Colonial dining room*)

SIZE: 4¼"W × 1⅝"D × 6¾"H

WOOD: ³⁄₁₆" balsa sheet, ⅛" balsa sheet, ³⁄₃₂" balsa sheet, ¹⁄₁₆" balsa sheet, ¹⁄₁₆" scribed sheathing with scribes ½" apart

SUGGESTED FINISH: maple

BASIC TOOLS AND SUPPLIES, plus 2 small round beads, gold paint

PIECE FROM ³⁄₁₆" BALSA SHEET
   A: 1" × 4⅜" piece

PIECES FROM ⅛" BALSA SHEET
   B: two pieces from pattern, diagram 1
   C: 1⅝" × 4¼" piece
   D: eight pieces from pattern, diagram 2
   E: 1⁹⁄₁₆" × 4⅛" piece
   F: two 1½" × 2⅜" pieces

PIECES FROM ³⁄₃₂" BALSA SHEET
   G: three ¾" × 3⅞" pieces
   H: ¼" × 4⅛" piece
   I: two ⅜" × 2⅛" pieces
   J: ¼" × 3⅜" piece
   K: two 1¹¹⁄₁₆" × 1⅞" pieces
   L: 1¼" × 3⅞" piece

PIECES FROM ¹⁄₁₆" BALSA SHEET
   M: two 1³⁄₁₆" × 1⅜" pieces
   N: 2⅜" × 3⅞" piece

PIECE FROM ¹⁄₁₆" SCRIBED SHEATHING
   O: 3½" × 3⅞" piece

CUTTING
   1. Cut wood on lengthwise grain except for pieces (N) and (O), which are cut on crosswise grain.
   2. Your X-acto knife blade must be very sharp to cut the ³⁄₁₆" balsa wood required for piece (A). This piece could be cut from ⅛"-thick balsa wood.
   3. For side pieces (B), see under "wood cutting" to make a decorative edge.
   4. For legs (D), see directions on page 33 for cutting a curved line. Cut ¼" off short side edge of four of the eight leg pieces; see broken line in diagram 2.
   5. If you cannot purchase scribed sheathing for piece (O), use ¹⁄₁₆" balsa sheet instead.

SANDING AND STAINING
   1. Sand wood.
   2. For cupboard top (A) and bottom (C), bevel front and side edges.
   3. For door panels (M), bevel all four edges.
   4. Stain wood.

ASSEMBLING TOP CUPBOARD SECTION, diagram 3
   1. Glue long straight edges of side pieces (B) to side edges of back piece (O) so edges of (B) are flush with outside surface of (O).
   2. Divide back (O) into four equal parts by putting pencil dots ⅞" apart on vertical line. Divide and mark inside surface of side pieces (B) ⅞" apart; see diagram 1. Glue shelves (G) to pencil dots so shelves are level, evenly spaced, and perfectly perpendicular to back (O).
   3. Center top (A) on top edges of assembly from steps 1 and 2 and glue upside down so beveled edges are on the bottom. The straight back edge of (A) is flush with outside surface of back (O).

ASSEMBLING BOTTOM CUPBOARD SECTION, diagram 3
   1. Center and glue door panels (M) to doors (K) and place suitable weight on top.
   2. Glue a short edge of each piece (I) to top long edge of piece (H) at the corners so short side edges of (H) are flush with long edges of pieces (I). Glue piece (J) between pieces (I) so

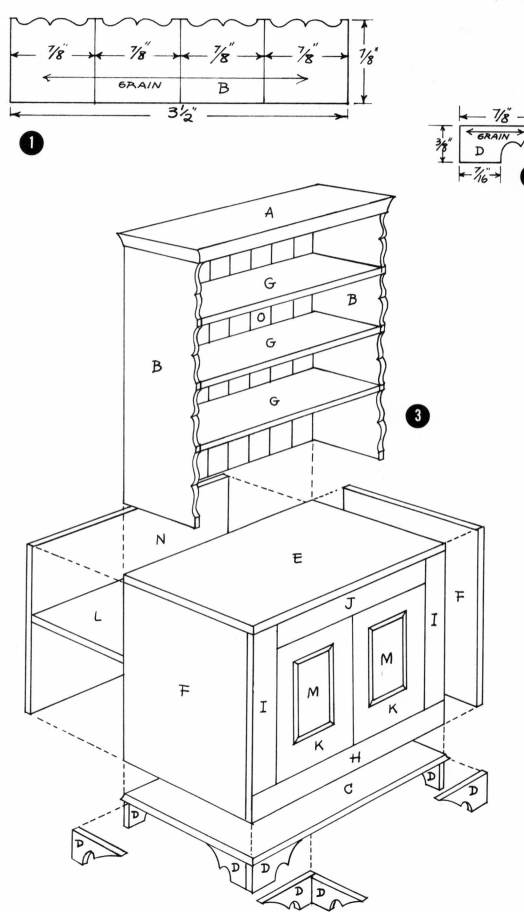

1

7/8" | 7/8" | 7/8" | 7/8" | 7/8"

GRAIN

B

3 1/2"

2

7/8"

GRAIN

D

3/8"

7/16"

3

A

G

O

G

B

B

G

N

E

L

J

F

I

F

M

M

I

K

K

H

C

D

D

D

D

D

D

D

top edges of both pieces are flush. These four pieces must form a perfect 2⅜″ × 4⅛″ rectangular frame in order for doors (K) to fit inside perfectly. Make any necessary adjustments.

3. Hinge doors (K), using straight pin hinges, to assembly from step 2.

4. Glue front piece assembly from steps 1–3 to underside of top piece (E) so front edge of (E) is flush with front surface of assembly.

5. Trim back edge of side piece (F) so that it is flush with back edge of top (E). Glue side (F) to top (E) and front piece assembly, with outside surface of (F) flush with side edge of (E) and side edge of front piece assembly; repeat for other side (F).

6. Glue assembly from step 5 to bottom piece (C); beveled surface of (C) is right side up and straight back edge of (C) is flush with back edges of sides (F).

7. Put glue along side edges of shelf (L) and glue to inside surfaces of sides (F) 1″ from top edges of (F) and a fraction of an inch away from front piece assembly; the correct positioning of shelf (L) is important for the doors (K) to open and close easily and smoothly.

8. Measure back opening in bottom cupboard section and make any adjustments necessary for correct fit of back piece (N). Place glue along four edges of back (N) and along back edge of shelf (L). Glue (N) to bottom cupboard section so outside surface of (N) is flush with back edges of (E) and (F), and place suitable weight on top.

9. Apply glue to top long edges of two of the longer legs (D); glue to bottom of cupboard along front edge of (C), with short straight edges of (D) flush with outside surface of sides (F). Repeat procedure for other two longer legs (D), gluing along back edge of (C).

Apply glue to top long edges and short side edges of two of the shorter legs (D); glue to bottom of cupboard along side edges of (C) as well as to front legs so each short-long leg combination forms a perfect right angle. Repeat procedure for other two shorter legs (D), gluing to bottom of (C) and to longer back legs.

10. Glue top cupboard section to bottom cupboard section so outside surfaces of backs (N) and (O) and sides (B) and (F) are flush.

FINISHING

1. Shellac; one coat is sufficient. Open doors to shellac them and keep open until dry.

2. Varnish, excluding inside of cupboard. Open doors to varnish them and keep open until dry.

3. For door knobs, use two gold beads, two smooth-surfaced beads painted gold, or two map pins painted gold. Paint heads of two straight pins gold, and with pins and a little glue, attach beads to each door (K) near the center and halfway between pieces (H) and (J).

Variation: SERVING BOARD

The bottom cupboard section is a suitable serving board for a dollhouse dining room or kitchen. It may also be used in a bedroom or hall as a storage piece. Stain in mahogany for a more formal finish.

ICEBOX
(Victorian kitchen)

Size: 2½"W × 1⅝"D × 4"H

Wood: ⅛" balsa sheet, ³⁄₃₂" balsa sheet, ¹⁄₁₆" balsa sheet, ¼" sq. balsa strip, ¹⁄₁₆" × ¼" balsa strip, ⅛" dowel

Suggested finish: none

Basic tools and supplies, plus scrap of imitation leather (optional), silver or pewter paint, sewing loop, sewing hook, aluminum foil, pliers, plastic eye make-up box

Pieces from ⅛" balsa sheet
    A: 2" × 2⅛" piece
    B: 1" × 2⅛" piece

Pieces from ³⁄₃₂" balsa sheet
    C: two pieces from pattern, diagram 1
    D: piece from pattern, diagram 2
    E: 2" × 3¾" piece
    F: 1⅛" × 2" piece
    G: two 1⁵⁄₁₆" × 2³⁄₁₆" pieces

Pieces from ¹⁄₁₆" balsa sheet
    H: 1⅝" × 2½" piece
    I: ⅜" × 2" piece

Pieces from ¼" sq. balsa strip
    J: four 3⅞" pieces

Pieces from ¹⁄₁₆" × ¼" balsa strip
    K: four 2" pieces
    L: four 1⅛" pieces
    M: two 2¹⁄₁₆" pieces
    N: two 1¾" pieces
    O: two 2⁵⁄₁₆" pieces
    P: two ⅝" pieces

Piece from ⅛" dowel
    Pipe: 2½"

Cutting
    1. Cut wood on lengthwise grain.
    2. For pieces (C) and (D), see directions under wood cutting to make a decorative edge.
    3. Cut out a 1" × 2⅛" rectangle directly in center of piece (H).

Sanding and staining
    1. Sand wood.
    2. Although pine or oak are suitable finishes for an icebox, the natural color of the balsa wood is the best choice for this piece of furniture.

Assembly, diagram 3
    1. Glue a piece (L) to side piece (C) so top edges of both pieces are flush. Glue a piece (L) to same side (C) so bottom edge of (L) is ³⁄₁₆" from the floor. Repeat procedure for other pieces (L) and other side (C).
    2. Glue one side (C) assembly from step 1 between two legs (J) so top edges of all pieces are flush and the outside surfaces of pieces (L) and legs (J) are flush. Repeat for other side (C) assembly and other legs (J).
    3. Glue a piece (K) to icebox back (E) so top edges of both pieces are flush. Glue a second piece (K) to back (E) so bottom edges of both pieces are flush.
    4. Glue a third piece (K) to top front piece (F) so top edges of both pieces are flush. Glue a fourth piece (K) to piece (F) so bottom edges of both pieces are flush.
    5. Glue piece (I) to bottom front piece (D) so top edges of both pieces are flush.
    6. Glue back (E) between back legs (J) so top edges of (E) and (J) are flush and outside surfaces of (J) and pieces (K) are flush.
    7. Glue top front piece (F) between front legs (J) so top edges of (F) and (J) are flush and front surfaces of (J) and pieces (K) are flush.
    8. Glue bottom front piece (D) between front legs (J) so top edge of (D) is ⅝" from floor and front surfaces of (J) and piece (I) are flush.
    9. Trim each corner of bottom piece (G) so it fits snugly around four legs (J). Glue (G) to back, sides, and front assemblies ⅛" from floor. Repeat for middle piece (G), except underside of middle piece is flush with bottom edge of top front piece (F).

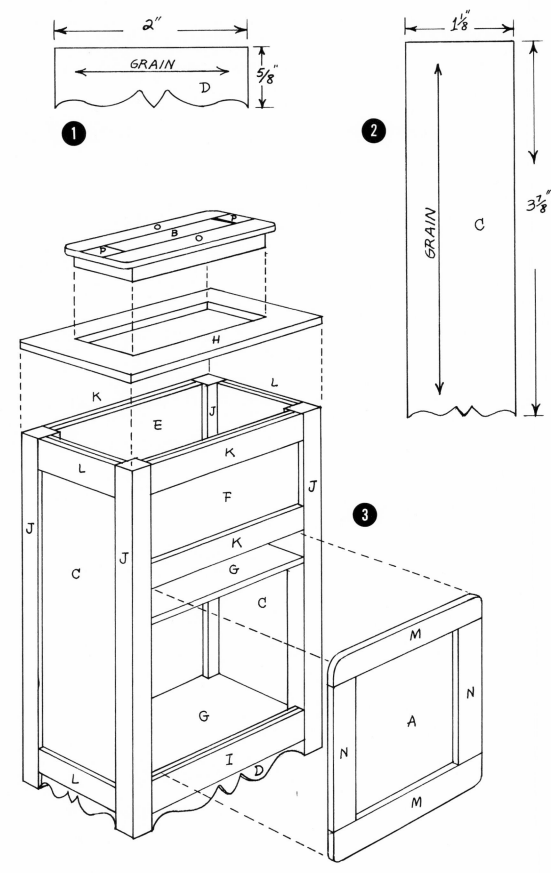

10. Glue icebox top (H) to top edges of the back, sides, and front assemblies and place suitable weight on top.

11. Glue two pieces (P) between two pieces (O) to form a rectangular frame. Glue frame to top surface of icebox lid (B); the frame will extend ⅛" on all four edges. When lid assembly is dry, round each corner of frame.

12. Glue two pieces (N) between two pieces (M) to form a rectangular frame. Glue frame to front surface of icebox door (A); the frame will extend 1⁄16" on all four edges. When door assembly is dry, round each corner of frame.

13. The icebox lid and door assemblies from steps 11 and 12 may be glued into their respective openings on the icebox. If you do this, paint hinges on icebox with silver or pewter paint; paint two hinges along back edge of lid and two hinges along left side of door. Make painted hinges more realistic by using pinheads to simulate the nails of the hinges.

If you want the icebox lid and door to open and close, make four strap hinges out of imitation leather, each measuring about 3⁄16" × ⅝", and attach with half-inch straight pins.

FINISHING

1. Shellac, then varnish.

2. For icebox lid handle, bend a sewing loop in an upright position and secure it with straight pins to front center edge of lid.

3. For icebox door latch, glue small piece of aluminum foil to middle of piece (N) for a metal plate; then cut two circular ends off a sewing hook and glue the hook-latch to aluminum foil plate.

4. Paint interior of both sections of icebox with silver or pewter paint. Cut, fit, and glue a ⅛" dowel to inside back of bottom section to resemble a pipe that carries melted ice from top section to drip pan on bottom of icebox. For drip pan, paint a plastic eye make-up container with silver or pewter paint. Paint pipe also.

CHAPTER *20* *Desks*

DAVENPORT DESK
(Victorian living room)

SIZE: 1¾"W × 1⅝"D × 2½"H

WOOD: ⅛" balsa sheet, 1/16" balsa sheet, 1/32" balsa sheet, ⅛" sq. balsa strip, 2 round wooden toothpicks

SUGGESTED FINISH: dark walnut

BASIC TOOLS AND SUPPLIES, plus 3/16"-wide embossed paper strip, gold paint, 20 tiny round beads, 4 round beads, woodtone paint, scrap piece of thin velvet or vinyl leather

PIECE FROM ⅛" BALSA SHEET
   A: piece from pattern, diagram 1

PIECES FROM 1/16" BALSA SHEET
   B: two 1½" × 1¾" pieces
   C: two ⅞" × 1½" pieces
   D: two pieces from pattern, diagram 2
   E: 1½" × 1⅝" piece
   F: ⅛" × 1⅝" piece
   G: 7/16" × 1⅝" piece
   H: ⅝" × 1⅝" piece
   I: 1 3/16" × 1¾" piece

PIECES FROM 1/32" BALSA SHEET
   J: eight 5/16" × ⅞" pieces

PIECES FROM ⅛" SQ. BALSA STRIP
   Decorative posts: two ⅛" pieces

CUTTING
1. Cut wood on lengthwise grain except for pieces (A), (B), and (C), which are cut on crosswise grain. Cut pieces from ⅛" sq. balsa strip later.
2. For desk bottom (A), first cut a 1⅝" × 1¾" rectangle, then cut out a ⅝" × 1¼" rectangle from the center front crosswise edge; see diagram 1. This will leave ¼" on each side of front edge of (A).

SANDING AND STAINING
1. Sand wood.

2. For bottom (A), round the ¼" front edges; see diagram 1.
3. For desk top (I), bevel all four edges in a round bevel.
4. Stain wood.

ASSEMBLING DESK TOP SECTION, diagram 3
1. Glue desk sides (D) to longer side edges of desk bottom (E).
2. Place glue along bottom edge of desk front (F) and glue to top surface of bottom (E) between short 3/16" front edges of sides (D). The front surface of (F) is flush with front edge of (E).
3. Place glue along back edge of bottom (E) and side edges of back piece (H), and glue (H) between sides (D) so back surface of (H) is flush with back edges of (D).
4. For brass gallery, cut embossed paper strip to fit inside the top edge of back (H) and ½" top edges of sides (D). Paint paper strip with brass or gold paint and glue it to extend ⅛" above (D) and (H).
5. Fit and glue gallery desk top piece (G) between sides (D) so top surface of (G) is flush with top edges of (D) and back (H). Piece (G) will hold embossed paper gallery in place.
6. Glue desk top (I) to slanted edges of sides (D), front edge of gallery desk top (G), and top edge of desk front (F).

ASSEMBLING DESK BOTTOM SECTION, diagram 3
1. Glue four drawers (J) to side piece (C). Leave 1/16" space between top drawer and top edge of (C), between bottom drawer and bottom edge of (C), and between each drawer. Sand side edges of drawers so they are perfectly flush with side edges of (C). Repeat procedure for other four drawers (J) and side (C). Place suitable weight on top of both assemblies.
2. Glue a drawers-and-side assembly from step 1 between shorter side edges of front and back pieces (B) so drawers are flush with side

edges of pieces (B). Repeat procedure for other drawers-and-side assembly.

3. Glue assemblies from steps 1 and 2 to bottom (A) so outside surface of back (B) is flush with back edge of (A).

4. Glue desk top section to desk bottom section so outside surfaces of backs (H) and (B) are flush.

FINISHING

1. Shellac, then varnish.

2. Make two decorative posts 1½" in length. Each post consists of a toothpick cut in half and trimmed, two tiny beads, and a ⅛" cube cut from ⅛" sq. balsa strip; see diagram 3. Paint post pieces with woodtone paint to match stain, and when dry, glue together. Then place dots of glue on tops of top beads and bottoms of bottom beads, and glue posts to bottom surface of (D) and top surface of (A) about ⅛" out from front (B).

3. For drawer knobs, paint 16 tiny beads and 16 pinheads with woodtone paint. Center and glue two beads to each drawer (J) ¼" from side edges.

4. For desk top, cut a 1" × 1⁹⁄₁₆" piece of velvet or vinyl leather; center and glue it to desk top (I).

5. For ball feet, paint four beads with woodtone paint and glue under the four corners of bottom (A).

Variation: CAPTAIN'S DESK

A captain's desk is the same style as a davenport desk but less formal. Eliminate embossed paper rail and fabric desk top cover. Stain desk in oak and paint beaded drawer knobs as well as the posts with woodtone paint to match stain.

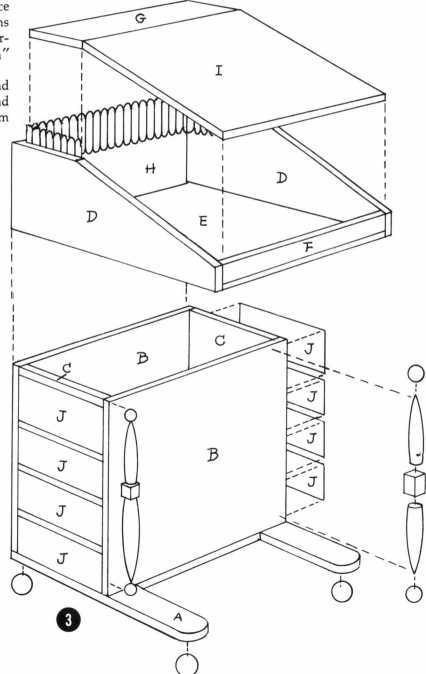

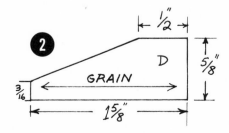

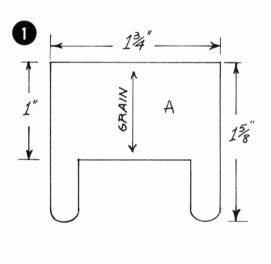

PARTNERS' DESK
(Georgian library)

SIZE: 4½"W × 3¼"D × 2½"H

WOOD: ⅛" balsa sheet, ³⁄₃₂" balsa sheet, ¹⁄₃₂" balsa sheet, ¹⁄₁₆" × ¼" balsa strip

SUGGESTED FINISH: mahogany

BASIC TOOLS AND SUPPLIES, plus 17" of ⅛"-thick picture hanging wire, pliers, woodtone paint, 12 map pins, 12 small round beads, gold paint

PIECE FROM ⅛" BALSA SHEET
  A: 3¼" × 4½" piece

PIECES FROM ³⁄₃₂" BALSA SHEET
  B: two 2⅜" × 4⅜" pieces
  C: two 2⅜" × 3¹⁄₁₆" pieces
  D: two 2" × 3¹⁄₁₆" pieces
  E: 2¼" × 3¹⁄₁₆" piece

PIECES FROM ¹⁄₃₂" BALSA SHEET
  F: twelve ½" × 1" pieces
  G: four ¼" × 1" pieces
  H: two ¼" × 2⅛" pieces

PIECES FROM ¹⁄₁₆" × ¼" BALSA STRIP
  I: four 1¼" pieces
  J: four 3¼" pieces

CUTTING
1. Cut wood on lengthwise grain.
2. Pieces (B) are both fronts for the partners' desk, which is actually two-desks-in-one for two people to use. For the kneehole, cut out a rectangle 2⅛" long and 2" high from center

bottom edge of each front piece (B), leaving 1⅛" on each side of rectangular opening.

SANDING AND STAINING
1. Sand wood.
2. For desk top (A), round all four edges inwards (concave) so rope molding made from picture hanging wire will fit snugly; use sandpaper wrapped around a ¹⁄₁₆" dowel. If you do not want rope molding around your desk top, bevel all four edges.
3. For drawers (F), (G), and (H), bevel all four edges.
4. For bottom moldings (I) and (J), bevel top edges.
5. Stain wood.

ASSEMBLY, diagram 1
1. Paint picture hanging wire with woodtone paint to match stain. When dry, bend wire with pliers into a rectangle the same size as desk top (A); cut overlapping wire with wire cutters. Glue wire to concave edges of desk top and hold in place with your hands until glue is set. Place suitable weight on top of desk top.
2. Glue three drawers (F) to each side of one front piece (B). Leave ½" space between top drawers and top edge of (B); leave ⅜" space between bottom drawers and bottom edge of (B); leave ¹⁄₁₆" space between drawers; leave ¹⁄₁₆" space between sides of drawers and side edges of (B).
3. Center and glue drawer (H) to front (B) between top edge of (B) and kneehole edge.
4. Glue drawers (G) to front (B) at same level as drawer (H), leaving ¹⁄₁₆" space between drawers and outside side edges of (B).
5. Repeat procedure in steps 2–4 for other drawers (F), (G), and (H) and other front (B). Place suitable weight on top of both assemblies from steps 2–5.
6. Glue one drawer-and-front assembly to front edges of two side pieces (C); repeat for other drawer-and-front assembly and other side edges of (C).
7. Glue front and back edges of kneehole side pieces (D) along inside edges of both drawer-and-front assemblies at kneehole openings.
8. Glue kneehole top piece (E) to top edges of kneehole sides (D).
9. Center and glue desk top (A) to drawer and front, and side assemblies with desk top extending evenly on all four edges.

10. Glue two moldings (J) to sides (C) so beveled edges of (J) are on top and bottom edges of (J) are flush with bottom edges of (C).

11. Glue other moldings (J) to kneehole sides (D) following procedure in step 10.

12. Glue four moldings (I) to front pieces (B) following procedure for moldings (J) in steps 10 and 11. Place suitable weight on top of entire assembly.

FINISHING

1. Shellac, then varnish.

2. For drawer hardware, paint heads of 12 map pins, 12 beads, and heads of 12 straight pins gold. Center and insert one map pin into each drawer (F). Insert straight pins through beads and attach beads $\frac{3}{16}''$ from side edges of drawers (G) and $\frac{3}{8}''$ from side edges of drawers (H).

Variation: KNEEHOLE DESK

If you want to make this a desk at which only one person can sit, cut rectangular opening in only one of the pieces (B); the other (B) becomes the desk back piece. Bottom back molding (I) is one $4\frac{1}{2}''$ piece. Entire desk is 1'' shorter in depth requiring the following changes in measurements: desk top (A) is $2\frac{1}{4}'' \times 4\frac{1}{2}''$, sides (C) are $2\frac{1}{16}'' \times 2\frac{3}{8}''$, kneehole sides (D) are $2\frac{1}{16}'' \times 2''$, kneehole top (E) is $2\frac{1}{16}'' \times 2\frac{1}{4}''$, moldings (J) are $2\frac{1}{4}''$. Number of drawers is reduced to six (F), two (G), and one (H).

QUICK GUIDE TO
Supplies
Balsa wood, 27
Basic tools, 27
Hardware, 29
Upholstery, 30

Method
Assembling, 35
Finishing, 36
Sanding, 34
Shellacking, 36
Staining, 34
Varnishing, 36

Woodworking
Beveling, 38
Carving, 38
Cutting, 33
Drilling, 39
Marking, 31
Mitering, 39
Molding, 39
Scoring, 39
Turning, 37

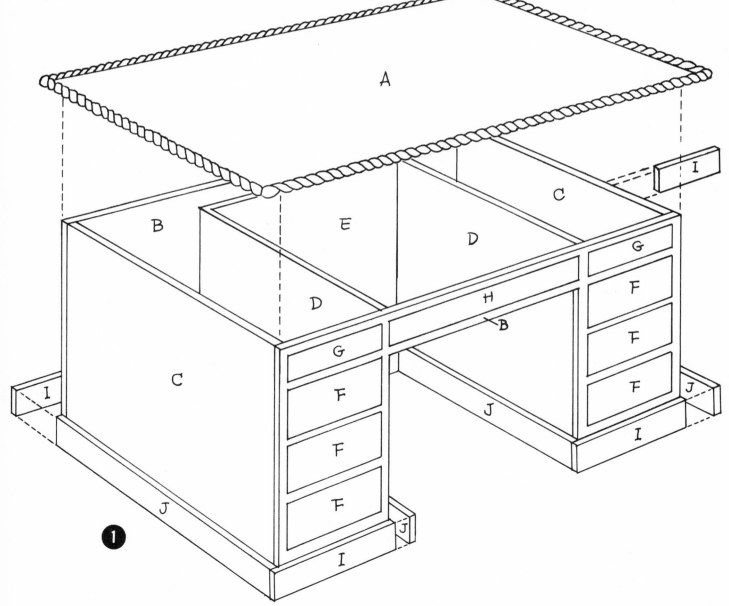

SLANT TOP DESK
(*Colonial living room*)

SIZE: 3½"W × 1⅞"D × 3½"H

WOOD: ⅛" balsa sheet, 3/32" balsa sheet, 1/32" balsa sheet

SUGGESTED FINISH: mahogany

BASIC TOOLS AND SUPPLIES, plus 8 sewing loops, prong (for holding rhinestone), gold paint, 2 pairs of pliers

PIECES FROM ⅛" BALSA SHEET
A: two pieces from pattern, diagram 1

PIECES FROM 3/32" BALSA SHEET
B: piece from pattern, diagram 2
C: 3" × 3¼" piece
D: 1½" × 3⅜" piece
E: 1" × 3¼" piece
F: 1 11/16" × 3¼" piece

PIECES FROM 1/32" BALSA SHEET
G: ¼" × 3¼" piece
H: two ⅜" × 3¼" pieces
I: ½" × 3¼" piece

CUTTING
1. Cut wood on lengthwise grain except for piece (C), which is cut on crosswise grain.
2. For desk front (B) and sides (A), see directions for cutting a curved line.
3. For drawer (G), cut away a ⅛" piece from each side edge and save these pieces. Cut away a 1/16" piece from each side edge of (G) so dimensions of (G) are ¼" × 2⅞".
4. For two back feet, use the feet that are part of decorative edge in diagram 1 for a pattern; each foot should be ½" long on top edge and ⅜" high when cut.

SANDING AND STAINING
1. Sand wood.
2. For desk top (D), bevel all four edges in a round bevel.
3. For drawers (G), (H), and (I), bevel all four edges.
4. Stain wood.

ASSEMBLY, diagram 3
1. Center and glue drawer (G) to desk front (B) 1/16" from top edge of (B). Glue the ⅛" × ¼" pieces that you cut away from drawer (G) 1/16" from top edge of (B) and side edges of (G) with ¼" edge flush with side edges of (B); these pieces are desk stops.
2. Glue drawers (H) to front (B), leaving 1/16" space between drawers (H) and (G); the side edges of (H) are flush with side edges of (B).
3. Glue drawer (I) to front (B), leaving 1/16" space between (I) and bottom drawer (H); the side edges of (I) are flush with side edges of (B). Place suitable weight on top of assembly from steps 1–3.
4. Glue side edges of assembly from steps 1–3 to side pieces (A) so short front edges of (A) are flush with front (B).
5. Glue desk top (E) between short top edges of sides (A) so top surface of (E) is flush with top edges of sides (A).
6. Glue side edges of back piece (C) to sides (A) so outside surface of (C) is flush with back edges of (A). The top edge of (C) is glued to underside of top (E) along back edge of (E).
7. Center and glue slanted top (D) to slanted edges of sides (A) and to front edge of top (E).
8. Glue desk bottom (F) in place so underside of (F) is flush with bottom edge of back (C) and straight bottom edges of (A) and (B).
9. Glue a back foot to each corner of bottom edge of back (C) and sides (A).

FINISHING
1. Shellac, then varnish.
2. For desk stop knobs, paint heads of two straight pins gold; center and insert pins in each desk stop.
3. For keyhole, paint a rhinestone prong gold; center and insert prong ⅛" from top edge of slanted top (D).
4. Make drawer handles out of sewing loops and attach as directed on page 40. Place handles ⅝" from side edges of front (B) and centered between top and bottom edges of each drawer.

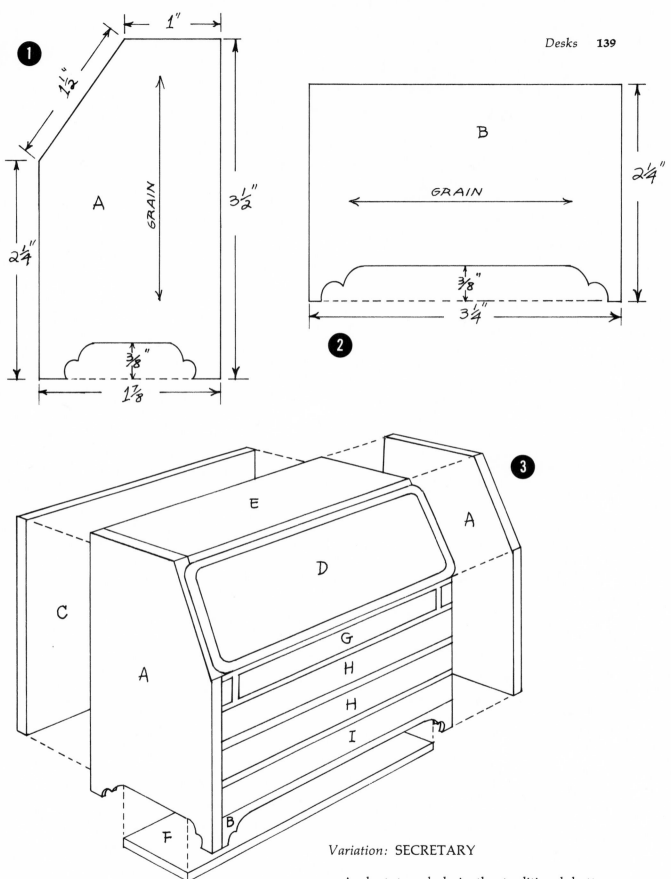

Variation: SECRETARY

A slant top desk is the traditional bottom half of a secretary. See page 84 for the top half, which is the secretary bookcase.

CHAPTER *21* *Sideboards*

QUEEN ANNE HUNT BOARD
(Colonial dining room)

SIZE: 4⅞″W × 1⅝″D × 2¾″H

WOOD: ⅛″ balsa sheet, ³⁄₃₂″ balsa sheet, ¹⁄₁₆″ balsa sheet, ¹⁄₃₂″ balsa sheet, ³⁄₁₆″ sq. balsa strip, ⅜″ × ³⁄₁₆″ balsa strip

SUGGESTED FINISH: cherry

BASIC TOOLS AND SUPPLIES, plus 4 sewing loops, gold paint, 2 pairs of pliers

PIECE FROM ⅛″ BALSA SHEET
  A: 1⅝″ × 4⅞″ piece

PIECES FROM ³⁄₃₂″ BALSA SHEET
  B: piece from pattern, diagram 1
  C: 1″ × 4¼″ piece
  D: two pieces from pattern, diagram 2
  E: 1⅛″ × 4½″ piece

PIECES FROM ¹⁄₁₆″ BALSA SHEET
  F: two 1″ × 1⅛″ pieces
  G: two ⅜″ × 1¾″ pieces

PIECES FROM ¹⁄₃₂″ BALSA SHEET
  H: two ⅝″ × ¾″ pieces

PIECES FROM ³⁄₁₆″ SQ. BALSA STRIP
  I: two 2⅝″ pieces

PIECES FROM ⅜″ × ³⁄₁₆″ BALSA STRIP
  J: two pieces from pattern, diagram 3

CUTTING
  1. Cut wood on lengthwise grain except for pieces (H), which are cut on crosswise grain.
  2. For front piece (B), cut a curved line.
  3. For legs (J), cut cabriole legs.

SANDING AND STAINING
  1. Sand wood.
  2. For top (A), bevel front and side edges.
  3. For pieces (F), (G), and (H), bevel all four edges.
  4. Stain wood.

ASSEMBLY, diagram 4
  1. Glue doors (F) to front (B) ⅛″ from top edge of (B); the shorter, side edges of (F) are flush with side edges of (B).
  2. Center and glue door panels (H) to doors (F) with wood grain of (H) running in the opposite direction of (F).
  3. Center and glue drawer (G) to front (B) ⅛″ from top edge of (B). Glue other drawer (G) ⅛″ below top drawer (G). Place suitable weight on top of assembly from steps 1–3.
  4. Glue legs (I) to each side of back piece (C) so top edges and back surfaces of both pieces are flush.
  5. Glue legs (J) to each side of front (B) in the same manner as you glued legs (I) to back (C).
  6. Glue a side piece (D) between leg (I) and leg (J) with top edges and outside surfaces of all pieces flush; repeat for other side (D) and legs (I) and (J).
  7. Center and glue top (A) to assembly from steps 4–6 so back edge of (A) is flush with outside surface of back (C).
  8. Glue bottom piece (E) between sides (D) ¼″ from curved bottom edges of (D). Place suitable weight on top of entire assembly.

FINISHING
  1. Shellac, then varnish.
  2. For door knobs, paint heads of two straight pins gold; insert between side edges of doors (F) and panels (H) near hunt board center, and centered between top and bottom edges of doors.
  3. Make drawer handles out of sewing loops and attach. Place handles ⅛″ from side edges of drawers (G) and centered between top and bottom edges of each drawer.

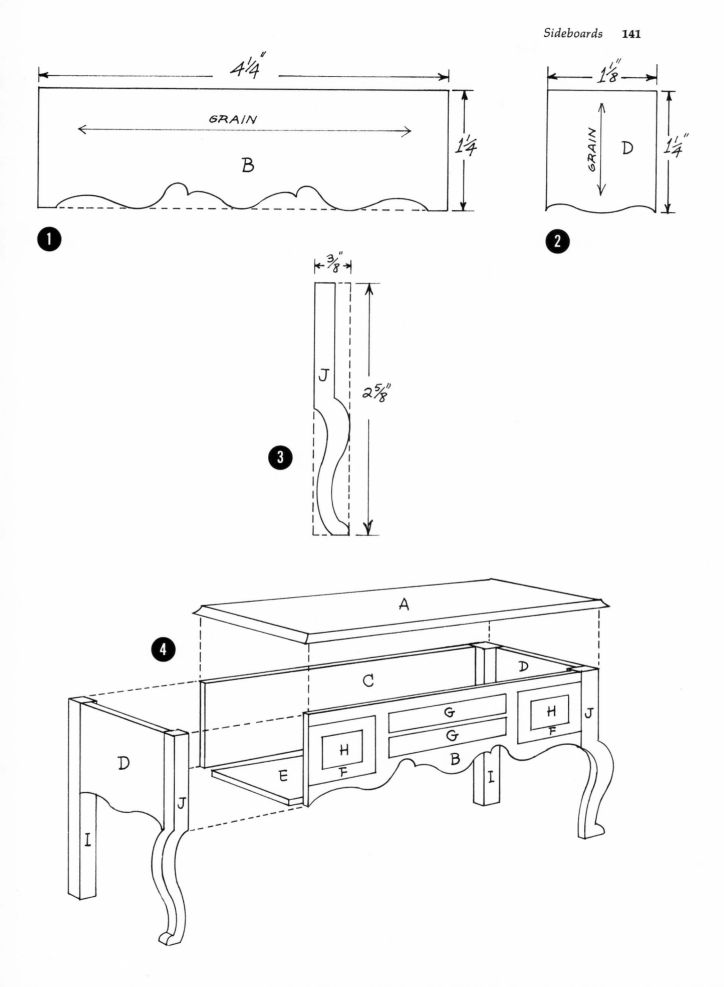

HEPPLEWHITE SIDEBOARD
(Georgian dining room)

SIZE: 6″W × 1⅞″D × 3″H

WOOD: ⅛″ balsa sheet, ³⁄₃₂″ balsa sheet, ¹⁄₃₂″ balsa sheet, ³⁄₁₆″ sq. balsa strip

SUGGESTED FINISH: mahogany

BASIC TOOLS AND SUPPLIES, plus 2 sewing loops, 2 pairs of pliers, two prongs (for holding rhinestones), gold paint

PIECE FROM ⅛″ BALSA SHEET
  A: piece from pattern, diagram 1

PIECES FROM ³⁄₃₂″ BALSA SHEET
  B: piece from pattern, diagram 2
  C: four 1¼″ × 1¼″ pieces
  D: two 1¼″ × 1⅜″ pieces
  E: 1¼″ × 5⅜″ piece

PIECES FROM ¹⁄₃₂″ BALSA SHEET
  F: ½″ × 2⅜″ piece
  G: two 1⅛″ × 1⅛″ pieces

PIECES FROM ³⁄₁₆″ SQ. BALSA STRIP
  H: six 2⅞″ pieces

CUTTING
  Cut wood on lengthwise grain.

SANDING AND STAINING
  1. Sand wood.
  2. For drawer (F) and doors (G), bevel all four edges.
  3. Stain wood.

ASSEMBLY, diagram 3
  1. Glue drawer (F) to front center piece (B), leaving ¹⁄₁₆″ space between top and side edges of (F) and top and side edges of (B). Place suitable weight on top.
  2. Center and glue doors (G) to front side pieces (C) with grain of wood of all pieces running horizontally. Place suitable weight on top of each door and front side piece assembly.

  3. Glue a side piece (C) between two legs (H) with top edges and outside surfaces of each piece flush and the grain of (C) running vertically; repeat for other side (C) and two legs (H).
  4. Glue drawer-and-front-center assembly from step 1 between two more legs (H) so top edges and front surfaces of piece (B) and legs (H) are flush.
  5. Glue a door-and-front-side assembly from step 2 to a side-and-legs assembly from step 3, forming a right angle corner of the sideboard; repeat for other door-and-front-side assembly and other side-and-legs assembly. Make sure that the right angle corners formed are opposite each other. Top edges of all pieces are flush, and outside surfaces of front pieces (C) are flush with outside surfaces of the two corner legs (H).
  6. Glue assembly from step 4 between the two assemblies from step 5. Top edges of all pieces are flush, and front surfaces of front pieces (C) are flush with front surfaces of two center legs (H).
  7. Glue back piece (E) between the rear legs (H) so top edges and back surfaces of all pieces are flush. A 1⅝″ × 5¾″ rectangular assembly should be formed.
  8. Trim and glue a piece (D) between back surface of front center leg (H) and perpendicular to back (E), with top edges of (D), (H), and (E) flush; repeat for other piece (D).
  9. Center and glue sideboard top (A) to assembly from steps 1–8 so back edge of (A) is flush with outside surface of back (E). Place suitable weight on top of entire assembly.

FINISHING
  1. Shellac, then varnish.
  2. Make drawer handles out of sewing loops and attach. Place handles ⅜″ from side edges of drawer (F) and centered between top and bottom of drawer.
  3. For keyholes for doors (G), paint two prongs gold; center and insert a prong in each door ¹⁄₁₆″ from top edge.

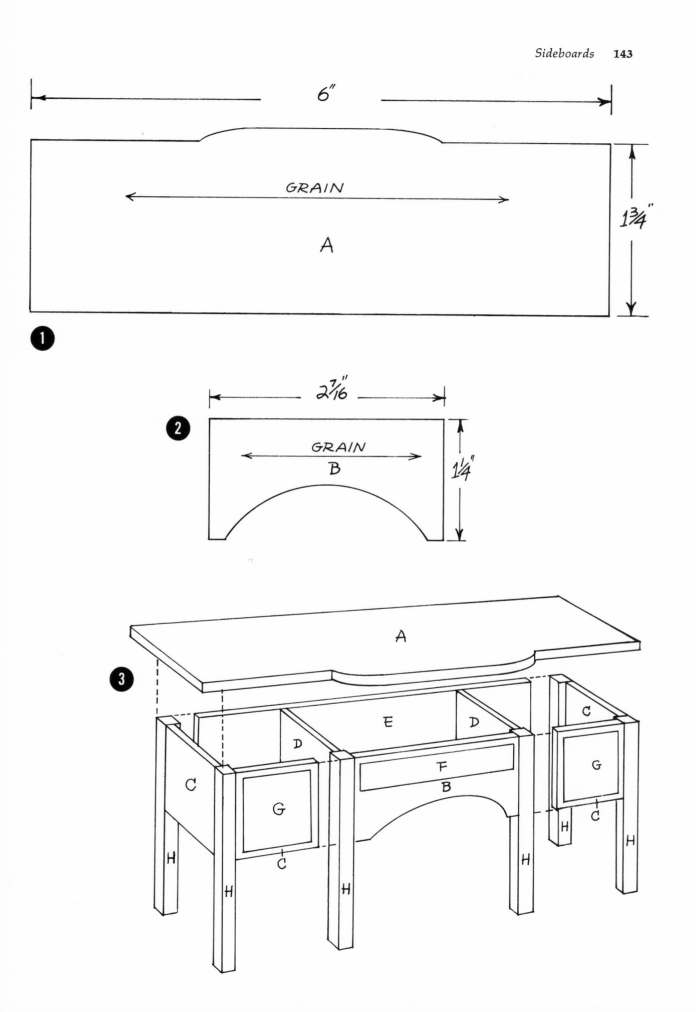

6"

GRAIN

A

1¾"

1

2⁷⁄₁₆"

GRAIN

B

1¼"

2

A

3

E

D

D

C

F

B

C

G

G

H

C

H

H

H

C

H

SERVING BOARD
(Victorian dining room)

Size: 5¼″W × 2⅛″D × 5¾″H

Wood: ⅛″ balsa sheet, ³⁄₃₂″ balsa sheet, ¹⁄₁₆″ balsa sheet, ¹⁄₃₂″ balsa sheet, ³⁄₁₆″ sq. balsa strip, ¹⁄₁₆″ × ³⁄₃₂″ balsa strip, ¹⁄₁₆″ × ⅛″ balsa strip, ¹⁄₁₆″ × ³⁄₁₆″ balsa strip, ¹⁄₁₆″ × ¼″ balsa strip, ⅝″ ogee molding, ³⁄₁₆″ dowel

Suggested finish: walnut

Basic tools and supplies, plus 2″ × 5¼″ mirror, ³⁄₁₆″-wide gold embossed paper strip, 7 sewing loops, gold paint, 2 pairs of pliers, 4 large round beads, woodtone paint

Pieces from ⅛″ balsa sheet
   A: ¾″ × 5″ piece
   B: 2⅛″ × 5¼″ piece

Pieces from ³⁄₃₂″ balsa sheet
   C: 2¾″ × 5¼″ piece
   D: two 2⅞″ × 4⅝″ pieces
   E: two 1⅝″ × 2⅞″ pieces
   F: 1¹¹⁄₁₆″ × 4⅝″ piece

Pieces from ¹⁄₁₆″ balsa sheet
   G: two 1″ × 1⅛″ pieces

Pieces from ¹⁄₃₂″ balsa sheet
   H: two ¼″ × 1⅜″ pieces
   I: three ¼″ × 1½″ pieces
   J: two ⁹⁄₁₆″ × 1½″ pieces
   K: two ⅜″ × 2¼″ pieces

Pieces from ³⁄₁₆″ sq. balsa strip
   L: four 2⅞″ pieces

Pieces from ¹⁄₁₆″ × ³⁄₃₂″ balsa strip
   M: three 4⅝″ pieces

Piece from ¹⁄₁₆″ × ⅛″ balsa strip
   N: 4⅝″ piece

Pieces from ¹⁄₁₆″ × ³⁄₁₆″ balsa strip
   O: ½″ piece
   P: two 1½″ pieces
   Q: two ⁷⁄₁₆″ pieces

Pieces from ¹⁄₁₆″ × ¼″ balsa strip
   R: four 1⅝″ pieces
   S: four 2⅜″ pieces
   T: two 2″ pieces
   U: two 4¾″ pieces

Piece from ⅝″ ogee molding
   V: 5½″ piece

Pieces from ³⁄₁₆″ dowel
   W: two 2″ pieces

Cutting
   1. Cut wood on lengthwise grain.
   2. Try to keep pieces (G) through (U) separate from rest of pieces.

Sanding and staining
   1. Sand wood.
   2. For door panels (G), bevel all four edges.
   3. For pieces (A) and (B), bevel front and side edges.
   4. For molding (V), sand sides with round file in a curve so top width of molding is 5½″ and bottom width is 5¼″.
   5. Stain wood.

Assembling serving board front and side sections, diagram 1
   1. Glue piece (N) to front piece (D) so bottom edges of both pieces are flush.
   2. Glue piece (O) to front (D) vertically at center of top edge of piece (N); the center is 2⁵⁄₁₆″ from side edges of (N).
   3. Glue first piece (M) to front (D) so top edge is ¾″ from bottom edge of (D).
   4. Glue two pieces (P) to front (D) vertically at top edge of piece (M) from step 3 and 1⅜″ from side edges of (D).

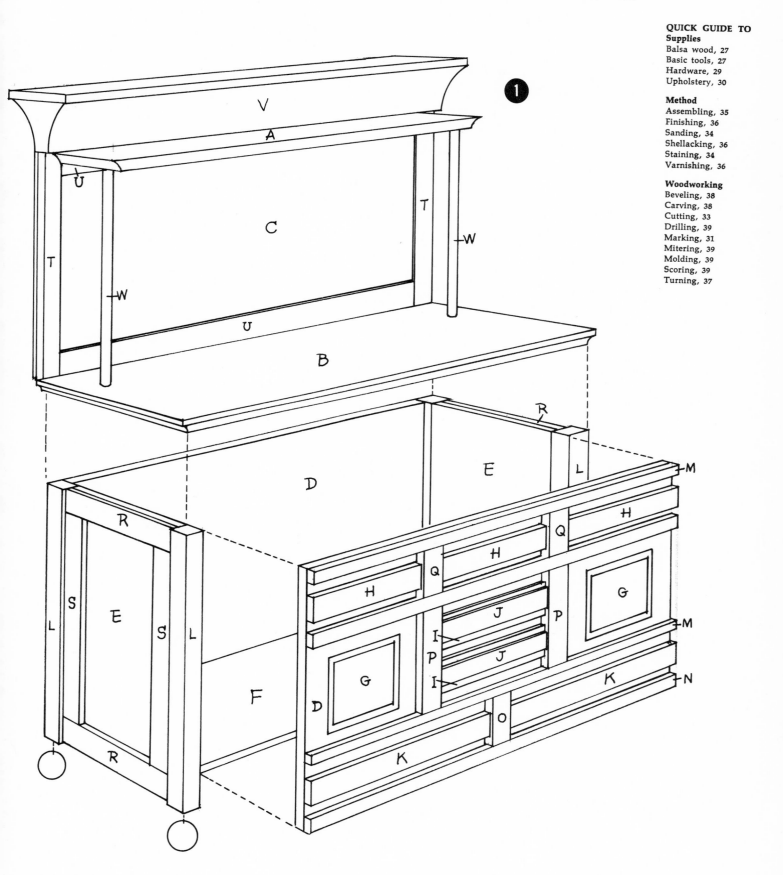

5. Glue second piece (M) to front (D) so bottom edge is ⅝″ from top edge of (D).

6. Glue pieces (Q) to front (D) vertically at top edge of second piece (M) and 1⅜″ from side edges of (D).

7. Glue third piece (M) to front (D) so top edges of both pieces are flush.

8. Glue door panels (G) to front (D), centering each panel between side edge of (D), piece (P), and first and second pieces (M).

9. Glue drawers (K) to front (D), centering each drawer between piece (N) and first piece (M). Glue inside edges of drawers to side edges of piece (O), and trim outside edges so they are flush with side edges of (D).

10. Glue drawers (H) to front (D), centering between second and third pieces (M) to right and left of pieces (Q). Glue inside edges of drawers to side edges of each piece (Q).

11. Glue top drawer (I) to front (D), centering between second and third pieces (M) and pieces (Q).

12. Glue two middle drawers (I) to front (D), spacing drawers evenly apart between first and second pieces (M) and each other; side edges of drawers are glued to side edges of pieces (P).

13. Center and glue pieces (J) to middle drawers (I).

14. Glue a piece (R) to a side piece (E) so top edges of both pieces are flush. Glue a second piece (R) to same side (E) so bottom edges of both pieces are flush.

15. Glue a piece (S) to side (E) from step 14 so front edges of both pieces are flush. Glue a second piece (S) to same side (E) so back edges of both pieces are flush.

16. Repeat steps 14 and 15 for other side piece (E) and other pieces (R) and (S).

ASSEMBLING SERVING BOARD BOTTOM AND TOP SECTIONS, diagram 1

1. Glue two legs (L) to each side of front assembly section so back surface of each leg is flush with back surface of front (D).

2. Glue two legs (L) to each side of back piece (D) so outside surface of each leg (L) is flush with back surface of back (D).

3. Glue a side (E) between a front leg (L) and a back leg (L) so inside surfaces of legs and side (E) are flush; repeat for other side (E) and other front and back legs (L).

4. Glue wide top (B) to top edges of back and front pieces (D) and sides (E) so back edge of (B) is flush with outside surface of back (D). Glue (B) upside down so beveled edge is on the bottom.

5. Glue bottom piece (F) in place so underside of (F) is flush with bottom edges of back and front pieces (D) and sides (E). Place suitable weight on top of entire assembly.

6. Glue molding (V) to mirror back piece (C); top surface of (V) is flush with top edge of (C) and side edges of (V) extend ⅛″ beyond sides of (C).

7. Glue back edge of narrow top (A) to piece (C) along bottom edge of molding (V), with beveled edge of (A) on the bottom.

8. Glue posts (W) to front corners of underside of top (A).

9. Glue assembly from steps 6–8 to top surface of wide top (B) along back edge of (B). Glue other ends of posts (W) to surface of (B).

FINISHING

1. Shellac, then varnish.

2. Glue mirror to mirror back piece (C). Glue frame pieces (T) and (U) to mirror so outside edges of (T) and (U) are flush with edges of mirror.

3. Make seven ⅜″ escutcheons for the seven drawers from embossed paper; center and glue escutcheons to drawers.

4. Make drawer handles out of sewing loops in Victorian style and attach to escutcheons.

5. For door keyholes, paint two pinheads gold. Center and insert pinheads between door panels (G), pieces (P), and first and second pieces (M).

6. For ball feet, paint four beads and four pinheads with woodtone paint to match stain. Pin beads to bottoms of legs (L).

BELTER VICTORIAN SOFA
(*Victorian living room*)

SIZE: 5"L × 1⅞"D × 4⅛"H

WOOD: ³⁄₁₆" balsa sheet, ⅛" balsa sheet

SUGGESTED FINISH: walnut

BASIC TOOLS AND SUPPLIES, plus 2 small frozen orange juice cans, wide elastic bands or masking tape, embossed paper picture frame, woodtone paint, oaktag cardboard, ³⁄₁₆"-thick cotton padding, ⅛ yard fabric, soutache braid, dye or felt tip pen, embroidery floss

PIECE FROM ³⁄₁₆" BALSA SHEET
A: piece from pattern (solid outline only), diagram 1

PIECES FROM ⅛" BALSA SHEET
B: two pieces from pattern (solid outline only), diagram 2
C: two pieces from pattern (solid outline only), diagram 3
D: two pieces from pattern, diagram 4
E: two pieces from pattern, diagram 5

PIECE FROM OAKTAG CARDBOARD
C: piece from pattern and reverse pattern (dotted curved outline to solid sloped outline), diagram 3

PIECES FROM COTTON PADDING
B: two pieces from pattern (solid curved outline plus dotted outline), diagram 2
C: two pieces from pattern and reverse pattern (dotted curved outline to solid sloped outline), diagram 3

PIECES FROM FABRIC
A: piece from pattern (solid curved outline plus dotted outline), diagram 1
C: piece from pattern and reverse pattern (dotted outline only), diagram 3
C: piece from pattern and reverse pattern (solid outline only), diagram 3

CUTTING WOOD
1. Cut pieces on lengthwise grain except pieces (C), which are cut on crosswise grain. Because the balsa sheet is only 6" wide, pieces (C), which form the sofa back, have to be cut in two parts and glued together later.
2. The four rectangles on piece (A) are cut out later.
3. Glue together two ⅛" pieces (B) to form chair seat ¼" thick; or you may cut one piece for seat (B) out of ¼" balsa sheet.
4. For legs (D) and (E), cut a curved line.

CUTTING OAKTAG, COTTON PADDING, AND FABRIC
Cut the eight pieces, cutting fabric crosswise. Since both halves of the sofa back (C) are identical, simply turn the (C) patterns to the reverse side to complete cutting of (C) pieces.

SANDING AND STAINING
1. Sand wood.
2. Round curved edges of sofa back pieces (C) very slightly. Soak one piece (C) in warm water for five minutes. Then bend (C) carefully around orange juice can with grain running vertically; start with curved armrest part of (C) and bend until you are within ¾" of straight side edge; do not bend this edge. Hold wood in place with elastic bands used vertically or masking tape; don't let elastic bands indent the soft wet wood. Let wood dry at room temperature or in a low oven for ten minutes. Repeat pro-

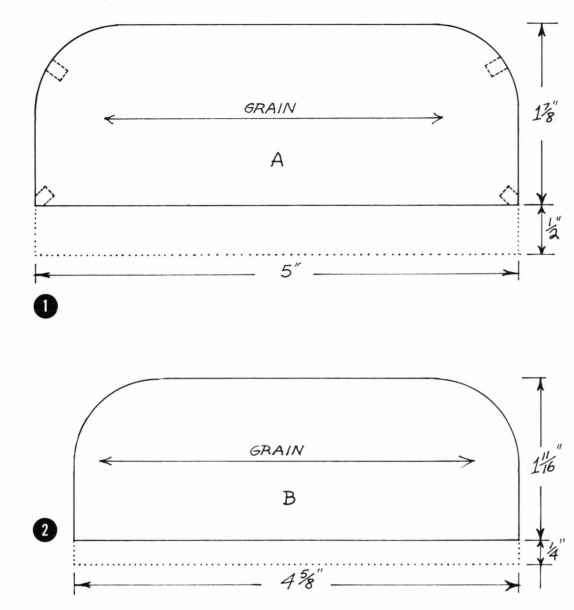

cedure for other piece (C), but be sure to bend wood in the opposite direction. When both pieces (C) are dry, glue straight side edges together to form one unit, the sofa back.

3. Stain wood.

ASSEMBLING AND FINISHING SOFA BASE, diagram 6

1. Carefully cut out four $\frac{1}{8}'' \times \frac{3}{16}''$ rectangles from base (A), as indicated by broken lines in diagram 1. Glue legs (D) into cut-outs on straight edge of (A), with top edges of (D) flush with top surface of (A), and the long, $\frac{1}{8}''$ edges of (D) curving out at top and in near bottom. Glue legs (E) into cut-outs on curved edge of

(A) in the same manner; the long, $\frac{1}{8}''$ edges of (E) curve out.

2. Shellac assembly from step 1. Use steel wool to smooth legs very carefully.

3. Varnish assembly from step 1.

FINISHING SOFA BACK

1. Shellac all surfaces of sofa back (C).

2. Varnish all surfaces of sofa back (C).

3. Cut three corners of the embossed paper picture frame so they fit together nicely around top curved edge of sofa back (C); place one embossed paper corner at center of curved edge and two corners to each side of the center. Some

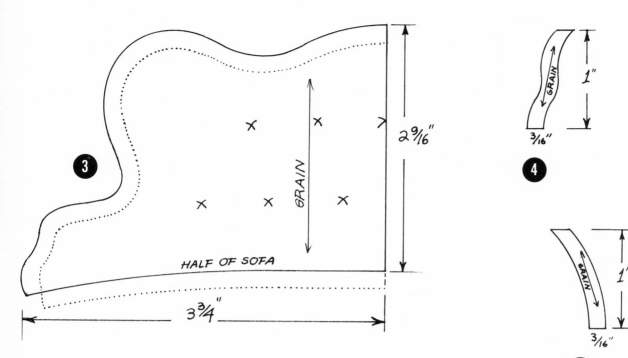

3

2⁹⁄₁₆"

GRAIN

HALF OF SOFA

3³⁄₄"

4

GRAIN

1"

³⁄₁₆"

5

GRAIN

1"

³⁄₁₆"

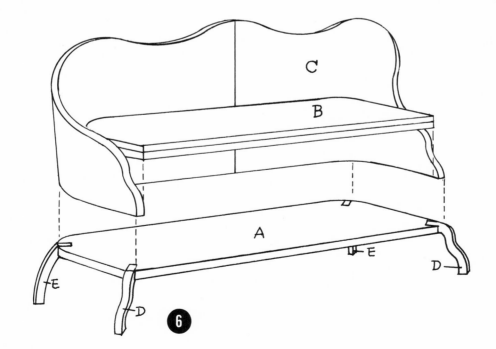

C

B

A

D

E

D

E

6

piecing and trimming will be necessary; the entire top curved edge of (C) should have embossed paper covering it in varying widths. Glue paper in place on back surface of (C) using a few straight pins to hold paper until glue begins to set. Paint embossed paper with woodtone paint to match stain.

4. Glue fabric (C) that was cut from dotted line pattern as follows; Put small amount of glue along curved edge of fabric (not sloping bottom edge) and glue to outside of sofa back (C), beginning $\frac{3}{16}$″ down from top curved edge; smooth out fabric over curved arms as much as possible without breaking arms. Put glue along molded bottom edge of sofa back (C) and turn $\frac{3}{16}$″ of fabric (C) under bottom edge of sofa back and glue; be sure fabric is smooth and taut.

5. Dye soutache braid to match fabric. Glue braid to raw edges of fabric from step 4, following contour of curved edge; turn braid ends under bottom edge of sofa back and glue.

ASSEMBLING AND FINISHING SOFA, diagram 6

1. Glue sofa base assembly to sofa back assembly: Bottom edge of (C) is glued to curved edge of (A), and outside surface of (C) is flush with curved edge of (A). This may require some refitting and re-gluing.

2. For carving on base (A), glue 4¾″ piece of embossed paper picture frame to straight edge of (A) between legs (D); some piecing may be necessary. Paint embossed paper with woodtone paint to match stain.

3. Fit oaktag (C) to inside surface of sofa back (C) so a $\frac{3}{16}$″ curved edge of back (C) shows evenly; you may have to trim oaktag. With oaktag on work surface, put small amount of glue along sloped bottom edge of oaktag and place two pieces of cotton padding (C) on top. Put small amount of glue along wrong side of sloped bottom edge of fabric (C)—cut from solid line pattern—and put fabric on top padding right side up. You may have to secure these bottom edges further with needle and thread.

Turn assembly over so oaktag is on top. Put glue along curved edge of oaktag and glue the $\frac{3}{16}$″ curved edge of fabric to back of oaktag. To facilitate gluing, make tiny cuttings on edges of seam allowance, especially at narrow curved portions of oaktag. Glue fabric as smoothly and tautly as possible, because when oaktag assembly is put in place, it will be curved.

4. Mark fabric (C) with straight pins for placement of French embroidery knots made to resemble the buttons used on heavily tufted furniture. Embroidery floss should match fabric. To make one French knot: Knot one end of embroidery floss and stitch from oaktag back to front of fabric, pulling needle and thread completely through; wind floss around tip of needle twice and return needle from fabric front to oaktag back as near as possible to the same hole. Repeat procedure for rest of French knots.

5. Glue entire oaktag assembly to inside surface of sofa back (C), making sure a $\frac{3}{16}$″ curved edge of (C) shows evenly.

6. Place both pieces of cotton padding (B) on top surface of sofa seat (B) so padding overlaps straight edge of seat. Place fabric (A) right side up on top of padding so curved edge of fabric overlaps $\frac{3}{16}$″ along curved edge of padding and straight edge of fabric overlaps ½″ along straight edge of seat. Glue fabric to bottom surface of seat ¼″ in from straight front edge; glue curved edge of fabric to curved edge of seat, making sure fabric is smooth and taut; turn in and fold fabric at two corners and glue to side edges of seat. Glue seat assembly to top surface of base (A) and to bottom edge of sofa back assembly so seat fits snugly.

Variation: VICTORIAN SOFA

A typical Victorian sofa may be made with the same directions by eliminating embossed paper carving.

CHIPPENDALE SOFA, CAMELBACK
(Colonial living room)

SIZE: $6\frac{3}{8}$"L × $1\frac{7}{8}$"D × 3"H

WOOD: $\frac{3}{32}$" balsa sheet, $\frac{3}{16}$" balsa sheet, $\frac{3}{16}$" sq. balsa strip, $\frac{1}{8}$" sq. balsa strip

SUGGESTED FINISH: mahogany

BASIC TOOLS AND SUPPLIES, plus $\frac{3}{16}$"-thick cotton padding, $\frac{1}{8}$ yard fabric, soutache braid, dye or felt tip pen, $1\frac{9}{16}$" × $5\frac{7}{8}$" cardboard

PIECES FROM $\frac{3}{32}$" BALSA SHEET
  A: piece from pattern (solid outline only), diagram 1
  B: two pieces from pattern (solid outline only), diagram 2
  C: $1\frac{7}{8}$" × $6\frac{3}{8}$" piece

PIECES FROM $\frac{3}{16}$" BALSA SHEET
  D: two $1\frac{11}{16}$" × 6" pieces

PIECES FROM $\frac{3}{16}$" SQ. BALSA STRIP
  E: two $1\frac{1}{4}$" pieces
  F: four $\frac{3}{4}$" pieces
  G: four $1\frac{3}{16}$" pieces

PIECES FROM $\frac{1}{8}$" SQ. BALSA STRIP
  H: four $1\frac{9}{16}$" pieces
  I: three $1\frac{15}{16}$" pieces

PIECES FROM COTTON PADDING
  A: two pieces from pattern (solid outline only), diagram 1
  B: six pieces from pattern (solid outline only), diagram 2
  D: two $1\frac{9}{16}$" × $5\frac{7}{8}$" pieces

PIECES FROM FABRIC
  A: piece from pattern (dotted outline only), diagram 1
  B: piece from pattern (dotted outline only), diagram 2
  B: piece from reverse side of pattern (dotted outline only), diagram 2
  D: piece from pattern, diagram 3
  B–A–B: piece from pattern, diagram 4
  Cushion fabric: 2" × $6\frac{5}{8}$" piece

CUTTING WOOD
1. Cut pieces on lengthwise grain.
2. Instead of using two $\frac{3}{16}$" pieces for sofa bottom (D), you can use any combination of thickness of wood you have on hand and cut to obtain required $\frac{3}{8}$" thickness.
3. Cut away top and bottom edges of back legs (G) on an angle of about 20°; see detail in diagram 5. Make sure the slanted top and bottom edges are exactly parallel.
4. For stretchers (H) and (I), you may want to cut one $10\frac{1}{2}$" strip and later cut the seven pieces exactly to size.

CUTTING COTTON PADDING AND FABRIC
1. Cut pieces of cotton padding, using same cardboard patterns as for marking wood pieces (A), (B), and (D). Two or three layers of thin cotton padding are suggested for this sofa, though the amount of padding varies depending on thickness of fabric. For pieces (B), cut four of the layers according to patterns; these layers are stretched to cover the armrests. Cut other two pieces (B) $\frac{3}{16}$" longer along top edge than pattern indicates in order to make a top smooth padding for each armrest.
2. Cut fabric crosswise. Because sofa sides (B) face each other, be sure to reverse pattern on the same side of the fabric when cutting.

SANDING AND STAINING
1. Do not sand or stain wood pieces (A), (B), (D), and (E) because they will be covered with fabric.
2. Sand and stain rest of wood.

ASSEMBLING SOFA BASE, diagram 5
1. Glue front legs (F) to bottom of sofa base (C) along front edge of (C), with two legs at each corner and two $1\frac{7}{8}$" in toward center; this should leave another $1\frac{7}{8}$" space in the center. Reinforce legs with straight pins from top surface of (C). Repeat procedure for back legs (G), gluing them along back edge of (C).
2. If you haven't already cut stretchers (H), measure exact distance between front and back legs (F and G) and cut stretchers to fit. Slant one end of each stretcher to fit properly against back legs. Glue stretchers in place about midway between floor and base (C).
3. Measure exact distance between stretchers (H) and cut stretchers (I) to fit between them. Glue stretchers (I) between stretchers (H) $\frac{5}{8}$" from front edge of base (C).

ASSEMBLING UPHOLSTERED PART OF SOFA, diagram 5
1. Glue together sofa seat pieces (D) to form one piece. After drying, put glue on both top and bottom surfaces of (D), $\frac{1}{2}$" in from front edges but not on the $\frac{3}{8}$" front edge. Glue fabric (D) to sofa seat (D), tucking $\frac{3}{8}$" fabric extensions to each side edge.

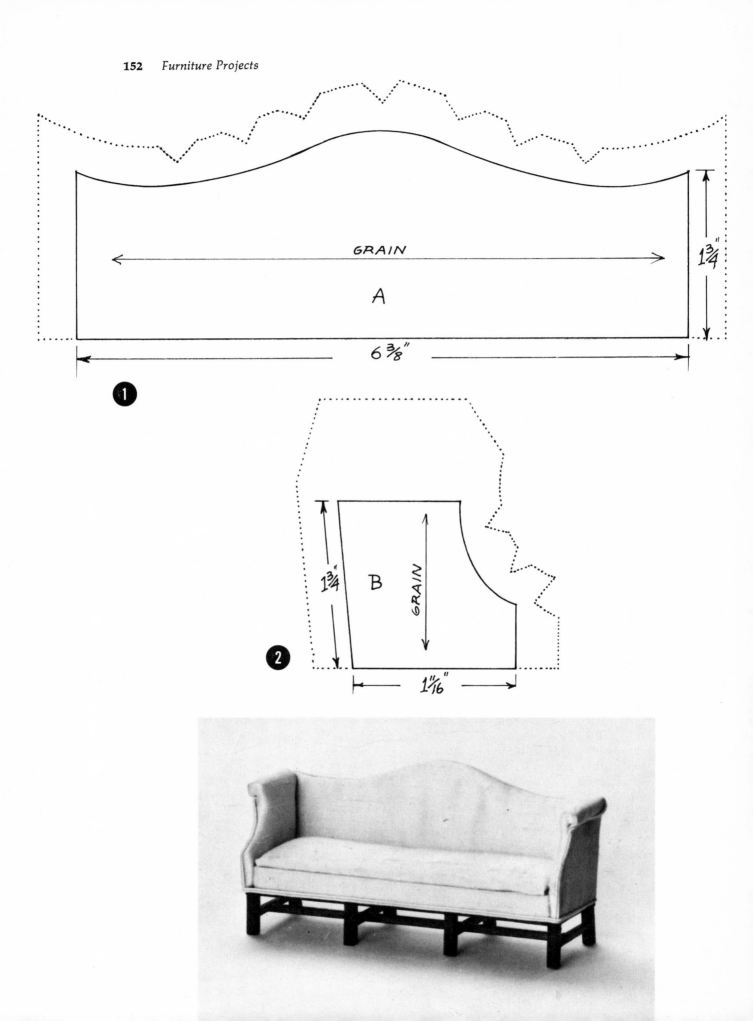

GRAIN

A

$1\frac{3}{4}$"

$6\frac{3}{8}$"

1

$1\frac{3}{4}$"

B

GRAIN

$1\frac{1}{16}$"

2

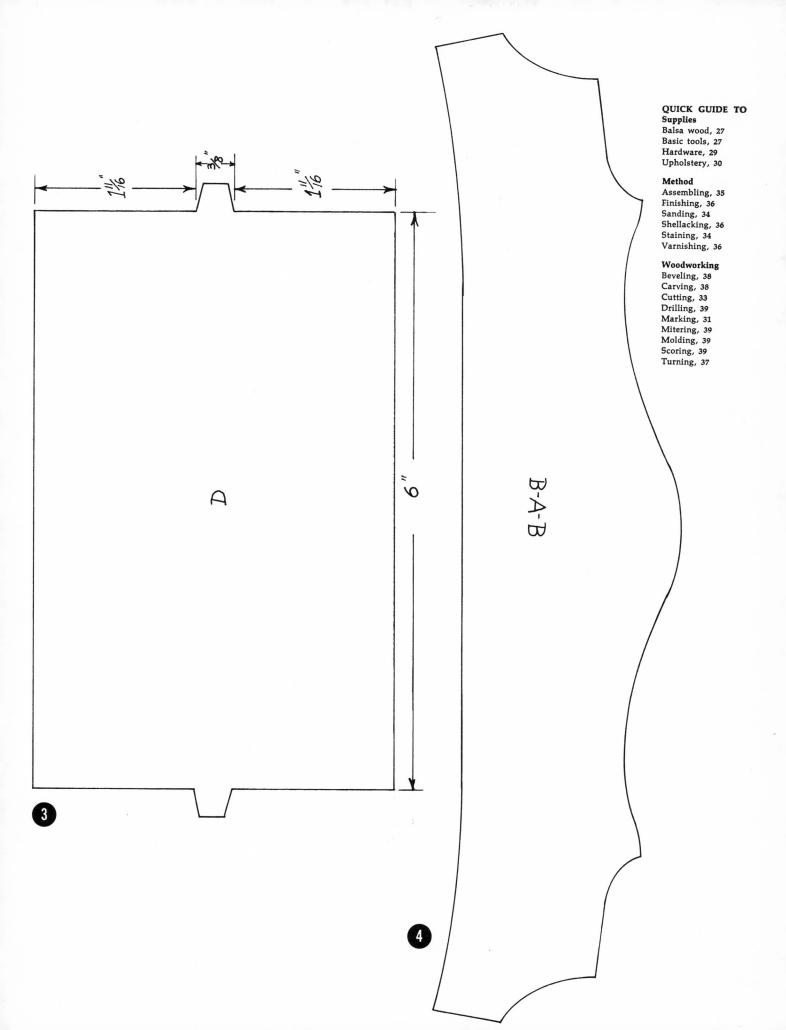

D

3

B-A-B

4

2. Place sofa back (A) on work surface and secure both pieces of cotton padding (A) to it with a few dots of glue. Place fabric (A) right side up on top of padding, with bottom edge of fabric flush with bottom edges of padding and sofa back; hold these edges in place with glue or pins. Turn over assembly and glue ⅜″ fabric seams to back side of sofa back (A), gluing straight side seams first and then curved, clipped top seam; trim seams if necessary to avoid extra thickness. Hold fabric in place with pins until glue is dry.

3. Center and glue fabric side of sofa back (A) to back edge of sofa seat (D) so bottom edge of (A) is flush with bottom surface of (D); the sofa back extends ³⁄₁₆″ on each side of sofa bottom. Reinforce gluing with straight pins.

4. Glue armrest (E) to top edge of sofa side (B) on outside surface of (B); the top edges of armrest and sofa side are flush. Repeat procedure for other side (B) and armrest (E).

5. Place one sofa side (B) on work surface with armrest (E) facing down and cover with three pieces of cotton padding (B): Stretch first and second layers over armrest and hold in place with dot of glue; place longer third layer over first two layers for smooth effect and secure with dot of glue. Place fabric (B) right side up on top of padding, with bottom edges flush; hold these edges in place with glue or pins. Turn assembly over to armrest side. Glue fabric seams to this side, gluing straight side seams first and then curved, clipped seam; trim seams if necessary to avoid extra thickness. Gluing fabric over armrest can be done smoothly if you tuck fabric over front edge of armrest first, holding it in place with glue or pins, and then draw fabric over top edge of armrest and glue seam to surface of sofa side (B) along bottom edge of armrest. Hold seam in place with glue or pins

until dry. Repeat procedure for other sofa side (B), padding (B), and fabric (B).

6. Glue fabric side of sofa sides (B) to sides of sofa seat (D) so bottom edges of (B) are flush with bottom surface of (D). Glue slanted back edges of sides (B) to sofa back (A) where it extends ³⁄₁₆″ out from seat (D). Armrests (E) will extend about ⅛″ out from (A) on each side so top edge of (A) and top edges of (E) form one continuous curved line. Reinforce gluing with straight pins.

7. Fit right side of fabric (B–A–B) to outside surface of sides (B) and back (A). Place tiny dots of glue as close to fabric edge as possible, an inch or so apart, and glue fabric along top, bottom, and side edges of sofa sides and back to cover wood and raw seams.

8. Glue upholstered sofa assembly to sofa base assembly so four edges from each are flush and matching in length.

FINISHING

1. Shellac sofa base assembly and varnish, but do not shellac or varnish side edges of base (C).

2. Dye soutache braid to match fabric. Glue braid to raw seam edges of fabric (B–A–B), following contour of edges. Glue braid around base (A) to cover raw edges of fabric and side edges of (A).

3. For sofa cushion, cut cardboard base and cotton padding ⅛″ smaller on all sides than the dimensions of sofa seat (D); this is to allow for thick padding on sides and back of sofa. Place cushion fabric right side down on work surface; place padding on top of fabric, and cardboard base on top of padding. Glue fabric side seams to cardboard base first, then glue front and back seams to base. Glue cushion to sofa seat (D).

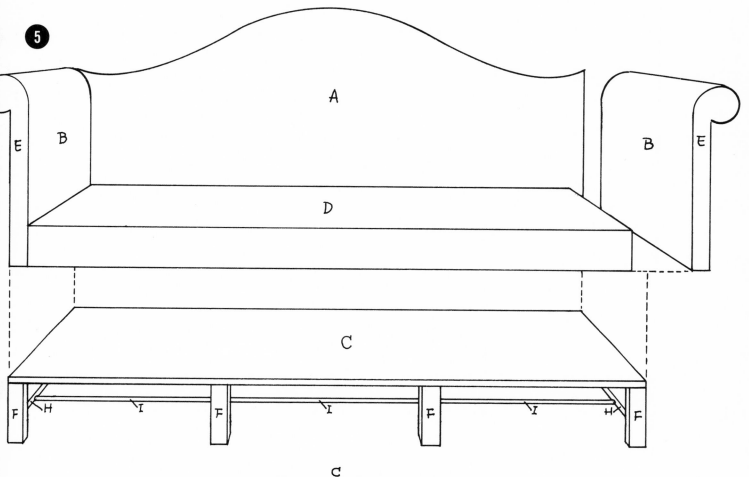

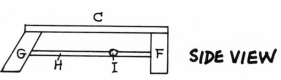

SIDE VIEW

6

DEACON'S BENCH
(Colonial keeping room)

SIZE: 5"L × 1⅜"D × 3"H

WOOD: ⅛" balsa sheet, ³⁄₃₂" balsa sheet, ³⁄₁₆" dowel, ⅛" dowel, 13 round wooden toothpicks

SUGGESTED FINISH: black paint

BASIC TOOLS AND SUPPLIES, plus black satin enamel paint, red model paint, yellow model paint, green model paint

PIECE FROM ⅛" BALSA SHEET
  A: piece from pattern, diagram 1

PIECES FROM ³⁄₃₂" BALSA SHEET
  B: ⅜" × 5" piece
  C: two pieces from pattern, diagram 2

PIECES FROM ³⁄₁₆" DOWEL
  D: six 1¼" pieces

PIECES FROM ⅛" DOWEL
  E: two 1¼" pieces
  F: two ⅝" pieces
  G: four 2⅛" pieces
  H: two 1" pieces

PIECES FROM TOOTHPICKS
  I: eleven 1⅜" pieces
  J: four ⅝" pieces

CUTTING
  1. Cut wood on lengthwise grain.
  2. Cut away top edges of three back legs (D) on an angle of about 15°. It is important that the amount cut away from each leg is the same.
  3. Cut one end from each toothpick (I) so each is 1¼" long. Cut four ⅝" pieces (J) by cutting out the middle section of remaining two toothpicks.

SANDING
  1. Sand wood.
  2. For bench seat (A) round all four corners slightly.
  3. For bench back (B), round corners at each end of top edge.

ASSEMBLY, diagram 3
  1. Put pencil dot in the middle of straight bottom edge of bench back (B); make ten more dots, ⅜" apart, along bottom edge, five to the right and five to the left of middle dot. Dip pointed ends of pieces (I) into glue one at a time, and insert each one about ⅛" into (B)

where indicated by pencil dots. Let dry firmly. Glue flat ends of pieces (I) to bench seat (A) ¹⁄₁₆" from back edge of (A) on dots indicated in diagram 1. This will require holding pieces (I) in place by hand as they are drying, and you may have to re-glue until all pieces (I) are firmly in place. While glue is drying, slant each piece (I) very slightly backwards so bench back assembly is not absolutely perpendicular to seat (A).
  2. Glue pieces (E) between bottom edge of back (B) and seat (A) so top edges of pieces (E) are ³⁄₁₆" from side edges of (B) and ⅛" from side edges of (A).
  3. Glue bottom edges of piece (F) ⅛" from side edges of seat (A) and ¼" from front edge of (A).
  4. Glue back edge of armrest (C) to piece (E) ⅝" from top surface of seat (A). Place glue on the top edge of piece (F) and glue to underside of front end of armrest. Repeat procedure for the other armrest (C).
  5. Glue two pieces (J) between one armrest (C) and bench seat (A) with pointed ends underneath (C); pieces (J) are ⅜" apart and ⅛" from side edge of (A). Repeat procedure for other pieces (J) on other side.
  6. Glue three slanted legs (D) to underside of seat (A) ¹⁄₁₆" from back edge of (A), with two legs at each corner and the third leg in center. Repeat procedure in front for three straight legs (D). Make sure bench seat is level. Legs must not slant too much.
  7. Glue bench rungs (G) between corner legs and center legs ½" from floor.
  8. Glue bench rungs (H) between front and back corner legs ½" from floor. For an accurate fit, slant one end of each rung by sanding it.

FINISHING
  1. Paint bench with two or three coats of black satin enamel paint. (Flat paint can be used if you let it dry and then add a coat of shellac or varnish for luster. Model paint can be used, too, but first give unprimed wood a coat or two of shellac so wood will not absorb paint too much.)
  2. Paint Pennsylvania Dutch motif on bench back (B); see diagram 4. Use small bottles of model paint in three or four colors of your choice.

1

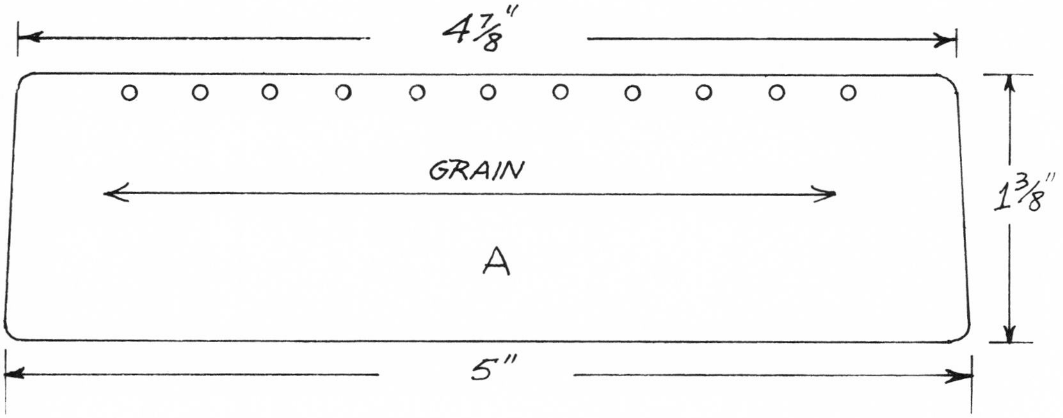

4⅞"

○ ○ ○ ○ ○ ○ ○ ○ ○ ○ ○

GRAIN ⟵⟶

A

1⅜"

5"

2

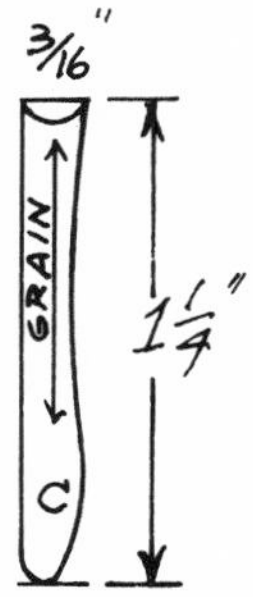

3/16"

GRAIN

C

1¼"

3

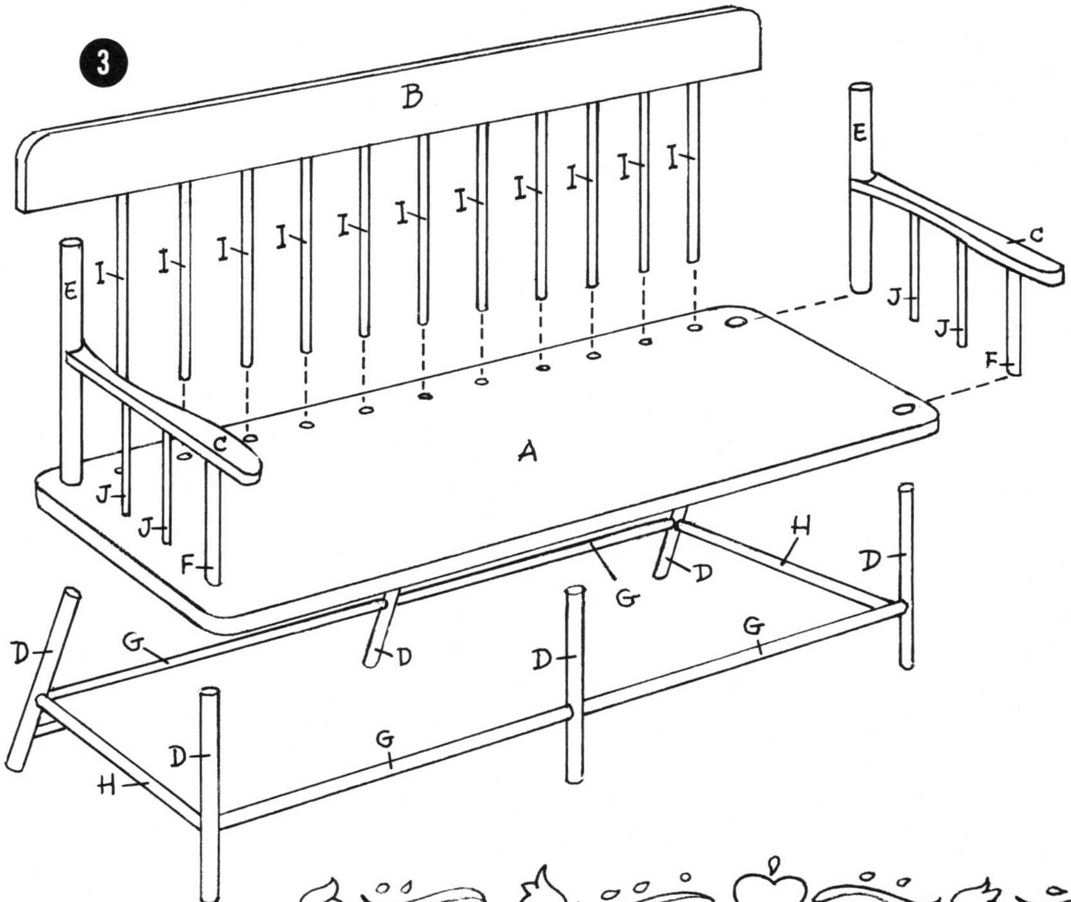

B

E

I I I I I I I I I

E I C

J

J F

A

C

J J F

H

G D

D

G D

D G

D G

H

D

G

4

SETTLE
(*Colonial keeping room*)

SIZE: $3\frac{3}{4}"$L $\times$ $1\frac{5}{8}"$D $\times$ $4\frac{1}{2}"$H

WOOD: $\frac{3}{32}"$ balsa sheet

SUGGESTED FINISH: pine

BASIC TOOLS AND SUPPLIES

PIECES FROM $\frac{3}{32}"$ BALSA SHEET
    A: $3\frac{1}{2}" \times 4\frac{1}{4}"$ piece
    B: two pieces from pattern, diagram 1

C: $1\frac{1}{2}" \times 3\frac{1}{2}"$ piece
D: $1\frac{1}{4}" \times 3\frac{1}{2}"$ piece

CUTTING
    1. Cut wood on lengthwise grain except for piece (A), which is cut on crosswise grain.

SANDING AND STAINING
    1. Sand wood.
    2. For seat (C), round the long front edge.
    3. Stain wood.

ASSEMBLY, diagram 2
    1. Glue long straight sides of sides (B) to long side edges of back (A).
    2. Glue long top edge of apron (D) to underside of seat (C) along rounded edge of (C), which overlaps (D) slightly.
    3. Glue assembly from step 2 to assembly from step 1; the bottom edge of apron (D) is glued $\frac{1}{4}"$ from the floor, and the side edges of (D) are recessed $\frac{1}{8}"$ from front edges of sides (B). When glue begins to set, lay entire assembly on its side and place suitable weight on top.

FINISHING
    Shellac, then varnish.

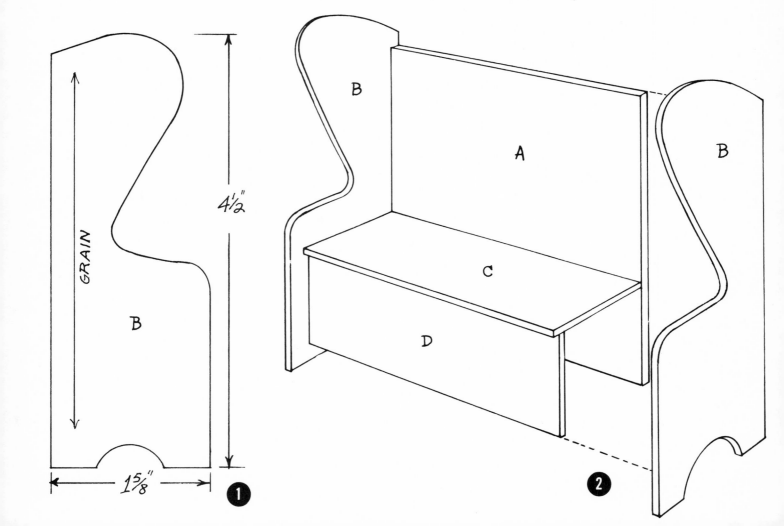

C H A P T E R **23** *Tables*

CLOVERLEAF CANDLE STAND
(*Georgian hall*)

SIZE: $1\frac{1}{4}$"W × $1\frac{3}{4}$"D × $2\frac{1}{4}$"H

WOOD: $\frac{1}{8}$" balsa sheet, $\frac{3}{32}$" balsa sheet, $\frac{1}{16}$" × $\frac{1}{4}$" balsa strip, $\frac{1}{4}$" dowel, $\frac{1}{16}$" dowel or round wooden toothpick

SUGGESTED FINISH: mahogany

BASIC TOOLS AND SUPPLIES, plus 1" lamp finial, woodtone paint

PIECES FROM $\frac{1}{8}$" BALSA SHEET
   A: three pieces from pattern, diagram 1

PIECE FROM $\frac{3}{32}$" BALSA SHEET
   B: piece from pattern, diagram 2

PIECES FROM $\frac{1}{16}$" × $\frac{1}{4}$" BALSA STRIP
   C: two pieces from pattern, diagram 3

PIECE FROM $\frac{1}{4}$" DOWEL
   D: $\frac{3}{8}$" piece

CUTTING
   1. Cut wood on lengthwise grain.
   2. For legs (A), see directions for cutting a curved line.

SANDING AND STAINING
   Sand wood, then stain.

ASSEMBLY, diagram 3
   1. Glue $\frac{3}{8}$" straight edges of legs (A) to $\frac{3}{8}$" round surface of piece (D). In order to space legs evenly, draw a triangle with each side $1\frac{1}{2}$"; the feet of the legs should fit into angles of the triangle. Make sure legs touch the floor evenly and piece (D) is level; the assembly should be $1\frac{1}{4}$" high. Let assembly dry completely, or it won't hold weight of finial.
   2. Paint finial with woodtone paint to match stain. When dry, center and glue flat end of finial to top of assembly from step 1, making sure finial is upright from all sides by turning it around on level surface.
   3. With pencil, mark exact center of under-

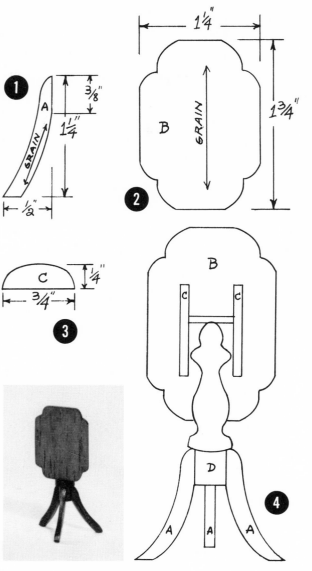

side of cloverleaf top (B). Glue pieces (C) to underside of top (B), parallel to each other and an equal distance apart from pencil dot; this distance is determined by size of round end of finial, which should fit snugly between pieces (C).
   4. For a *tilt-top* cloverleaf candle stand (as shown), measure distance between pieces (C); from center of $\frac{1}{16}$" dowel or a toothpick, cut a piece this measured distance and glue it between pieces (C) exactly at pencil dot. Glue round end of finial underneath dowel and between pieces (C).
   5. For a *level* cloverleaf candle stand, glue top (B) to round top end of finial; hold in place with hands until glue begins to set, making sure top is perfectly level.

FINISHING
   1. Shellac; one coat is sufficient for legs (A). Steel wool very carefully.
   2. Varnish.

INLAY CARD TABLE
(*Georgian dining room*)

SIZE: 3″W × 1⅝″D × 2½″H

WOOD: ⅛″ balsa sheet, ¹⁄₁₆″ × ⅜″ balsa strip, ³⁄₁₆″ sq. balsa strip, ¼″- or ⅜″-wide strip of inlay wood

SUGGESTED FINISH: mahogany

BASIC TOOLS AND SUPPLIES

PIECES FROM ⅛″ BALSA SHEET
  A: piece from pattern (solid outline only), diagram 1
  B: piece from pattern (solid outline only), diagram 1

PIECE FROM ¹⁄₁₆″ × ⅜″ BALSA STRIP
  C: 2½″ piece

PIECES FROM ³⁄₁₆″ SQ. BALSA STRIP
  D: four 2⅜″ pieces

PIECES FROM INLAY WOOD STRIP
  E: 2½″ piece
  F: two 1¹⁄₁₆″ pieces

CUTTING
  1. Cut wood on lengthwise grain.
  2. For piece (B), cut away ⅛″ along back edge as indicated by broken line in diagram 1.
  3. You need less than 5″ of wood for inlay strips (E) and (F). Try getting a scrap piece from a cabinet maker or refinisher rather than ordering a large quantity from a special wood supplier. If you can't obtain inlay wood, make entire card table with balsa wood.

SANDING AND STAINING
  Sand wood, then stain.

ASSEMBLY, diagram 2
  1. If inlay wood strip is ⅜″ wide, the width is correct. If inlay strip is ¼″ wide, glue a ¹⁄₁₆″-wide balsa strip to each side of inlay strip so total width is ⅜″.
  2. Glue inlay front piece (E) between two legs (D) so top edges and front surfaces of (E) and (D) are flush.
  3. Glue back piece (C) between other legs (D) in the same manner as in step 2.
  4. Glue an inlay side piece (F) between front and back leg (D) so top edges and outside surfaces are flush; repeat for other side piece (F) and legs (D).
  5. Center and glue assembly from step 4 to underside of table top (A) so back edge of (A) is flush with outside surface of back (C).
  6. Glue long straight edge of vertical table top (B) to top surface of table top (A) along back edge of (A).

FINISHING
  Shellac, then varnish.

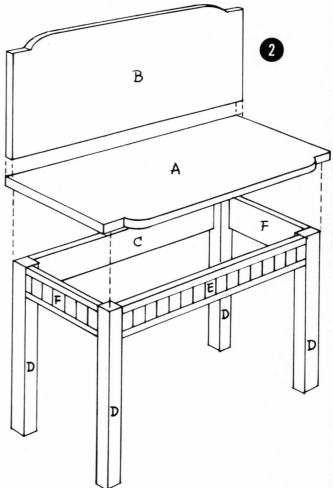

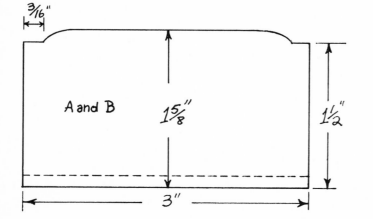

CIRCULAR COFFEE TABLE
(Victorian living room)

Size: 2⅝″W × 1½″H

Wood: 3/16″ balsa sheet, ⅛″ balsa sheet

Suggested finish: walnut

Basic tools and supplies, plus 2½″ to 2¾″ circular top (imitation woodgrain and/or imitation mother-of-pearl; or ivory inlay in the form of a button or compact cover; or imitation marble in the form of Formica or contact paper), compass, 1″ lamp finial, 3/16″-wide embossed paper strip, 3 small beads, woodtone paint

Piece from 3/16″ balsa sheet
    A: piece from pattern, diagram 1

Piece from ⅛″ balsa sheet
    B: circle approximately 2⅝″ in diameter

Cutting
    1. Cut wood, cutting piece (A) on lengthwise grain as nearly as possible.
    2. Diameter of table top (B) will depend on size of your cover material for it; top (B) should not be less than 2½″ or more than 2¾″ in diameter. If you do not want to cover top (B) with a decorative material, you will still use 3/16″ balsa for (B).

Sanding and staining
    Sand wood, then stain.

Assembly, diagram 2
    1. Glue decorative cover material to table top (B) so circular edges of both decorative and wood tops are flush.
    2. The overall height of the coffee table, including ball feet, should not exceed 1⅝″, so you may have to mount the lamp finial to reduce table height. Do this by cutting a hole the size of the end of the finial in either table top (B) or base (A) or both, so finial partly recedes. Center and glue flat end of finial to underside of top (B). Glue round end of finial to base (A). Paint finial with woodtone paint to match stain.

Finishing
    1. Shellac, then varnish.
    2. Glue embossed paper strip around edge of table top to resemble carving and paint with woodtone paint.
    3. Paint beads with woodtone paint. When dry, glue beads to underside of each leg of base (A).

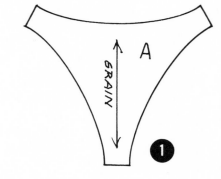

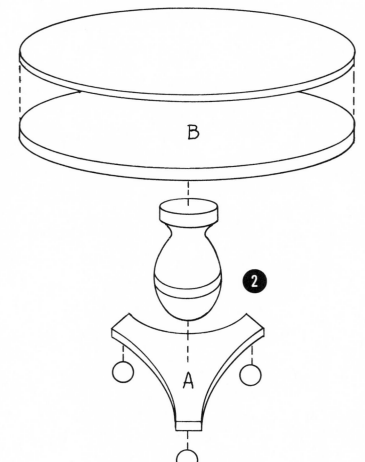

CONSOLE TABLE
(*Victorian dining room*)

Size: $3\frac{1}{4}$"W × $1\frac{1}{2}$"D × $2\frac{5}{8}$"H

Wood: $\frac{3}{16}$" balsa sheet, $\frac{3}{32}$" × $\frac{1}{4}$" balsa strip

Suggested finish: walnut

Basic tools and supplies, plus $\frac{3}{8}$"-wide embossed paper picture frame, Formica with marble pattern, white paint, decorative button about $\frac{3}{8}$" high and $\frac{3}{8}$" in diameter, woodtone paint

Pieces from $\frac{3}{16}$" balsa sheet
A: piece from pattern, diagram 1
B: two pieces from pattern, diagram 2
C: two pieces from pattern, diagram 3

Piece from $\frac{3}{32}$" × $\frac{1}{4}$" balsa strip
D: $3\frac{1}{4}$" piece

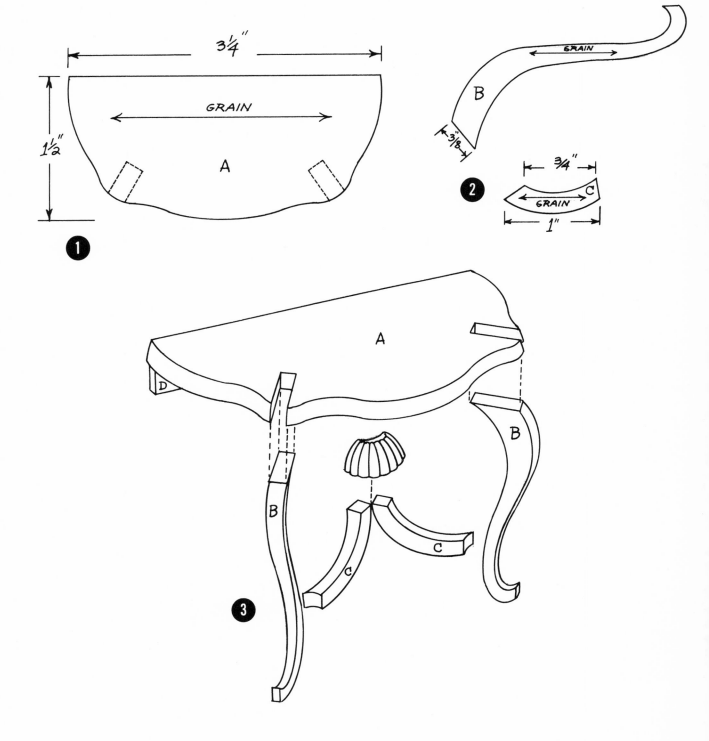

PIECE FROM FORMICA

Table top: piece from pattern, diagram 1

CUTTING

1. Cut wood on lengthwise grain.

2. For pieces (A) and (B), cut a curved line. The two rectangles in piece (A) are cut later.

3. The thickness of wood for piece (D) may vary depending on what wood you have on hand.

4. Cut Formica piece slowly and carefully, then smooth edges with metal file.

SANDING AND STAINING

1. Sand wood.

2. For table top (A), bevel entire curved edge in a round bevel. The bevel should be $\frac{1}{16}''$ deep. The top, unbeveled surface should measure $3\frac{1}{8}''$ along the back edge and $1\frac{7}{16}''$ from the back edge to the center front of beveled edge.

3. Stain wood.

ASSEMBLY, diagram 4

1. Carefully cut out two $\frac{3}{16}'' \times \frac{3}{8}''$ rectangles from top (A) as indicated by broken lines in diagram 1. Glue legs (B) into these cut-outs, with top edges of (B) flush with top surface of (A).

2. For table top carving, cut two corners from embossed paper picture frame and glue each paper corner to where legs (B) are glued to top (A). Trim excess paper so it is flush with surface of (A). Glue width of embossed picture frame to front and sides of top (A), following contour of beveled edge. Paint paper with woodtone paint to match stain.

3. Glue piece (D) to underside of top (A) so back surface of (D) is flush with back edge of (A).

4. With round sandpaper file, sand bottom ends of pieces (C) at opposite angles until they fit backs of legs (B) when glued and so top ends meet in the center; study diagram 4 carefully. Glue pieces (C) to backs of legs (B) $\frac{7}{16}''$ from floor.

5. Glue decorative button to top ends of pieces (C) at the center. Paint button with woodtone paint.

FINISHING

1. Shellac. Use steel wool to smooth fragile leg assembly very carefully.

2. Varnish.

3. Paint edges of Formica white and glue Formica to top (A).

CIRCULAR DINING TABLE
(*Victorian dining room*)

SIZE: $4\frac{5}{8}''$W × $2\frac{1}{2}''$H

WOOD: $\frac{3}{16}''$ balsa sheet, $\frac{3}{32}''$ balsa sheet, $\frac{1}{4}''$ dowel

SUGGESTED FINISH: walnut

BASIC TOOLS AND SUPPLIES, plus compass, $\frac{1}{2}''$ lamp finial, woodtone paint

PIECES FROM $\frac{3}{16}''$ BALSA SHEET
   A: circle $4\frac{3}{8}''$ in diameter
   B: piece from pattern, diagram 1

PIECE FROM $\frac{3}{32}''$ BALSA SHEET
   C: circle $4\frac{5}{8}''$ in diameter

PIECES FROM $\frac{1}{4}''$ DOWEL
   D: four $2\frac{1}{4}''$ pieces

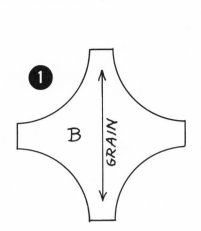

CUTTING

Cut wood, cutting piece (B) on lengthwise grain.

SANDING AND STAINING

1. Sand wood.
2. Round bottoms of legs (D).
3. Stain wood.

ASSEMBLY, diagram 2

1. Center and glue table top (A) to table top (C). To prevent warping, be sure the grain of one top runs at right angles to grain of other top. Place suitable weight on top of assembly.

2. Glue a leg (D) to one projection of base (B) so (B) is ⅜″ from floor; some propping will be necessary. Repeat for other legs (D), one at a time, propping and letting glue set before proceeding to next leg.

3. Center and glue legs assembly from step 2 to underside of table top assembly from step 1, making sure each leg is perfectly perpendicular to table top. Two of the legs should be placed in the same direction as the grain of the wood.

FINISHING

1. Shellac, then varnish.
2. Center and glue lamp finial to top surface of base (B) and paint with woodtone paint to match stain.

TWO-PEDESTAL DINING TABLE
(Georgian dining room)

SIZE: 4″W × 6″L × 2⅜″H

WOOD: ⅛″ balsa sheet, ¼″ dowel

SUGGESTED FINISH: mahogany

BASIC TOOLS AND SUPPLIES, plus two 1″ lamp finials, woodtone paint

PIECES FROM ⅛″ BALSA SHEET
A: 4″ × 6″ piece
B: six pieces from pattern, diagram 2

PIECES FROM ¼″ DOWEL
C: two ⅜″ pieces

CUTTING

1. For table top (A), use a 6″-wide piece of ⅛″ balsa sheet for best results and cut on crosswise grain; see diagram 1 for cutting four round corners. Then cut (A) into two equal parts, each 3″ × 4″, on lengthwise grain so when two parts are glued back together to resemble an extension dining table, they will fit perfectly.

2. Cut legs (B) on lengthwise grain. (See directions for cutting a curved line.)

SANDING AND STAINING
Sand wood, then stain.

ASSEMBLY, diagram 3

1. Glue two table top parts (A) back together at straight edges of both pieces. Put suitable weight on top.

2. Glue ⅜″ straight edges of three legs (B) to ⅜″ round surface of piece (C). In order to space legs evenly, draw a triangle with each side 2″ long; the feet of the legs should fit into angles of the triangle. Make sure legs touch the floor evenly and piece (C) is level; the assembly should be 1″ high. Let assembly dry completely or it won't hold weight of finial. Repeat procedure for other legs (B) and piece (C).

3. Paint lamp finials with woodtone paint to match stain. When dry, glue flat ends of finials to top center of each assembly from step 2. Make sure finials are upright from all sides by turning them around on a level surface.

4. The leg-and-finial assemblies from step 3 should be 2″ high. In order for completed table to be 2⅜″ high, make two ½″ squares out of a ¼″-thick balsa sheet to go between finials and table top (A). If your leg-and-finial assemblies are slightly more or less than 2″ high, adjust thickness of ½″ balsa squares accordingly. Glue squares to underside of (A) so center of each square is 2″ from sides of table and 1⅛″ from end of table.

5. The rounded ends of the finials don't glue easily to a flat surface, so you need to hollow out round indentations in the ½″ balsa squares for the finials; make indentations with X-acto knife, metal file, or sandpaper and make sure finials fit snugly. Glue finials into indentations in the squares so one leg of each leg-and-finial assembly faces the other under exact center of table.

FINISHING

1. Shellac; one coat is sufficient for legs. Use steel wool to smooth legs very carefully.

2. Varnish.

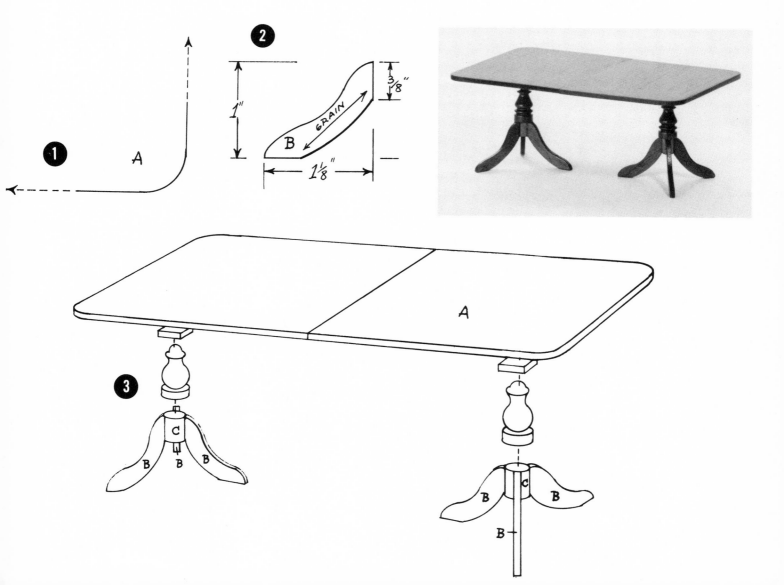

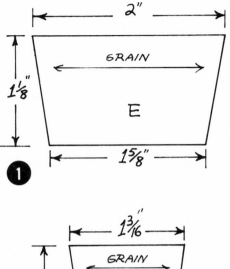

DOUGHBOX
(Colonial keeping room)

SIZE: 2¼″W × 1½″D × 2½″H

WOOD: ³⁄₃₂″ balsa sheet, ¹⁄₁₆″ × ¼″ balsa strip, ³⁄₁₆″ dowel

SUGGESTED FINISH: pine

BASIC TOOLS AND SUPPLIES, plus pair of ⅝″ decoupage hinges

PIECES FROM ³⁄₃₂″ BALSA SHEET
    A–B: 1½″ × 2¼″ piece
    C: ⅛″ × 2¼″ piece
    D: two ⅛″ × 1⅛″ pieces
    E: two pieces from pattern, diagram 1
    F: two pieces from pattern, diagram 2
    G: 1³⁄₁₆″ × 1¾″ piece

PIECES FROM ¹⁄₁₆″ × ¼″ BALSA STRIP
    H: two pieces from pattern, diagram 3
    I: two pieces from pattern, diagram 4

PIECES FROM ³⁄₁₆″ DOWEL
    J: four 1¼″ pieces

CUTTING
    1. Cut wood on lengthwise grain.
    2. For box top (A–B), cut off piece (A) ¼″ from long edge of rectangle (A–B).

SANDING AND STAINING
    1. Sand wood.
    2. For box bottom (G), round all four edges slightly.
    3. For legs (J), round one end of each.
    4. Stain wood.

ASSEMBLY, diagram 5
    1. Glue box front (E) and box back (E) to front and back edges of box sides (F).
    2. Center and glue assembly from step 1 to bottom (G) so (G) extends ¹⁄₁₆″ all the way around.

    3. Trim decoupage hinges to ⅜″ and insert between top pieces (A) and (B) so each hinge is ⅜″ from sides of (A–B); see directions under Hardware for "blind" hinging. Place glue along ³⁄₃₂″ edge of piece (C) and glue to underside of top (B) along front edge of (B). Place glue along ³⁄₃₂″ edges of pieces (D) and glue to underside of (B) along side edges of (B).
    4. Glue top (A) to top edge of back (E) and part of top edges of sides (F). Do not put any glue on top (B) or box top won't open.
    5. Glue pieces (H) to side edges of pieces (I), making sure assembly angles out slightly and dries firmly.
    6. Center and glue assembly from step 5 to underside of bottom (G). When glue begins to set, place suitable weight on top.
    7. Glue legs (J) to inside corners of assembly from step 5; if the latter has been cut and glued accurately, each leg will slope out at the correct angle. Make sure legs dry very firmly.

FINISHING
    1. Shellac; one coat is sufficient for legs. Use steel wool to smooth legs very carefully.
    2. Varnish.

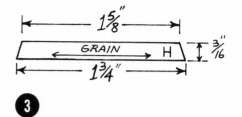

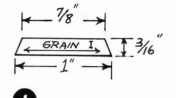

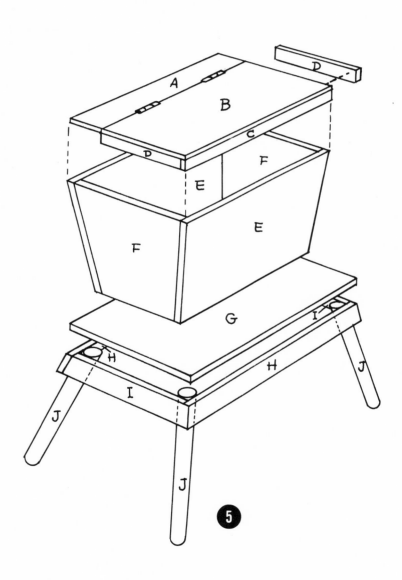

DRESSING TABLE
(Georgian bedroom)

SIZE: 4¼″W × 1⅝″D × 2⅜″H

WOOD: ⅛″ balsa sheet, ³⁄₃₂″ balsa sheet, ¹⁄₃₂″ balsa sheet, ³⁄₁₆″ sq. balsa strip

SUGGESTED FINISH: mahogany

BASIC TOOLS AND SUPPLIES, plus 4 sewing eyes, gold paint

PIECE FROM ⅛″ BALSA SHEET
   A: 1⅝″ × 4¼″ piece

PIECES FROM ³⁄₃₂″ BALSA SHEET
   B: two ¾″ × 3⅝″ pieces
   C: two ¾″ × 1⅛″ pieces
   D: two ¾″ × 1⅜″ pieces

PIECES FROM ¹⁄₃₂″ BALSA SHEET
   E: four ¼″ × ¾″ pieces
   F: ¼″ × 1¾″ piece

PIECES FROM ³⁄₁₆″ SQ. BALSA STRIP
   G: four 2¼″ pieces

CUTTING
   1. Cut wood on lengthwise grain.
   2. For front piece (B), cut out a rectangle 1⅞″ long and ⅜″ high from the center of one long edge; this will leave ⅞″ on each side of the rectangular space.

SANDING AND STAINING
   1. Sand wood.
   2. For table top (A), round four corner edges slightly.
   3. For drawers (E) and (F), bevel all four edges.
   4. Stain wood.

ASSEMBLY, diagram 1
   1. Glue drawers (E) to front piece (B); leave ¹⁄₁₆″ space between top drawers and top edge of (B), between bottom drawers and bottom edge of (B), and between side edges of drawers and side edges of (B).
   2. Center and glue drawer (F) to front (B) between top edge of (B) and rectangular open-ing. Place suitable weight on top of assembly from steps 1 and 2.
   3. Glue a side piece (C) between two legs (G) so top edges and outside surfaces of all pieces are flush and the grain of the wood of (C) runs horizontally; repeat for other side (C) and legs (G).
   4. Glue back piece (B) between back legs (G) so top edges and outside surfaces of all pieces are flush.
   5. Glue front (B) between front legs (G) so top edges and front surfaces of all pieces are flush.
   6. Trim and glue one piece (D) between front and back pieces (B) perpendicular to these pieces; one side edge of (D) is glued alongside rectangular opening in front (B) and top edge of (D) is flush with top edges of both pieces (B). Repeat procedure for other piece (D).
   7. Center and glue top (A) to assembly from steps 1–6 so back edge of (A) is flush with out-side surface of back (B). Place suitable weight on top of entire assembly.

FINISHING
   1. Shellac, then varnish.
   2. Make drawer handles out of sewing eyes and attach. Center handles on drawers (E).

Variation: WRITING TABLE

The dimensions of the dressing table are suit-able for a living room writing table. Change four small drawers (E) to two larger drawers, each measuring ⅝″ × ¾″. Paint two small round beads and straight pins gold for drawer knobs on drawers (E), and paint two more beads and straight pins gold for knobs on drawer (F).

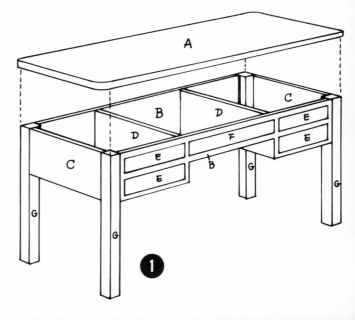

DROP-LEAF DINING TABLE
(Colonial dining room)

Size: 4″W × 6″L × 2½″H

Wood: ⅛″ balsa sheet, ³⁄₁₆″ sq. balsa strip, ¼″ × ¹⁄₁₆″ balsa strip

Suggested finish: cherry

Basic tools and supplies

Piece from ⅛″ balsa sheet
  A: 4″ × 6″ piece

Pieces from ³⁄₁₆″ sq. balsa strip
  B: six 2⅜″ pieces

Pieces from ¼″ × ¹⁄₁₆″ balsa strip
  C: two 1⅝″ pieces
  D: two 3⅜″ pieces
  E: two 1½″ pieces

Cutting

1. Cut wood on lengthwise grain except for piece (A), which is cut on crosswise grain.

2. For table top (A), use a 6″-wide piece of ⅛″ balsa sheet for best results and cut on cross- wise grain. Then cut (A) into three equal parts, each 2″ × 4″, on crosswise grain so when the three parts are glued back together to resemble a drop-leaf table, they will fit perfectly.

Sanding and staining
  Sand wood, then stain.

Assembly, diagram 1

1. Glue three table top parts (A) back to- gether at long edges to form a perfect 4″ × 6″ rectangle. Place suitable weight on top.

2. Glue a piece (C) between two legs (B) so top edges and outside surfaces of all pieces are flush; repeat for other piece (C) and two legs (B).

3. Glue one assembly from step 2 to under- side of center part of table top (A) ⅛″ from 2″ edge of (A); repeat for other assembly from step 2.

4. Put glue along ¹⁄₁₆″ edge of a piece (D) and glue (D) to underside of top (A) between two legs (B) where there's a seam joining two parts of (A); repeat for other piece (D).

5. Put glue along ¹⁄₁₆″ edge of a piece (E) and glue (E) to underside of top (A) and to middle of piece (D); (E) should be perpendicular to (D). Repeat for other piece (E).

6. Center and glue one leg (B) to underside of top (A) at outside edge of piece (E); repeat for remaining leg (B). Place suitable weight on entire assembly, taking care not to unglue legs (B).

Finishing
  Shellac, then varnish.

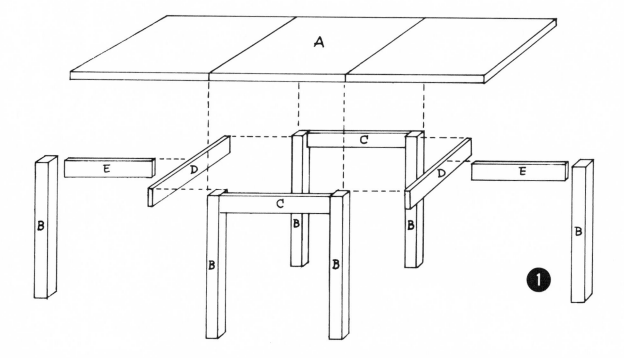

DRUM TABLE
(Georgian library)

SIZE: $2\frac{1}{2}''$W × $2\frac{3}{8}''$H

WOOD: $\frac{1}{8}''$ balsa sheet, $\frac{3}{32}''$ balsa sheet, $\frac{1}{16}''$ balsa sheet, $\frac{1}{4}''$ dowel

SUGGESTED FINISH: mahogany

BASIC TOOLS AND SUPPLIES, plus compass, 1'' lamp finial, woodtone paint, 2 small round beads, gold paint

PIECES FROM $\frac{1}{8}''$ BALSA SHEET
    A: three pieces from pattern, diagram 1

PIECES FROM $\frac{3}{32}''$ BALSA SHEET
    B: two circles $2\frac{1}{2}''$ in diameter

PIECES FROM $\frac{1}{16}''$ BALSA SHEET
    C: two $\frac{5}{16}'' \times 4''$ pieces

PIECE FROM $\frac{1}{4}''$ DOWEL
    D: $\frac{1}{4}''$ piece

CUTTING
    1. Cut wood on lengthwise grain except for pieces (C), which are cut on crosswise grain.
    2. For legs (A), cut a curved line.

SANDING AND STAINING
    Sand wood, then stain.

ASSEMBLY, diagram 2
    1. Before gluing pieces (C) to one table top piece (B), see where pieces (C) should begin and end as directed in step 2. Then glue pieces (C) to top (B) so outside surfaces of (C) are flush with edge of (B). Pieces (C) were cut on crosswise grain of the wood so they would bend easily to form a circle. Hold assembly in place with hands until glue begins to set, paying particular attention to gluing where pieces (C) meet. If you have a $2\frac{1}{2}''$ jar lid to use as a mold, this will facilitate the gluing.
    2. Cut two straight lines, opposite each other and $\frac{7}{8}''$ to the right of where pieces (C) meet; see broken lines in diagram 2. These cut lines, plus the lines where pieces (C) meet, are the edges of the drum table's drawers. These drawers should be opposite each other and centered in the same direction as the grain of the wood of top (B).
    3. Glue other table top piece (B) to pieces (C) in the same way as in step 1.
    4. Paint lamp finial with woodtone paint to match stain. When dry, center and glue flat rim

to underside of assembly from steps 1–3. If finial measures a little less than 1'', cut a small balsa square up to $\frac{1}{8}''$ thick, center and glue it to underside of drum table top, and then glue finial to small square.
    5. Glue $\frac{1}{4}''$ straight edges of legs (A) to $\frac{1}{4}''$ round surface of piece (D). In order to space legs evenly, draw a triangle with each side 2'' long; the feet of the legs should fit into angles of the triangle. Make sure legs touch the floor evenly and piece (D) is level; the assembly should be $\frac{3}{4}''$ high. Let assembly dry completely, or it won't hold weight of drum table top and finial.
    6. Glue drum table top and finial assemblies from steps 1–4 to assembly from step 5, with one of the drawers centered over one of the legs; some propping will be necessary.

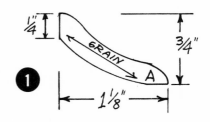

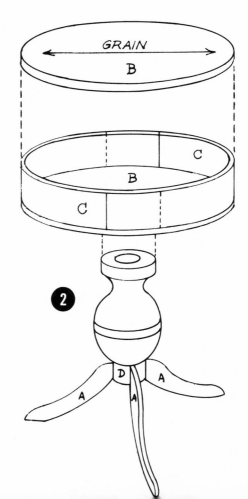

FINISHING

1. Shellac; one coat is sufficient for legs. Use steel wool to smooth legs very carefully.

2. Varnish.

3. For drawer knobs, paint beads and heads of two straight pins gold and attach to center of each drawer.

4. Paint tips of legs gold.

Variation: QUEEN ANNE TABLE

A round table in the Queen Anne style can be made easily with only one table top piece (B). Eliminate pieces (C) and use a 1½" lamp finial instead of a 1" finial.

MARBLE TOP KITCHEN TABLE
(Victorian kitchen)

SIZE: 3¼"W × 5"L × 2½"H

WOOD: ⅛" balsa sheet, 1/32" balsa sheet, ⅜" sq. balsa strip, ¼" dowel

SUGGESTED FINISH: oak

BASIC TOOLS AND SUPPLIES, plus Formica with marble pattern, 4 push pins, woodtone paint, small round white bead, white model paint

PIECES FROM ⅛" BALSA SHEET
A: 3¼" × 5" piece
B: two ⅜" × 4" pieces
C: two ⅜" × 2¼" pieces

PIECE FROM 1/32" BALSA SHEET
D: ¼" × 1⅜" piece

PIECES FROM ⅜" SQ. BALSA STRIP
E: four ½" pieces

PIECES FROM ¼" DOWEL
F: four 1¼" pieces

PIECE FROM FORMICA
A: 3¼" × 5" piece

CUTTING

1. Cut wood on lengthwise grain.

2. Cut Formica piece slowly and carefully, then smooth edges and round four corners slightly with metal file.

SANDING AND STAINING

1. Sand wood.

2. For wood and Formica table top (A), round four corners slightly.

3. Stain wood.

ASSEMBLY, diagram 1

1. Center and glue drawer (D) to one long side piece (B).

2. Center and glue piece (B) to underside of wood table top (A) 3/16" from long edge of (A); repeat for other piece (B) and other long edge of (A).

3. Glue four pieces (E) to four ends of pieces (B) so ⅜"-square top of each piece (E) is glued to underside of table top (A), and the two outside surfaces of each piece (E) are ⅛" from corner edges of (A).

4. Glue a short side piece (C) to underside of table top (A) between two pieces (E) 3/16" from short edge of (A); repeat for other piece (C) and other short edge of (A).

5. Center the pin of a push pin on surface of end of one leg (F) and push in; repeat for other legs (F). Center and glue other ends of legs (F) to underside of pieces (E).

FINISHING

1. Shellac, then varnish.

2. For drawer knob, attach bead to center of drawer (D) with a little glue and straight pin.

3. Paint edges of Formica top (A) white and glue to wood top (A).

4. Paint push pins with woodtone paint to match stain.

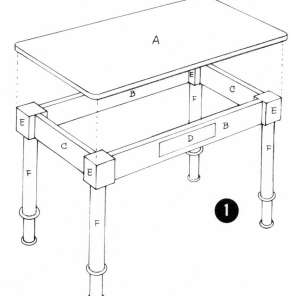

PEMBROKE TABLE
(Colonial living room)

SIZE: 2"W × 2⅝"L × 2¼"H

WOOD: 3⁄32" balsa sheet, 1⁄32" balsa sheet, 3⁄16" sq. balsa strip

SUGGESTED FINISH: mahogany

BASIC TOOLS AND SUPPLIES, plus sewing loop, gold paint, 2 pairs of pliers

PIECES FROM 3⁄32" BALSA SHEET
  A: piece from pattern, diagram 1
  B: two pieces from pattern, diagram 2
  C: two 7⁄16" × 1⅜" pieces

PIECE FROM 1⁄32" BALSA SHEET
  D: ¼" × 1⅜" piece

PIECES FROM 3⁄16" SQ. BALSA STRIP
  E: four 2¼" pieces

CUTTING
  1. Cut wood on lengthwise grain.
  2. For table leaves (B), cut a curved line.

SANDING AND STAINING
  Sand wood, then stain.

ASSEMBLY, diagram 3
  1. Center and glue drawer (D) to a table side piece (C). Then glue (C) between two legs (E) so top edges and outside surfaces of (C) and (E) are flush. Repeat for other side piece (C) and other legs (E). The assemblies must be the exact width of the table top (A) 1¾".
  2. Glue a side-and-legs assembly from step 1 to underside of table top (A) 1⁄16" from curved edge of (A), measuring from the corners. Repeat for other side-and-legs assembly and other curved edge of (A).
  3. Glue a table leaf (B) to straight side of top (A) so straight top edge of (B) is flush with *underside* of (A). To do this, place glue on side surfaces of two legs (E) for a distance of about 1" starting at top of legs; then glue leaf (B) to legs (E), matching corners of long straight edges of (B) and (A). Repeat procedure for other leaf (B).

FINISHING
  1. Shellac, then varnish.
  2. Make a drawer handle out of the sewing loop and attach handle to center of drawer (D).

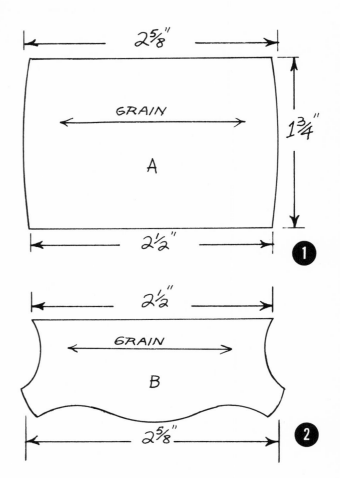

Variation: STRAIGHT-LEAF PEMBROKE TABLE

For a Pembroke table with straight leaves, cut each piece (B) 1" × 2½" and round bottom corner edges slightly.

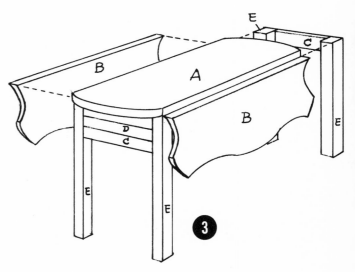

SEWING OR BEDSIDE TABLE
(Victorian living room)

SIZE: $1\frac{7}{8}$"W × $1\frac{1}{2}$"D × $2\frac{1}{2}$"H

WOOD: $\frac{1}{8}$" balsa sheet, $\frac{3}{32}$" balsa sheet, $\frac{1}{4}$" dowel

SUGGESTED FINISH: walnut

BASIC TOOLS AND SUPPLIES, plus $\frac{3}{4}$" lamp finial, woodtone paint, 4 tiny round beads, gold paint

PIECES FROM $\frac{1}{8}$" BALSA SHEET
A: four pieces from pattern, diagram 1

PIECES FROM $\frac{3}{32}$" BALSA SHEET
B: $1\frac{3}{8}$" × $1\frac{3}{4}$" piece
C: $1\frac{1}{2}$" × $1\frac{3}{4}$" piece
D: two $\frac{5}{8}$" × $1\frac{3}{4}$" pieces
E: two 1" × $1\frac{1}{2}$" pieces

PIECES FROM $\frac{1}{4}$" DOWEL
F: two $1\frac{1}{8}$" pieces
G: $\frac{5}{16}$" piece

CUTTING
1. Cut wood on lengthwise grain.
2. For legs (A), cut a curved line.
3. For front piece (D), cut out a rectangle $1\frac{1}{8}$" long and $\frac{1}{2}$" high from the center of one long edge; this will leave $\frac{5}{16}$" on each side of the rectangular space.

SANDING AND STAINING
1. Sand wood.
2. For table leaves (E), round the bottom corner edges.
3. Stain wood.

ASSEMBLY, diagram 2
1. Glue dowel drawers (F) together lengthwise. When dry, glue drawers (F) in the rectangular opening cut in front piece (D); glue on diameter of the dowels so drawers look semicircular or curved.
2. Glue bottom edge of assembly from step 1 to top surface of bottom piece (B) along $1\frac{3}{4}$" edge of (B); the front surface of piece (D) is flush with front edge of (B).
3. Glue back piece (D) along other $1\frac{3}{4}$" edge of bottom (B); back surface of (D) is flush with back edge of (B).
4. Glue table top (C) to top edges of pieces (D) so back edge of (C) is flush with back surface of back (D) and front edge of (C) extends $\frac{1}{8}$" beyond front (D).

5. Glue a table leaf (E) to short, $1\frac{1}{2}$" side of top (C) so straight top edge of (E) is flush with *underside* of (C). To do this, place glue on side edges of front and back pieces (D); then glue (E) to pieces (D), matching corners of the $1\frac{1}{2}$" edges of (D) and (C). Repeat procedure for other leaf (E).
6. Center and glue lamp finial to underside of bottom (B). Paint finial with woodtone paint to match stain.
7. Glue $\frac{5}{16}$" straight edges of legs (A) to $\frac{5}{16}$" round surface of piece (G). In order to space legs evenly, draw a $1\frac{1}{4}$" square; the feet of the legs should fit into angles of the square. Make sure legs touch the floor evenly and piece (G) is level; the assembly should be about 1" high. Let assembly dry completely or it won't hold weight of table top and finial.
8. Center and glue table-top-and-finial assembly to assembly from step 7.

FINISHING
1. Shellac; one coat is sufficient for legs. Use steel wool to smooth legs very carefully.
2. Varnish.
3. For drawer knobs, paint beads gold and glue two beads to each drawer (F) $\frac{3}{16}$" from side edges of (F).

Variation: OVAL END TABLE

Replace cabinet top with oval-shaped balsa piece.

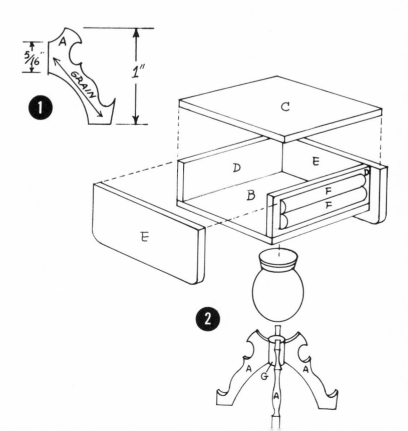

TEA TABLE
(Colonial living room)

SIZE: 1½"W × 3½"L × 2¼"H

WOOD: ⅛" balsa sheet, ³⁄₃₂" balsa sheet, ³⁄₃₂" quarter-round basswood strip

SUGGESTED FINISH: mahogany

BASIC TOOLS AND SUPPLIES, plus gold paint, 2 half-inch straight pins

PIECES FROM ⅛" BALSA SHEET
    A: two pieces from pattern, diagram 1
    B: two pieces from pattern, diagram 2
    C: 1¼" × 2¼" piece

PIECES FROM ³⁄₃₂" BALSA SHEET
    D: two ½" × ½" pieces

PIECE FROM ³⁄₃₂" QUARTER-ROUND WOOD STRIP
    E: 9" piece

CUTTING
    1. Cut wood on lengthwise grain except for pieces (A), which are cut on crosswise grain. Each piece (A) is a combination of the long table side and two legs. The grain of the wood will go in the wrong direction for the table side, but in the right direction for the legs, which is essential because the legs are very slender and delicate.
    2. For pieces (A) and (B), cut a decorative edge and a curved line. If a piece (A) breaks in the middle of cutting it, you may continue cutting, sanding, and staining the broken pieces and then glue them back together when stain is dry.
    3. Piece (E) is cut later. If you can't find quarter-round basswood for (E), use ³⁄₃₂" sq. balsa strip.

SANDING AND STAINING
    1. Sand wood, using only the finest grade of sandpaper and sanding very carefully.
    2. Stain wood.

ASSEMBLY, diagram 3
    1. Center and glue a piece (A) to long edge of table top (C) so top edge of (A) is flush with top surface of (C); repeat for other piece (A).
    2. Glue a table side (B) to short edge of top (C) and short, straight side edges of pieces (A); top edge of (B) is flush with top surface of (C) and outside surface of (B) is flush with side edges of (A). Repeat procedure for other side (B).
    3. Cut piece (E) in two 2¼" pieces and two 1½" pieces; miter corner edges of the four pieces. Glue pieces (E) to top ⅛" edges of pieces (A) and (B) so round edges face out. The mitered corners should fit together so top of table resembles a tray.
    4. Center and glue pieces (D) to sides (B) ⅛" from the top edges of (B).

FINISHING
    1. Shellac. Use steel wool very carefully.
    2. Varnish.
    3. For candlestick shelf knobs, paint heads of half-inch straight pins gold; center and insert a pin carefully into outside edge of each candlestick shelf (D).

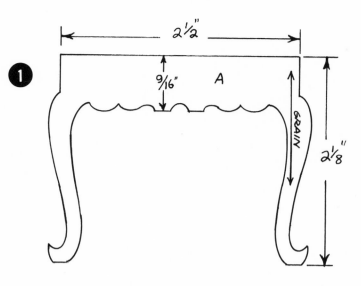

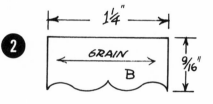

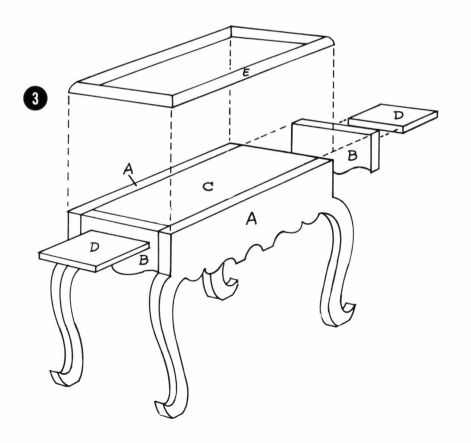

TRESTLE TABLE
(Colonial keeping room)

Size: 3"W × 6"L × 2½"H

Wood: ³⁄₁₆" balsa sheet, 2 round wooden toothpicks

Suggested finish: pine

Basic tools and supplies

Pieces from ³⁄₁₆" balsa sheet
A: 3" × 5⅝" piece
B: two ³⁄₁₆" × 3" pieces
C: ½" × 5½" piece
D: two pieces from pattern (solid outline only), diagram 1
E: two ¼" × 2" pieces

pieces from toothpicks
F: two ⅜" pieces

Cutting
1. Cut wood on lengthwise grain.
2. For table legs (D), cut a curved line. Cut out ³⁄₁₆" × ⁵⁄₁₆" rectangle from each leg, following broken line in diagram 1.
3. For each foot (E), leave a ⅞" straight edge in the middle of top edge and slope edges on either side slightly; hollow out a slight recess in the middle of bottom edge.
4. For stretcher (C), cut out a ³⁄₁₆" × ⁷⁄₁₆" rectangle at both top corners, with the ³⁄₁₆" edge vertical and the ⁷⁄₁₆" edge horizontal.
5. For pegs (F), cut ⅜" from middle of toothpicks.

Sanding and staining
Sand wood, then stain.

Assembly, diagram 2
1. Glue table top end pieces (B) to short edges of table top center piece (A).
2. Glue legs (D) to feet (E) matching the ⅞" straight edges.
3. Insert stretcher (C) through cut-out rectangles in legs (D); the stretcher should fit snugly and require no glue. Using a round metal file, drill a tiny hole in both ends of (C) and insert pegs (F) in these holes to lock stretcher in place.
4. Center and glue assembly from steps 2 and 3 to underside of top (A–B). When glue begins to set, place suitable weight on top of entire assembly.

Finishing
Shellac, then varnish.

Variation: SHAKER TRESTLE TABLE

For this simpler version of the trestle table, use ⅛" balsa sheet throughout. Narrow table top (A–B) to width of 2¼". Cut plain, straight legs ⅜" wide. Cut all other pieces the same and assemble table following same procedures as for the trestle table.

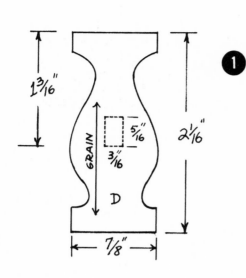

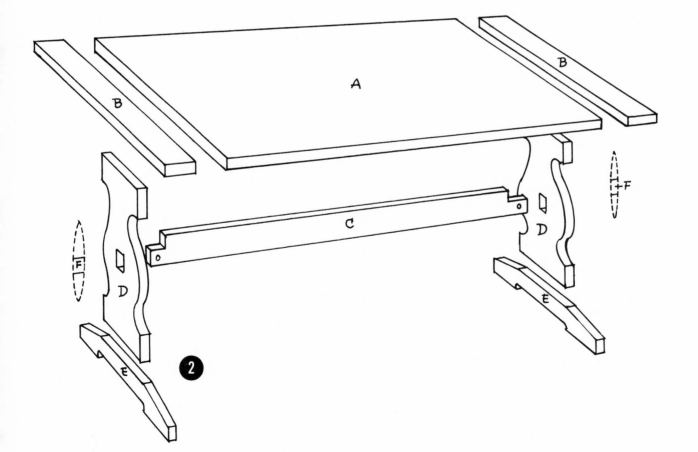

VICTORIAN WHAT-NOT
(Victorian living room)

SIZE: 3⅛″W × 1⅛″D × 5″H

WOOD: ¹⁄₁₆″ balsa sheet

SUGGESTED FINISH: dark walnut

BASIC TOOLS AND SUPPLIES, plus 92 round beads ³⁄₁₆″ in diameter, 16 oblong beads, 16 two-inch hat pins, woodtone paint

PIECES FROM ¹⁄₁₆″ BALSA SHEET
   A: two pieces from pattern, diagram 1
   B: piece from pattern, diagram 1
   C: piece from pattern, diagram 1
   D: piece from pattern, diagram 1

CUTTING
   Cut wood on lengthwise grain. Diagram 1 is actually four patterns from which you will cut five shelves. See directions for cutting the curved lines.

SANDING AND STAINING
   1. Sand wood, then stain.
   2. Shellac shelves (A), (B), (C), and (D). It is more convenient to do this before assembling.

ASSEMBLY, diagram 2
   1. With pencil, mark four dots on underside of each shelf (A) as follows: The dots are placed ⅛″ from front and back edges of (A); two dots in back are 2¾″ apart and so are two dots in front; each dot should be the same distance from side edges of (A). These dots indicate where to insert hat pins.
   2. In the next four steps, you will be stringing beads on hat pins to simulate wood spindle turnings. Place a round bead on a hat pin and push pin through underside of bottom shelf (A) at one corner. Place seven more beads on this pin and push pin through underside of top shelf (A) at matching corner. Place glue on pin and add an oblong bead to cover it. Repeat this procedure for other three corners of shelves (A), keeping assembly straight and level.
   3. Following procedure in step 1, mark four dots on top surface of top shelf (A) and four dots on top surface of shelf (B), only this time place dots 2½″ apart along front and back edges. Cut beaded ends from four hat pins so each is 1⁷⁄₁₆″ long. Push pointed end of a pin through top surface of shelf (B) at one corner. Place six more beads on this pin, put glue on the sixth bead, and push pin through top surface of top shelf (A) at matching corner, making sure pin does not go completely through (A). Put glue on cut-off end of the pin and add an oblong bead to cover it. Repeat procedure for other three corners of shelves (B) and (A), keeping assembly straight and level.
   4. Following procedure in step 1, mark four dots on top surface of shelf (B) and four dots on top surface of shelf (C), only this time place dots 2¼″ apart along front and back edges. Cut beaded ends from four hat pins so each is 1¼″ long. Push pointed end of a pin through top surface of shelf (C) at one corner. Place five more beads on this pin, put glue on the fifth bead, and push pin through top surface of shelf (B) at matching corner, making sure pin does not go completely through (B). Put glue on cut-off end of the pin and add an oblong bead to cover it. Repeat procedure for other three corners of shelves (C) and (B), keeping assembly straight and level.
   5. Following procedure in step 1, mark four dots on top surface of shelf (C) and four dots on top surface of shelf (D), only this time place dots 2″ apart along front and back edges. Cut beaded ends from four hat pins so each is

1⅛″ long. Push pointed end of a pin through top surface of shelf (D) at one corner. Place four more beads on this pin, put glue on the fourth bead, and push pin through top surface of shelf (C) at matching corner, making sure pin does not go completely through (C). Put glue on cut-off end of the pin and add an oblong bead to cover it. Repeat procedure for other three corners of shelves (D) and (C), keeping assembly straight and level.

FINISHING

1. Paint beads with woodtone paint to match stain.

2. Varnish.

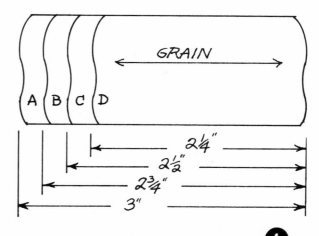

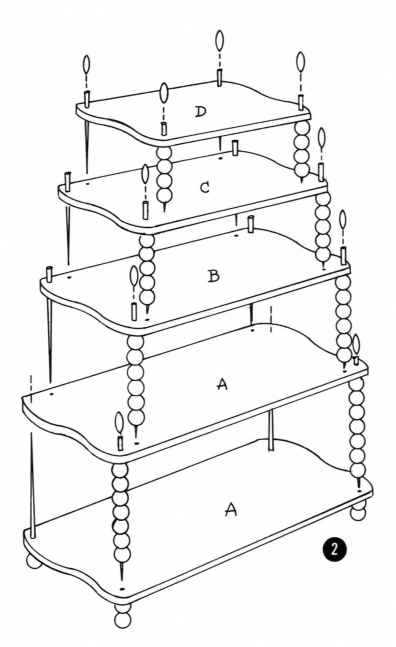

CHAPTER *24* *Miscellaneous*

SPINNING WHEEL
(Colonial keeping room)

SIZE: ¾″W × 6⅛″L × 5⅛″H

WOOD: ³⁄₁₆″ balsa sheet, ⅛″ balsa sheet, ¹⁄₁₆″ × ¼″ balsa strip, ¹⁄₃₂″ × ⁵⁄₁₆″ basswood strip, ³⁄₁₆″ dowel, 12 round wooden toothpicks

SUGGESTED FINISH: pine

BASIC TOOLS AND SUPPLIES, plus coffee can and plastic top 4″ in diameter, elastic bands or masking tape

PIECES FROM ³⁄₁₆″ BALSA SHEET
A: piece from pattern, diagram 1
B: circle ⁷⁄₁₆″ in diameter

PIECES FROM ⅛″ BALSA SHEET
C: ¼″ × 2⅜″ piece
D: circle ⁷⁄₁₆″ in diameter

PIECES FROM ¹⁄₁₆″ × ¼″ BALSA STRIP
E: two 2⅜″ pieces

PIECE FROM ¹⁄₃₂″ × ⁵⁄₁₆″ BASSWOOD STRIP
F: 14″ piece

PIECES FROM ³⁄₁₆″ DOWEL
G: 1½″ piece
H: two 1¼″ pieces

PIECES FROM TOOTHPICKS
I: twelve 1¾″ pieces

CUTTING
Cut wood pieces, cutting toothpick pieces (I) on one end only.

SANDING AND STAINING
1. Sand wood.
2. Round each corner of platform (A). With a round file, drill hole ³⁄₁₆″ in diameter in platform (A), placing it ¼″ from narrow end and centered; drill hole from top to bottom on outward slant. Drill two more holes ³⁄₁₆″ in diameter, placing them ½″ from corners of wide end of (A); these holes are also drilled from top to bottom on outward slant toward the corners.
3. For wheel (B), make a groove with a half-round file around center of circular edge.
4. Round the top edges of pieces (C) and (E). Slant bottom edges of (C) and (E) at an angle of about 15°. With a round or triangular file, notch both sides of (C) and (E) at ¼″ intervals to resemble spindle turning.
5. For wheel rim (F), soak piece (F) in warm water for five minutes. Then bend (F) carefully around coffee can (there will be some overlap) and hold in place with elastic bands or masking tape; do not let elastic bands indent the wet wood. Let wood dry at room temperature or in a low oven for ten minutes.
6. For legs (G) and (H), round one edge of each.
7. Stain wood.

ASSEMBLY, diagram 2
1. Insert flat edge of leg (G) into hole at narrow end of platform (A); it should fit snugly and require no glue. Trim top of leg (G) so it is flush with top surface of (A). Repeat procedure for legs (H) and holes at wide end of (A). Platform (A) should now tilt at an angle.
2. With a straight pin, make a hole through the center of wheel (B) and through the rounded ends of pieces (E) ¼″ from the end and centered. With wire cutters, cut a ⅜″ piece from the middle of a straight pin and insert the piece of pin through holes in piece (E), wheel (B), and other piece (E), in that order. Secure pin at each end with a little glue. The wheel should turn.
3. Glue assembly from step 2 to platform (A) ½″ from narrow end of (A), centered, and tilting outward. Hold assembly in place with hands until glue begins to set.
4. Glue piece (C) to platform (A) ⅛″ from a side edge, ¾″ from the wide end, and tilting outward. Reinforce piece (C) with a straight pin from underneath platform (A); see directions for reinforced gluing.

glue on pointed end of a spoke and insert about $\frac{1}{16}''$ into wheel hub (D); repeat this procedure for a second spoke, inserting into hub exactly opposite the first spoke so spokes point to 12 o'clock and 6 o'clock. Insert two more spokes at 3 o'clock and 9 o'clock, making sure you are forming a perfect circle divided evenly into quarters. Finish the circle by inserting spokes at 1, 2, 4, 5, 7, 8, 10, and 11 o'clock. Let spokes dry firmly.

7. Put wheel rim (F) back inside coffee can cover mold. Take hub-and-spokes assembly from step 6 and fit inside (F); where necessary, trim spokes on the end to insure a perfect fit. Place a dot of glue at flat end of each spoke and join the two assemblies. Let dry completely in the mold.

8. With a straight pin, make a hole through the center of wheel hub (D) and through rounded end of piece (C) $\frac{1}{4}''$ from the end and centered. With wire cutters, cut a straight pin to $\frac{1}{2}''$ and insert it through holes in hub (D) and piece (C) in that order. The wheel should turn.

FINISHING

1. Shellac. (Shellac wheel rim (F) only once and use steel wool to smooth it very carefully.)

2. Varnish.

5. Fit wheel rim (F) to inside rim of plastic coffee can cover. Make a slantwise cut through overlapping ends of (F); see detail in diagram 2. Glue slanted ends together, putting glue only on the inside of wheel rim. When completely dry, remove (F) carefully from mold and glue slanted ends on the outside.

6. The 12 spokes (I) on the spinning wheel represent the 12 hours of the day. Place a dot of

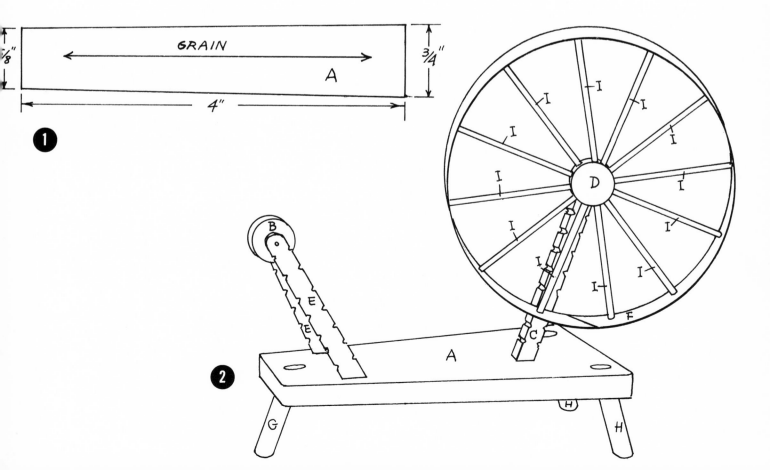

CAST-IRON STOVE
(Victorian kitchen)

SIZE: 4⅛″W × 2¼″D × 7″H

WOOD: 1″ × 2″ balsa strip, ³⁄₁₆″ balsa sheet, ⅛″ balsa sheet, ³⁄₃₂″ balsa sheet, ⅜″ sq. balsa strip, ⁵⁄₁₆″ dowel

SUGGESTED FINISH: black paint

BASIC TOOLS AND SUPPLIES, plus embossed paper, thumb or upholstery tack, black paint, oblong bead

PIECES FROM 1″ × 2″ BALSA STRIP
   A: two 3¾″ pieces
   B: ⅝″ piece

PIECES FROM ³⁄₁₆″ BALSA SHEET
   C: two 2¼″ × 4¼″ pieces

PIECE FROM ⅛″ BALSA SHEET
   D: piece from pattern, diagram 1

PIECES FROM ³⁄₃₂″ BALSA SHEET
   E: 1⅝″ × 2″ piece
   F: two ⅝″ × 1″ pieces

PIECES FROM ⅜″ SQ. BALSA STRIP
   G: four ½″ pieces

PIECE FROM ⁵⁄₁₆″ DOWEL
   H: 3½″ piece

CUTTING
1. Saw wood on lengthwise grain.
2. Glue pieces (A) together to form one solid block of wood, 2″ × 2″ × 3¾″. However, if you have a 2″-sq. block of wood on hand, cut it 3¾″ long and use for (A) instead of gluing together the two 1″ × 2″ blocks of wood.
3. For oven door (E), make two wooden hinges by cutting away a ¼″-sq. piece from top and bottom corners of a 2″ side and cutting away a ¼″ × ¾″ rectangular piece from the middle of the same 2″ side.

SANDING
1. Sand wood.
2. For stove top and bottom pieces (C), bevel front and side edges in a round bevel.
3. For doors (E) and (F), round edges on all four sides very slightly.
4. With a dowel sandpaper file or half-round file, sand two adjacent leg surfaces of a leg (G) at a slight angle so top edge of leg is reduced from a ⅜″ square to a ¼″ square; repeat for other legs (G).

ASSEMBLY, diagram 2
1. Glue oven door (E) to a 2″ × 3¾″ surface of stove body (A), centering (E) between the top and bottom edges of (A) and gluing wooden hinges of (E) ⅛″ from right edge of (A).
2. Glue fire drawer door (F) and ash drawer door (F) to front surface of stove body (A) directly over each other and on a line with oven door (E); outside edges of doors (F) are ¼″ from left edge of (A).
3. Center and glue assembly from steps 1 and 2 to stove bottom (C) so back edge of (C) is flush with back surface of stove body (A).
4. Center and glue stove top (C) to assembly from step 3 so back edge of top (C) is flush with back surface of stove body (A). Place suitable weight on top of entire assembly.
5. Glue legs (G) to underside of bottom (C) at each corner so the ¼″-sq. top edge of each leg is ³⁄₁₆″ from corner edges and curved surfaces of all legs face outward.
6. Center and glue piece (D) to top surface of stove top (C) along back edge of (C); the back surface of (D) is flush with back surface of stove body (A).
7. Center and glue warming oven (B) to piece (D) so the ⅝″ × 2″ top surface of (B) is flush with top edge of (D).
8. Stove pipe (H) will vary in length depending on size and layout of your dollhouse kitchen.

Cut two pieces of pipe (H) to fit together in middle at an exact 45° angle, and so one end touches warming oven (B) and the other end touches wall behind stove. Glue the two pieces of pipe together to form 90° angle, then center and glue flat edge of shorter piece of pipe to top surface of warming oven; you may or may not glue other end of pipe to wall.

FINISHING

1. Cut out interesting curlicues of embossed paper for all doors and glue paper on them in a pleasing arrangement. You can also insert an upholstery or thumbtack in center of oven door (E) to resemble a rivet.

2. For a knob on each door (F), center and insert a straight pin between top and bottom edges of door near a side edge.

3. For latch on oven door (E), center and glue an oblong bead between top and bottom edges of door near side edge at stove center.

4. For stove top lids, make four circular indentations on stove top (C) with a round object, such as a bottle top; see directions for scoring.

5. Paint entire stove with two or three coats of flat black enamel paint. Then paint embossed paper details wtih a coat of shellac.

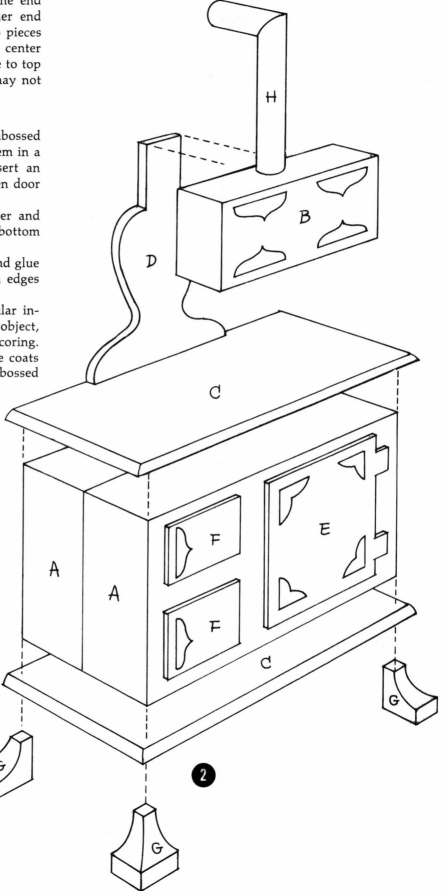

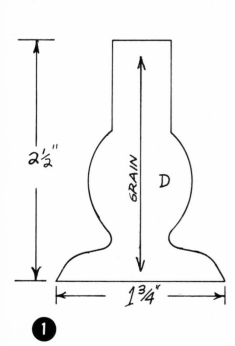

PART V

Accessories Projects

The accessories in this part of the book are designed merely to get you started accessorizing your own dollhouse. You may want to use some of the accessories here; you may want to alter some of them; and you will no doubt want to create some accessories of your own.

We have kept the instructions simple. Wherever possible, we have suggested an alternative part that works as well, realizing you may not be able to locate the exact bottle top, button, or whatever called for in the directions.

We recommend you have the following tools and supplies on hand for making dollhouse accessories: wire cutter, scissors, tweezers, white resin glue, liquid solder, small jars of paint, small artist's brushes, floral clay, nylon thread, a spool of #28 wire, fabric scraps, ribbon scraps, lace scraps, lamp finials, corrugated cardboard, various sizes of screws, bottle caps of all kinds, broken jewelry, buttons, sequins, drapery hooks, fish hooks, jewelry chain, toothpicks, belt eyelets, pocket mirrors, upholstery samples, beads. Some items don't appear on this list because you are certain to have them in your home, anyway, such as needles, safety pins, and paperclips. Other items don't appear on the list because not many projects require them.

We do not give detailed directions for all but one of the several needlepoint projects that are accessories. If you are not accustomed to doing needlepoint, check out a good basic book on the subject from your library or borrow one from a friend. Our needlepoint patterns are simple enough for even a novice to do.

As with the furniture projects, each accessory project is labeled according to the model dollhouse room in which it appears.

CHAPTER **25** *Bedding*

BOLSTER PILLOW
(*Colonial bedroom*)

Cut a 1″ × 4½″ piece out of ¼″-thick foam rubber. Coat one side with glue and roll up to form a bolster; secure with pins until glue dries. Cut a 1½″ × 4½″ piece of white embroidered organdy edging, roll around bolster and secure with dots of glue. Cut two circles ¾″ in diameter from embroidered edging and glue in place on ends of bolster.

CANOPY
(*Colonial bedroom*)

Cut a 4½″ × 6½″ piece of white net and glue to top of bed canopy frame, letting edges hang over frame sides ⅛″. Glue a piece of 2″-wide lace (about 20″ of lace) all around the edge of canopy frame, pleating softly to make gathers; see diagram.

VARY DESIGN DEPENDING ON BIAS TAPES AND TRIMS ON HAND

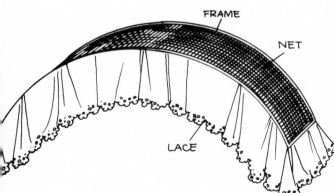

CANOPY BED COVERLET
(*Colonial bedroom*)

To make this you need: 8½″ × 7″ piece of thin, plain cotton; 4 packages of colored cotton bias tape; 1 yard each of ½″-wide embroidered cotton trim in two coordinating patterns that go well with colors of bias tapes. (Our coverlet was made with yellow, white, medium blue, and light blue bias tape, and red and orange embroidered trims.) Cut tape and embroidered trim into 7″ strips, arrange attractively on cotton fabric vertically, and pin down; see diagram. Weave remaining strips through vertical strips. Cut out bottom corners, as indicated by broken lines in diagram, turn under raw edges ¼″, and glue down hem. Glue all strips to fabric. Place coverlet on bed and tack cut-out corners together with needle and thread to ensure a smooth fit.

CRADLE COVERLET AND MATTRESS
(*Colonial bedroom*)

For the mattress, cut a $3\frac{1}{8}'' \times 1\frac{1}{4}''$ piece out of $\frac{3}{4}''$-thick foam rubber. For the coverlet, cut a $2'' \times 4''$ piece out of plain or tiny patterned fabric. Glue coverlet to mattress, turning down top edge as when making a regular bed.

DUST RUFFLE
(*Colonial bedroom*)

To make a dust ruffle, you need 28'' of $1\frac{1}{2}''$-wide white embroidered organdy edging. Glue edging to inside surfaces of bed side rails, head, and footboard, pleating softly to make gathers.

MATTRESS FOR CANOPY BED
(*Colonial bedroom*)

Cut a $4'' \times 6''$ piece of 1''-thick foam rubber.

BEDSPREAD
(*Georgian bedroom*)

Cut an $8\frac{1}{2}'' \times 6\frac{1}{4}''$ bedspread out of fabric, shaping edges of sides and foot according to diagram. Glue soutache braid to raw edges of sides and foot. Make up bed, tucking spread under pillow, as you would make up a regular bed.

CANOPY AND SIDE CURTAINS
(*Georgian bedroom*)

From $\frac{1}{8}''$ balsa sheet, cut $4\frac{3}{4}'' \times 6\frac{1}{4}''$ piece for canopy top; cut and shape two $1\frac{1}{2}'' \times 6\frac{1}{4}''$ pieces for long sides and two $1\frac{1}{2}'' \times 4\frac{3}{4}''$ pieces for short sides of canopy top; see diagram. Cut fabric to cover canopy top and sides, making each piece of fabric $\frac{1}{4}''$ larger on all sides than wood pieces; turn under raw edges of fabric and glue down hem. Glue fabric to wood, using small amounts so glue won't soak through fabric. Glue soutache braid to edges of fabric. Glue together canopy top and sides and set on top of bed.

For side curtains, cut two $4'' \times 8''$ pieces of fabric to match canopy top. Fold each piece in half lengthwise, turn under raw edges $\frac{1}{4}''$, and glue edges together; glue soutache braid to other long edge of each curtain. Glue curtains to long side pieces of canopy top underneath canopy fabric, with soutache braid facing foot of bed.

For back curtain behind headboard, cut a $9'' \times 8''$ piece of matching fabric. Fold in half along 8'' length, turn under raw edges $\frac{1}{4}''$, and glue edges together. Glue back curtain to $4\frac{3}{4}''$ back edge of canopy top.

DUST RUFFLE
(*Georgian bedroom*)

For dust ruffle sides, cut two $2\frac{1}{2}'' \times 5\frac{3}{4}''$ pieces of fabric to match canopy curtains and top. Fold each piece in half along $5\frac{3}{4}''$ edge and bind raw edges with small amount of glue. For dust ruffle at foot of bed, cut a $2\frac{1}{2}'' \times 4''$ piece of fabric, fold along 4'' edge, and bind raw edges with glue. Glue dust ruffle pieces to sides and foot of bed.

MATTRESS AND PILLOW
(*Georgian bedroom*)

For a pillow, cut a $1\frac{1}{2}'' \times 4''$ piece out of $\frac{1}{2}''$-thick foam rubber. For a mattress, cut a $4'' \times 6''$ piece out of 1''-thick foam rubber.

BEDSPREAD
(*Victorian bedroom*)

Cut an $11'' \times 8''$ piece of fabric and shape bottom edges of sides and foot with scallop edge; see diagram. Do not turn under hem. Glue very narrow trim or soutache braid to bedspread where indicated in diagram. Make up bed, tucking spread under pillow, as you would make up a regular bed.

MATTRESS AND PILLOW
(*Victorian bedroom*)

For a pillow, cut a $1\frac{1}{4}'' \times 4''$ piece out of $\frac{1}{2}''$-thick foam rubber. For a mattress, cut a $4'' \times 6\frac{3}{4}''$ piece out of 1''-thick foam rubber.

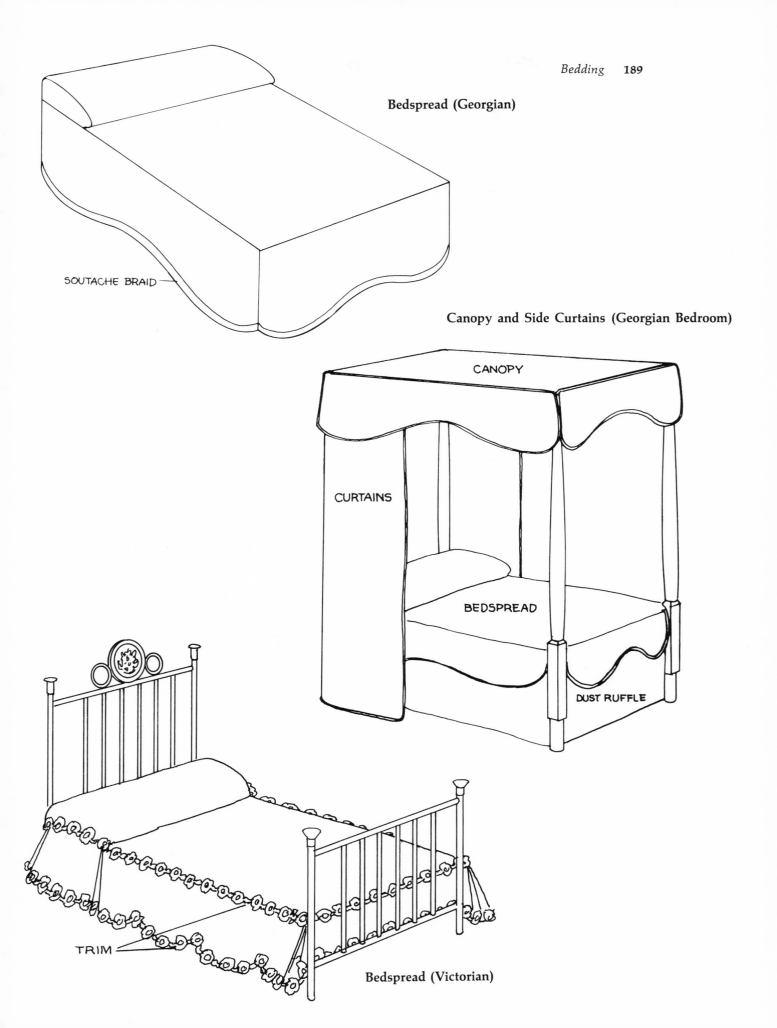

Bedspread (Georgian)

SOUTACHE BRAID

Canopy and Side Curtains (Georgian Bedroom)

CANOPY

CURTAINS

BEDSPREAD

DUST RUFFLE

TRIM

Bedspread (Victorian)

CHAPTER **26** *Draperies*

EMBROIDERED ORGANDY CURTAINS
(*Colonial bedroom*)

for 3½″ × 4¾″ windows

Use embroidered organdy trim for curtain fabric so most edges will be finished. For each pair of curtains, cut two 4″ × 5½″ pieces of fabric. For valence, cut a 4″ × 1½″ piece of fabric; for tie-backs, cut two 1¾″ × ¾″ pieces of fabric. Pleat curtains softly at top, turn top edges under ¼″, and glue to ½″ × 3½″ piece of balsa sheet, which is the backing for valence; see diagram. Turn raw edges of valence fabric to back of balsa sheet and glue, letting finished edge hang gracefully over curtains. Fold tie-backs in thirds lengthwise to conceal any raw edges; pull curtains to sides, secure with tie-backs, and glue tie-backs together behind curtains. Secure unit to top of window frame with double-faced masking tape or glue.

HOMESPUN CURTAINS
(*Colonial dining room*)

for 3½″ × 4¾″ window

Use cotton fabric with no pattern. For each pair of curtains, cut two 1″ × 4¾″ pieces out of corrugated cardboard; cut two 1½″ × 4¾″ pieces of fabric; cut ten pieces of soutache braid, each measuring ½″; cut 3½″ piece of ⅛″ dowel. Bind all raw edges of fabric with a little glue rubbed along edges with a toothpick. Attach curtain pieces to cardboard pieces by coating cardboard lightly with glue and pushing fabric into folds of cardboard with artist's brush handle. Make ¼″-deep loops out of soutache pieces and glue to back of each curtain fold; run dowel through loops and glue a small round bead to ends of dowel to complete curtain rod; see diagram. Secure unit to top of window frame with double-faced masking tape or glue.

SWAG AND JABOT DRAPERIES
(*Colonial living room*)

for 3½″ × 6″ window

A thin fabric, such as silk or satin, works best for these draperies. For each pair, cut an 8½″-sq. piece of fabric. Fold square in half on the diagonal and cut apart so you have two triangles; see diagram. Turn under edges of both triangles ¼″ and press with steam iron. Pleat each triangle toward center, making folds ½″ deep, and glue to 1″ × 3½″ piece of balsa sheet. For the swag, cut a 4½″-sq. piece of fabric, fold it in half diagonally, position on top of jabots, and glue to balsa. Secure unit to top of window frame with double-faced masking tape or glue.

DRAPERIES AND CHINESE CHIPPENDALE CORNICE
(*Georgian library*)

for 4½″ × 10″ window

For each pair of draperies, cut two 1½″ × 10″ pieces out of corrugated cardboard; cut two 2½″ × 10″ pieces of fabric. Attach drapery fabric to cardboard pieces by coating cardboard lightly with glue and pushing fabric into folds of cardboard with artist's brush handle. Cut a cornice out of 1/16″ balsa sheet, according to pattern in diagram; following same pattern, cut fabric covering for cornice, making it ¼″ larger all around than cornice. Make tiny cuts in cornice fabric, following broken lines in diagram. Glue fabric covering to cornice, turning raw edges to back of cornice (the tiny cuts facilitate this step); do not use too much glue or it may soak through fabric. Secure unit to window frame with double-faced masking tape or glue.

SWAG AND JABOT DRAPERIES WITH LACE UNDERCURTAINS
(*Georgian bedroom*)

for 3″ × 7″ window

A thin fabric, such as antique satin or silk, works best for these draperies. For each pair, cut two 7″-sq. pieces of fabric. Fold each one in half on the diagonal and pleat toward center, making folds ½″ deep; see diagram. If necessary, trim any excess fabric on outside edges. Glue jabots to ½″ × 3″ piece of ⅛″ balsa sheet. For the swag, cut a 1″ × 3″ piece of balsa sheet and cut a piece of fabric to fit, allowing an additional ¼″ all around to turn to back of balsa and glue down; glue swag to jabot unit. For lace undercurtains, cut two pieces of lace measuring 2″ × 7″ and glue across top edge of window, pleating slightly. Secure swag and jabot unit to top of window frame, over lace undercurtains, with double-faced masking tape or glue.

GOLD CORNICES
(*Victorian living room, dining room*)

To make a cornice, cut a ¾″-wide piece of ⅛″ balsa sheet to the width of your window, and glue onto this a 1½″-wide strip of gold embossed paper; see diagram. So cornice will project slightly, cut two ¾″ × ⅜″ pieces from ⅛″ balsa sheet; glue these to the front piece and cover with gold embossed paper. Glue cornice to wall at top of window frame.

LACE CURTAINS
(*Victorian living room, dining room*)

These curtains can be hung alone or under draperies. For each pair, cut two pieces of 1½″-wide lace trim to length of the window. You don't have to hem because lace does not ravel. Glue curtains to top of window frame without gathering them; be sure to line up each curtain if there is a pattern or scalloped edges.

VICTORIAN DRAPERIES
(*Victorian living room, dining room, bedroom*)

for 3½″ × 7½″ window

Silk, satin, and thin velvet are appropriate fabrics for Victorian draperies. For each pair, cut two 4″ × 7½″ pieces of fabric, leaving inside and bottom edges plain or making scallops. Pleat draperies softly at top, turn top edges under ¼″, and glue to ½″ × 3½″ piece of balsa sheet. Secure balsa to top and sides of window frame with double-faced masking tape or glue. Pull draperies to sides, secure with tie-backs made of tiny embroidered trim or dyed cord, and glue tie-backs together behind draperies; add tassels to tie-backs if made out of cord. Add a gold cornice above draperies, or make a 1½″-deep valence out of drapery fabric.

VICTORIAN WINDOW SHADES
(*Victorian bedroom*)

These window shades can be made with unbleached muslin, off-white linen, or an Indianhead fabric. Cut shade to width of window and whatever length you desire, allowing an additional 1″ at bottom for hem; turn under hem and glue only along raw edge. About ¼″ down from glued edge of hem, stitch a casing by hand or machine, following broken line in diagram; insert a wooden slat in casing made from ⅛″ × 1/16″ balsa strip cut to width of shade. Glue trim of your choice to bottom of shade, and a tassel, too, if you wish. Glue shade to top of window frame under draperies.

(Diagrams for these projects will be found on pages 192–195.)

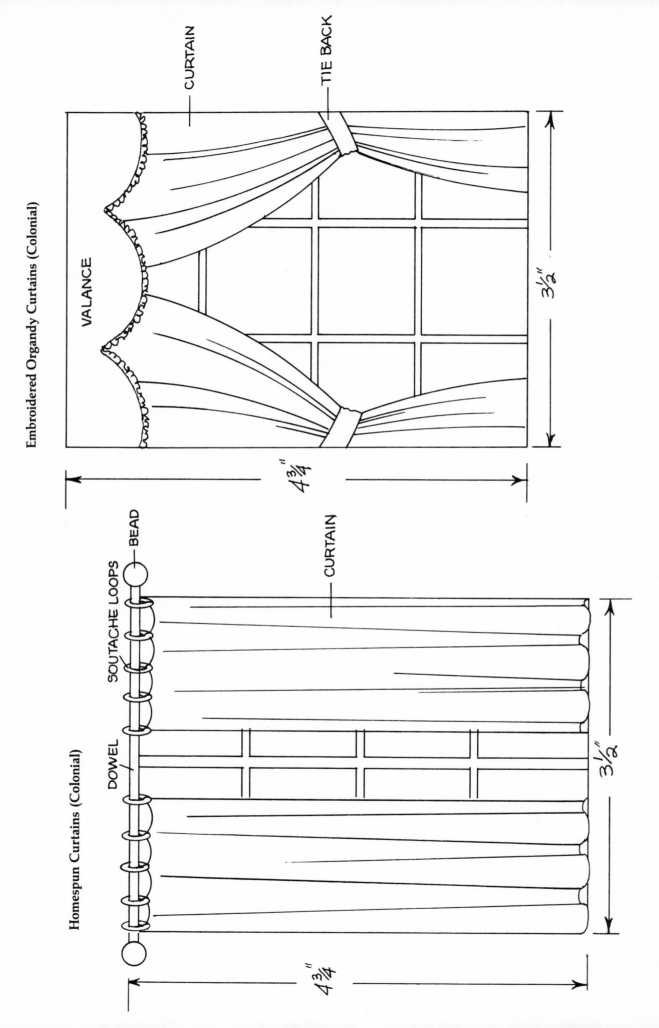

Embroidered Organdy Curtains (Colonial)

VALANCE

CURTAIN

TIE BACK

3½"

4¾"

Homespun Curtains (Colonial)

BEAD

SOUTACHE LOOPS

DOWEL

CURTAIN

3½"

4¾"

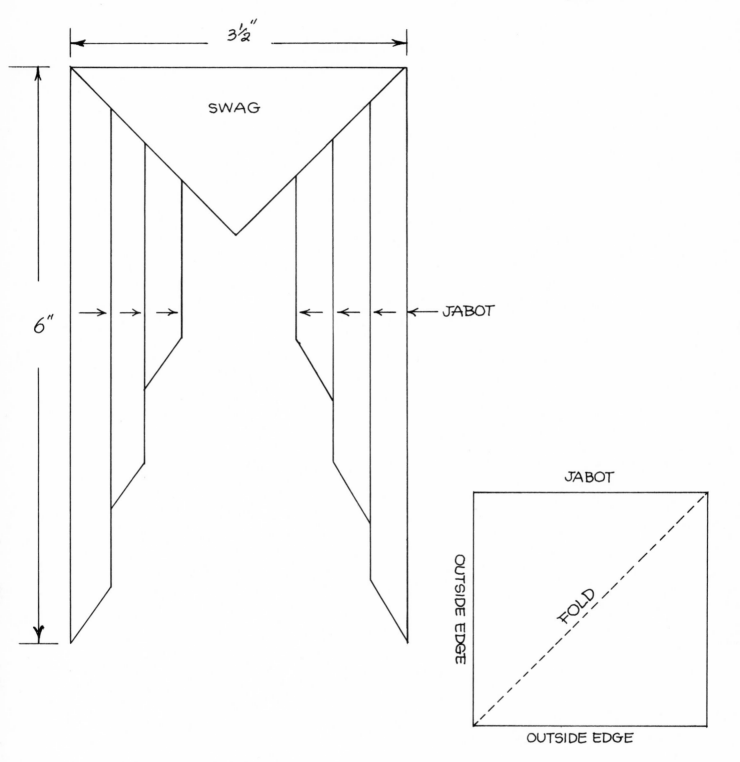

Swag and Jabot Draperies (Colonial)

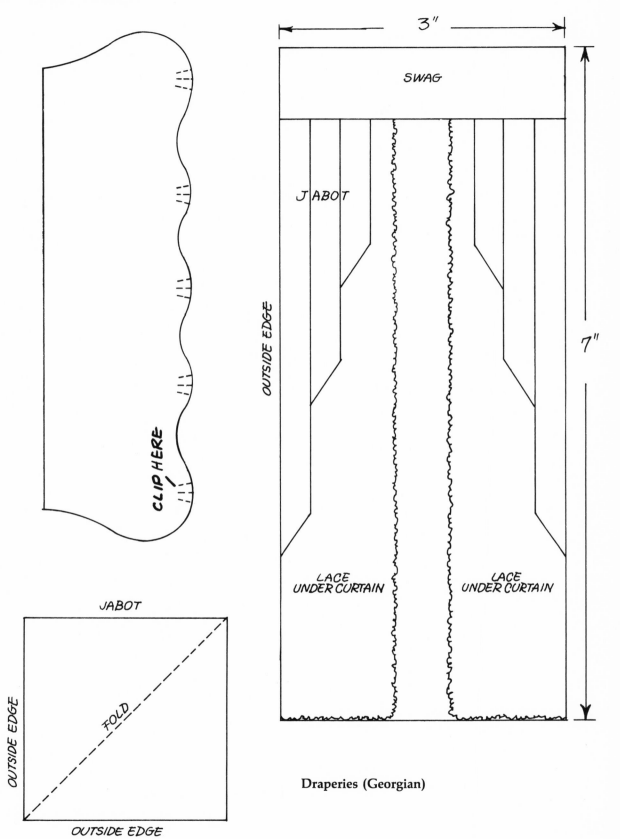

CLIP HERE

JABOT

OUTSIDE EDGE

FOLD

OUTSIDE EDGE

OUTSIDE EDGE

3"

SWAG

JABOT

OUTSIDE EDGE

7"

LACE
UNDER CURTAIN

LACE
UNDER CURTAIN

Draperies (Georgian)

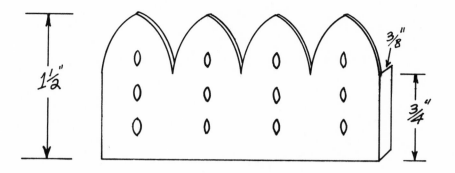

Gold Cornice (Victorian)

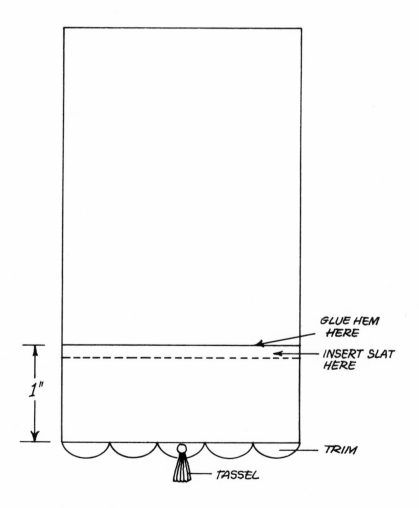

Window Shade (Victorian)

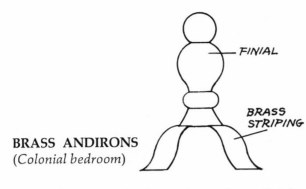

BRASS ANDIRONS
(Colonial bedroom)

For these you need two brass lamp finials and two ¼″ × 1½″ pieces of brass stripping, available at hobby or model train shops. Bend brass stripping with pliers, as shown in diagram, then attach stripping to base of finials with liquid solder.

BEDWARMER
(Colonial bedroom)

Glue a 3″ piece of ⅛″ dowel to a broken locket that is gold or painted gold; see diagram. Fill in back of locket with piece of balsa sheet cut to fit. At other end of dowel, glue two tiny gold colored rivets, or if unavailable, a ¼″ piece of gold embossed paper.

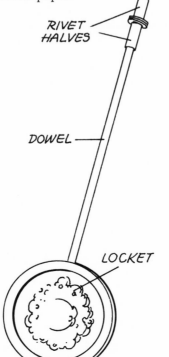

HEARTH BROOM
(Colonial keeping room)

Take a tiny brush used for cleaning electric razors, or for cleaning a sewing machine, and paint the handle black. Hang broom from a straight pin pushed nearly all the way into front of fireplace.

LOGS
(Colonial keeping room)

Pick up twigs from your own back yard for fireplace logs.

WROUGHT-IRON ANDIRONS
(Colonial keeping room)

To make a pair of andirons, cut two coat-hangers ½″ above twisted wire part and 1½″ below twisted wire; see diagram. With liquid

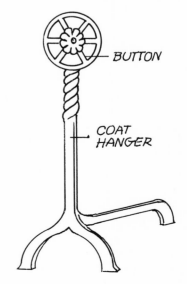

solder, attach two buttons to top of twisted wire, pushing shank of buttons down over end of wire. For each andiron, cut a 1¾" piece out of top hook of coathanger, bend as shown in diagram, and attach with liquid solder to bottom of andiron to form a long third leg. Paint andirons black.

TRAMMEL
(*Colonial keeping room*)

The trammel hangs from the crane to hold a cooking kettle or teapot over the fire; see diagram. Cut the trammel from a paper clip and paint black.

SOUP LADLE
(*Colonial keeping room*)

Our soup ladle was made from an old stick pin with a shell design at the end. You can also liquid solder a large sequin or paillette to a piece of wire. Paint entire piece black or gold, or paint ladle gold and handle black. Hang from straight pin pushed nearly all the way into side of fireplace.

CRANE
(*Colonial keeping room*)

Screw two picture screws into one side of fireplace opening; see diagram. Bend 6" piece of thick wire, such as coat hanger wire, into two parts, one 4" and the other 2"; insert 2" part of wire into picture screws so 4" part swings in and out. Paint screws and wire with flat black paint.

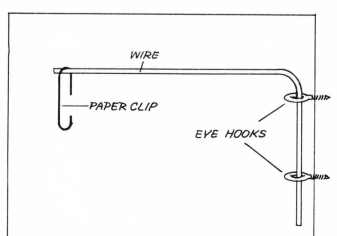

WROUGHT-IRON COOKING KETTLE
(*Colonial keeping room*)

For this you need one half of a plastic gum ball container, the kind that dispenses tiny prizes to children at supermarkets and dimestores. For legs, cut three ¼" pieces from ⅛"-sq. balsa strip and glue to bottom of plastic container so it stands straight; see diagram. Cut handle from thin wire and glue to container. Paint inside and outside of entire kettle black.

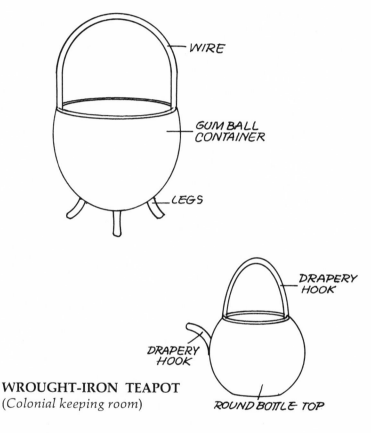

WROUGHT-IRON TEAPOT
(*Colonial keeping room*)

For this you need a round metal bottle top about 1" in diameter (perfume bottle tops work well). Cut handle and spout from a drapery hook and attach to bottle top with liquid solder; see diagram. Paint entire teapot black.

BRASS FIREPLACE FAN
(*Georgian library*)

The fan is a small plastic party-favor fan with its decorative silk tassel removed. Spray paint with brass paint and glue into fireplace opening.

BRASS FIREPLACE FENDER
(Georgian library)

Cut a ½"-wide strip of gold embossed paper to enclose three sides of fireplace hearth, and glue clear plastic acetate to back of paper so it will hold its shape. If desired, two additional cut-outs of embossed paper can be glued to front of fender for more decoration; see diagram.

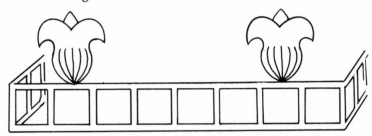

FIRESCREEN
(Victorian living room)

To make a firescreen, you need the following: 2"-sq. piece of needlepoint, petit point, or beading; 2"-sq. piece of balsa sheet; twisted wire, such as handle of pastry brush or radiator brush; two brass staples; two ¼" beads; ¼"-sq. balsa strip; embossed paper. Glue needlepoint to balsa sheet. Cut four 2¼" pieces of balsa strip and miter corners; glue strips together to form frame and glue to needlepoint. Trim top of frame with embossed paper cut-out. Make holder for screen out of twisted wire, and with liquid solder, attach brass staples to wire for feet; see diagram. Cut off two straight pins and attach to wire holder and screen with liquid solder. Trim tops of wire with beads. Paint entire assembly, except needlepoint, with woodtone paint in gloss finish.

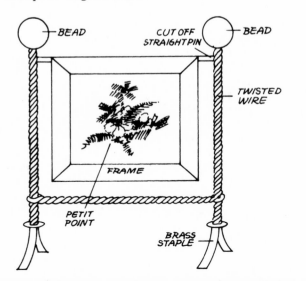

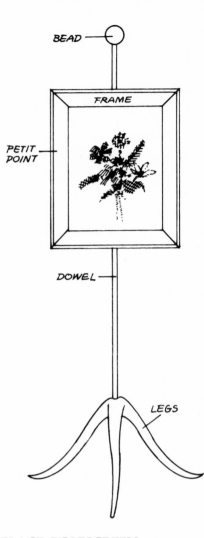

FIREPLACE POLESCREEN
(Georgian dining room)

To make a fireplace polescreen, you need the following: ⅛" balsa sheet, ¹⁄₁₆" balsa sheet, ¹⁄₁₆" × ³⁄₁₆" balsa strip, ⅛" dowel, 1¾" × 2" piece of petit point or beading from old handbag, small round bead, woodtone paint, and gold paint.

To make the screen, cut a 1¾" × 2" rectangle from ¹⁄₁₆" balsa sheet and stain. When dry, glue petit point or beading onto screen. Cut four pieces of balsa strip to form frame around screen; miter corners of strips; stain strips and glue together. Glue frame onto petit point.

To make the pole, cut a 5¼" piece of dowel; sand and stain. Make three legs from ⅛" balsa sheet, following pattern for legs on page 159; sand and stain legs, then mount to bottom of pole.

Glue screen to other end of pole about ½" from top and centered over one of the legs; see diagram. Glue bead to top of pole and paint with woodtone paint. Paint ends of legs with gold or brass paint to resemble brass feet.

CHAPTER **28** *Lights and Lighting Accessories*

CANDLESTICKS WITH TURNED CANDLES
(Colonial living room)

All sizes of candlesticks and candles can be easily made with small flat-headed screws ranging from 1″ to 1¾″. For candlesticks on a tea table, use 1″ screws with ¼″ flat heads; see diagram. Paint the turned part of the screw in any desired color to create the candle. For the candlestick, leave the rest of the screw the color it is—either silver or brass—or paint it another desired color.

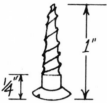

FLUTED TINWARE SCONCES
(Colonial keeping room)

To make a sconce, you need a soda bottle cap, part of a drapery hook, sequin, and round wooden toothpick. Flatten fluted edge of bottle cap with pliers to make it look handmade. Attach one end of drapery hook to back of bottle cap with liquid solder and glue a small sequin to other end of hook on the front; see diagram. For a candle, glue half a toothpick onto the sequin and paint it in color of your choice. Paint the sconce silver or black, and fasten to wall with double-faced masking tape.

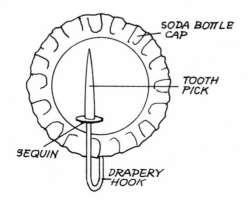

PEWTER CANDLEHOLDER WITH CANDLE
(Colonial bedroom)

Make the candleholder from a belt eyelet and its handle from the end of a small gold safety pin, which is attached with liquid solder; see diagram. Paint candleholder silver to resemble pewter, or paint it another color, if you wish. Cut a small birthday candle to 1″ and trim base to fit into candleholder; put a small amount of floral clay into candleholder, then insert candle.

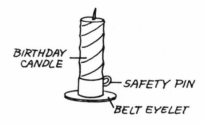

QUILLWORK SCONCES
(Colonial living room)

Real quillwork is simulated in these sconces by white costume jewelry earrings. For each sconce, remove earring back and flatten in a vise, protecting the earring with a clean rag. Remove glass from a miniature picture frame (obtained in a craft store) and glue earring to center of frame backing. Cut one hook off a small, three-part fish hook, and glue remaining double hook to back of miniature frame so hooks are in front; see diagram. Glue two small sequins to hooks, pushing them down a little over tips of hooks to secure. For candles, push two halves of round wooden toothpicks onto tips of hooks and secure with tiny bit of glue. Lay sconce on back while glue dries; you may have to prop

199

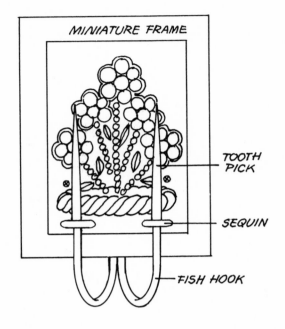

MINIATURE FRAME

TOOTH PICK

SEQUIN

FISH HOOK

toothpicks with piece of thin cardboard so they dry straight. Paint hooks and sequins gold and paint toothpicks in desired color. Fasten sconce to wall with double-faced masking tape. (Use wire cutter for cutting fish hook.)

WOOD SPINDLE CHANDELIER
(*Colonial dining room*)

To make this chandelier, you need two lamp finials in different shapes; a circle cut from ¼" balsa sheet to go between finials; six drapery hooks, sequins, and small birthday candles; woodtone paint; gold paint; two paper clips; a small hook. Glue flat ends of finials to each side of balsa circle; see diagram. It will be help-

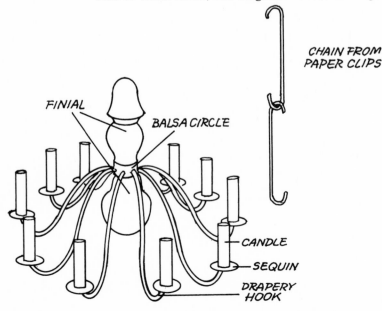

CHAIN FROM PAPER CLIPS

FINIAL

BALSA CIRCLE

CANDLE

SEQUIN

DRAPERY HOOK

ful to use a straight pin or a pointed cocktail pick to "drill" holes before inserting the drapery hooks. Push drapery hooks, evenly spaced, into balsa and secure with glue. Glue sequins to ends of drapery hooks. Paint finials and balsa with woodtone paint; paint hooks and sequins gold. Cut birthday candles to ¾" and glue to sequins. Make chain of paper clips, as shown in diagram. Attach one end of chain to hook and other end to chandelier with thin wire by wrapping wire around groove in top finial; screw hook into ceiling.

WROUGHT-IRON CHANDELIER
(*Colonial keeping room*)

To make this chandelier, you need a large frozen orange juice can, round wooden toothpicks, eight tiny rivet halves, a piece of jewelry chain, and a small hook. With X-acto knife, remove metal edge of orange juice can and discard can. Divide inside of metal edge into eighths with toothpicks cut in half; glue toothpicks to metal edge and together at center with dots of glue; see diagram. At the points of

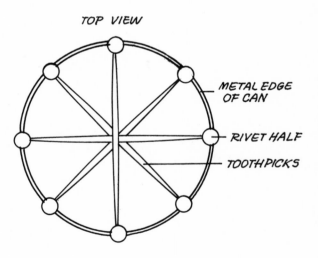

TOP VIEW

METAL EDGE OF CAN

RIVET HALF

TOOTHPICKS

division, glue on top of metal edge the electrical sockets and insert toothpicks into sockets to resemble candles (if you can't find sockets, glue toothpicks directly to metal edge). Attach jewelry chain to center of chandelier with piece of thin wire, twist wire to secure it, and trim ends of wire very close. Paint chandelier with

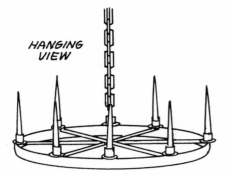

HANGING VIEW

flat black paint, and paint candles in desired color. Wire hook to top of chain and screw hook into ceiling. If chandelier does not hang straight, glue a few small lead beebees to it at strategic points until it hangs properly.

BRASS CHANDELIER
(*Georgian library*)

To make this chandelier, you need a lamp finial; a Christmas tree ball; a circle cut from ¼" balsa sheet to go between finial and tree ball; six drapery hooks, sequins, and small birthday candles; gold paint; a piece of jewelry chain; a small hook. Assemble chandelier according to directions for wood spindle chandelier; also see diagram. Spray paint chandelier gold. Cut birthday candles to ¾" and glue to sequins. Attach jewelry chain to top of finial with thin wire by wrapping wire around groove in finial; attach hook to other end of chain and screw into ceiling.

CANDELABRA
(*Georgian bedroom*)

To make this candelabra, attach the following items with liquid solder in the order given and as shown in diagram: flat button, flat-head screw, three-part fish hook (cut off down to hooks), small rounded button, tiny bead. Glue three small sequins to fish hooks, pushing them down a little over tips of hooks to secure. Cut three round wooden toothpicks to 1¼", push onto tips of hooks, and secure with tiny bit of glue. Paint candelabra and toothpick candles in colors of your choice.

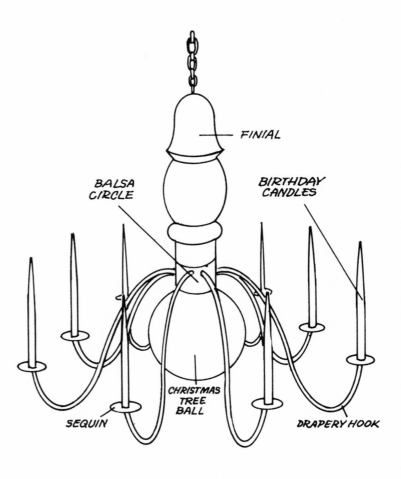

FINIAL

BALSA CIRCLE

BIRTHDAY CANDLES

SEQUIN

CHRISTMAS TREE BALL

DRAPERY HOOK

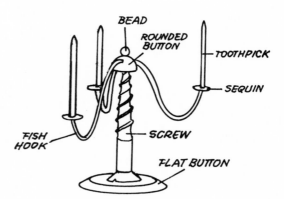

BEAD

ROUNDED BUTTON

TOOTHPICK

SEQUIN

FISH HOOK

SCREW

FLAT BUTTON

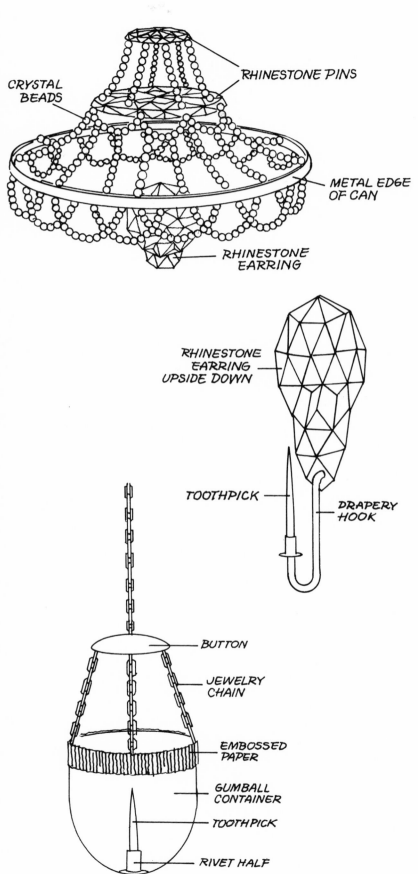

CRYSTAL BEADS

RHINESTONE PINS

METAL EDGE OF CAN

RHINESTONE EARRING

RHINESTONE EARRING UPSIDE DOWN

TOOTHPICK

DRAPERY HOOK

BUTTON

JEWELRY CHAIN

EMBOSSED PAPER

GUMBALL CONTAINER

TOOTHPICK

RIVET HALF

CRYSTAL CHANDELIER
(Georgian dining room)

The base of this chandelier is a round rhinestone earring with the back removed. The rim above the base is the metal edge of a large frozen orange juice can (separated from can with an X-acto knife), covered with about 9" of ¼" rhinestone beading. The top two tiers of the chandelier are the broken parts of a rhinestone pin, plus swags of #11 crystal beads strung on nylon thread (use only nylon thread; any other will sag). Since everyone's rhinestone jewelry parts will vary in size and shape, we give no specific directions for assembly; but a study of diagram should indicate how to proceed.

CRYSTAL SCONCES
(Georgian dining room)

These sconces are made from a pair of rhinestone drop earrings. For each sconce, remove earring back, and with liquid solder, attach one end of drapery hook to back of earring so the hook end is in front; see diagram. Attach tiny gold rivet halves or small sequin to tip of hook. For the candle, cut a round wooden toothpick to ¾" and insert in rivet, pushing down onto tip of hook. Paint sconce arm in gold or silver, and paint candle in desired color.

SMOKE BELL LANTERN
(Georgian hall)

To make this lantern, you need a flat or slightly rounded clear plastic button; one half of a plastic gum ball container, the kind that dispenses prizes to children in supermarkets and dimestores; one-half of a tiny gold rivet (optional); round wooden toothpick; ¼"-wide strip of gold embossed paper; some jewelry chain; a small hook. Cut toothpick to ¾" and paint in desired color. Glue rivet inside gum ball container and insert toothpick candle; see diagram. Glue embossed paper around top outside edge of gum ball container. Glue three very short pieces of jewelry chain to inside top edge of gum ball container, spacing pieces evenly; wire together other ends of these pieces with thin wire, run wire through hole in button, and attach wire to another, longer piece of jewelry chain. Attach hook to other end of chain and screw into ceiling.

ASTRAL LAMP
(Victorian living room)

To make this lamp, glue together the following items in the order given: a button, a small brass lamp finial, a cup-style jewelry clasp, a tiny gold color rivet or a ¼″ piece of plastic drinking straw. See diagram. Paint the various parts, except the straw, in colors of your choice.

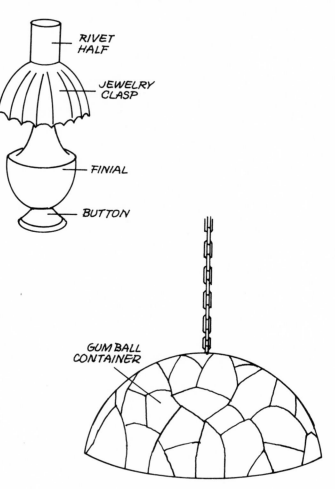

TIFFANY HANGING LAMP
(Victorian kitchen)

This is made with one half of a plastic gum ball container, the kind that dispenses prizes to children in supermarkets and dimestores. Apply lines of liquid solder to outside of container to resemble lead between pieces of stained glass; when dry, paint inside these lines of liquid solder with different colors of glass stain (available at craft stores). See diagram. Pierce a small hole in top of lamp, push some thin wire through hole, and attach wire to a piece of jewelry chain; attach other end of chain to a small hook and screw hook into ceiling.

GASLIGHT CHANDELIER
(Victorian dining room)

To make this chandelier, you need a lipstick tube; a 15″ piece of #18 or #20 wire; five round beads ½″ in diameter; a piece of costume jewelry, such as a pin or earring, ½″ in diameter; jewelry chain; floral clay; gold paint; a small hook. Cut wire into five 3″ pieces and wrap each piece around a *round* pencil to create a rounded circle in the center; see diagram. Push beads onto one end of each wire piece to make chandelier arms with lamps. Pack bottom of lipstick tube with floral clay—about ¾″—and insert arms of chandelier into clay for about ½″. Insert pin or earring into clay. Paint chandelier, except lamps, with gold paint, and paint lamps in desired color. Attach a short length of jewelry chain to lipstick tube with liquid solder; attach other end of chain to small hook and screw hook into ceiling medallion.

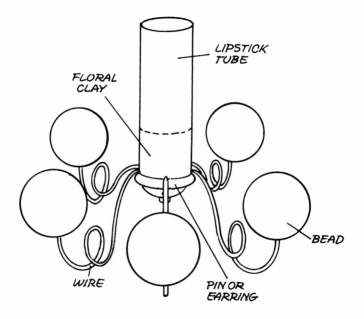

BAROQUE GASLIGHT CHANDELIER
(Victorian living room)

To make this chandelier, you need the following: five frosted white, round plastic beads about ¾″ in diameter; five drapery hooks; one or two gold embossed paper picture frames; ½″ lamp finial; a piece of jewelry chain; a large finger ring with a very ornate setting of metal (available in dimestores); ¾″ sq. balsa strip; ³⁄₃₂″ dowel; gold paint; a small hook.

Bend drapery hooks so rounded part forms curved chandelier arms, and cut off straight, pointed part, leaving only ¼″ for attaching arms to chandelier; see diagram. Glue embossed paper to both sides of chandelier arms in a baroque design; paper on arms does not have to match exactly.

Cut a ¾″ cube out of balsa strip. Cut away corners on a slant and round the prisms with metal file and sandpaper until you have a completely round ball. Cut setting away from dimestore ring and glue balsa ball inside setting. With jeweler's round metal file, drill five tiny, evenly spaced holes into balsa ball. Insert chandelier arms into holes and secure with glue.

Glue finial to top of balsa ball; you may have to reinforce the gluing with a piece of dowel inserted inside the finial and into surface of ball. Paint chandelier gold. Glue beads to ends of chandelier arms. Attach chain to top of finial with thin wire; attach hook to other end of chain and screw hook into ceiling medallion.

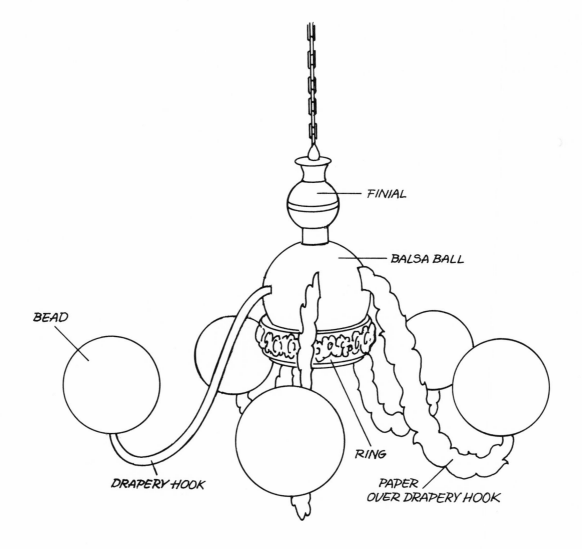

FINIAL

BALSA BALL

BEAD

RING

DRAPERY HOOK

PAPER OVER DRAPERY HOOK

GONE WITH THE WIND LAMP
(*Victorian living room*)

Glue together the following items in the order given: filigree cup-style jewelry clasp, two round beads ¾" in diameter in matching or contrasting color, ¼" piece of clear plastic drinking straw. See diagram. You will probably need to reinforce the beads before gluing by joining them with a toothpick; the toothpick won't show after beads are glued together.

TIFFANY TABLE LAMP
(*Victorian living room*)

Wash and dry nozzle from empty white resin glue bottle. Paint nozzle gold, along with a small flat button and a 1" piece of ⅛" dowel; then antique with burnt umber. Glue button to nozzle and dowel to button; see diagram. Glue rounded button or earring, in desirable color, to dowel to create Tiffany-style lamp shade.

GASLIGHT WALL LAMPS
(*Victorian kitchen*)

For these lamps, use a pair of earrings and cut away the screws; see diagram. Paint earrings in desired color. With an icepick, make holes in the wall where you want lamps to go, coat cut ends of earrings with glue, and insert in holes. You will have to prop lamps until glue is dry.

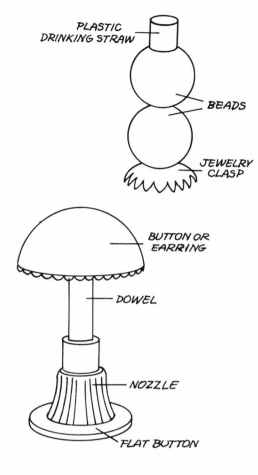

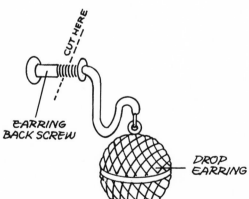

CHAPTER **29** *Objets d'Art and Other Finishing Touches*

CANDY DISH
(*Colonial living room*)

A small covered dish for candy or nuts is made from two buttons of the same diameter; the top button is flat or slightly rounded, is the shank type, and should be decorative; while the bottom button is quite rounded and is not a shank type. If button colors do not match, or are not compatible, give them a coat of enamel paint in desired color. Glue buttons together; see diagram.

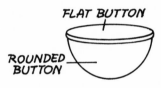

CHINA TEA SERVICE
(*Colonial living room*)

To make a teapot, use liquid solder to attach part of a drapery hook to a metal perfume bottle top to form a spout and another part of drapery hook to form a handle; see diagram. Glue small, slightly rounded button to perfume bottle top to form a lid, and glue a tiny bead to center of lid. Paint entire teapot with white enamel paint.

To make each tea cup, cut an eye drop bottle cap to correct size with a small saw; see diagram. Glue on a flat button to form a saucer. Cut off end of a small gold safety pin and glue to side of cup at top edge to form a handle. Paint cup, except for handle, with white enamel paint.

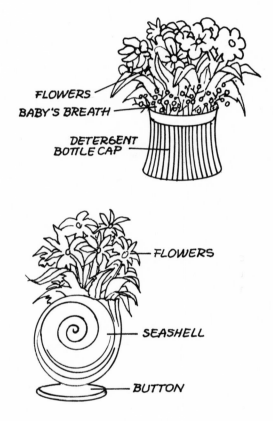

FLOWER VASES
(*Colonial dining room, living room*)

An exquisite vase for flowers, or pair of vases, can be made from a soap detergent bottle cap; see diagram. Wash cap and paint it with enamel paint in desired color. Fill center of cap with a small amount of floral clay to weight it and insert in clay tiny artificial flowers (available at dimestores) and some dried baby's-breath.

An equally pretty vase can be made from a small cone-shaped seashell; see diagram. Glue a button to bottom of the shell to steady it and fill shell with a small amount of floral clay; insert in clay a bouquet of tiny artificial flowers.

PEWTER PLATES
(Colonial keeping room)

Make a set of pewter plates with plain or patterned silver metal, flat shank-type buttons either ¾" or 1" in diameter.

PORCELAIN PLATES WITH FLORAL DESIGN
(Colonial dining room)

The plates are actually white plastic, shank-type, flat buttons ¾" in diameter, with a floral design already painted on them. You can also use plain buttons and paint flowers, or some other motif, on them.

SOLDIER FIGURINES
(Colonial bedroom)

A pair of figurines for the fireplace mantel can be made with any small figures measuring approximately 1½" tall. We borrowed two soldiers from a set of antique soldiers. You can use plastic figures from a train set, a game, or the figures that decorate elaborate cakes.

SOUP LADLE
(Colonial dining room)

Make a ladle with the back of a screw-type earring. Cut off the screw, where indicated by broken line in diagram, remove the front of the earring, and bend the remainder into the shape of a ladle. Leave the ladle gold or silver, or paint with enamel paint in desired color to simulate china.

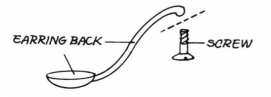

SOUP TUREEN
(Colonial dining room)

Make a soup tureen out of a large, squarish cap to an after-shave lotion bottle. Glue a rounded shank-type button on top for a lid and glue a tiny bead to center of lid; see diagram. Two sewing loops are glued to edges of tureen for handles. Paint entire tureen in desired color or combination of colors. You can make a tureen from a round cap, too, but you'll have to glue a button underneath to steady it.

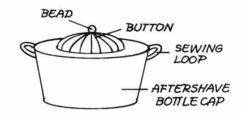

TRIVET
(Colonial living room)

Make a brass trivet from either a flat, pierced gold earring disc or a very small, flat, pierced gold pin; see diagram. Remove any stones in earring or pin with tweezers, and remove any backing that interferes; discard. Leave trivet gold, or paint silver or black.

WOODEN BOWL WITH APPLES
(Colonial keeping room)

To make a wooden bowl, cut off the plastic cork from a plastic champagne bottle cap, using a small saw, and paint the cap with brown paint. Fill center of cap with a small amount of floral clay to weight it. Glue small red artificial berries on top of cap to simulate apples; see diagram.

SPICE CABINET
(Colonial dining room)

To make a spice cabinet, you need the following: one antique daguerreotype picture frame, ⅛″ balsa sheet, eight round wooden toothpicks, 20 tiny round beads, four round beads ¼″ in diameter, and woodtone paint. A daguerreotype picture frame is easily found in antique shops and should be inexpensive. The parts of the frame can be used in many ways in a dollhouse; in this project, you will use either the front or back cover. Unhinge the covers carefully from the frame and remove the latch. Choose the cover in the best condition and stain the entire surface with the stain you plan to use on the rest of the cabinet.

Cut the following pieces from balsa sheet on lengthwise grain: one piece for cabinet back the same size as daguerreotype cover; two pieces for cabinet sides 1″ deep and the same height as daguerreotype cover; two pieces for top and bottom of cabinet 1¼″ deep and the same width as daguerreotype cover *plus* ¼″. Bevel front and side edges of top and bottom pieces in a round bevel. Sand and stain wood pieces.

Glue cabinet sides between cabinet back and daguerreotype cover to form a right-angle rectangular assembly. Center and glue this assembly between top and bottom pieces with straight edges of top and bottom pieces flush with back surface of cabinet; see diagram.

For feet, paint four tiny beads and four larger beads with woodtone paint to match and attach to cabinet corners with straight pins and glue. For decorative posts, stain eight toothpicks and glue four to each side of cabinet; paint 16 tiny beads with woodtone paint and glue to top and bottom of each toothpick.

Shellac and varnish entire cabinet.

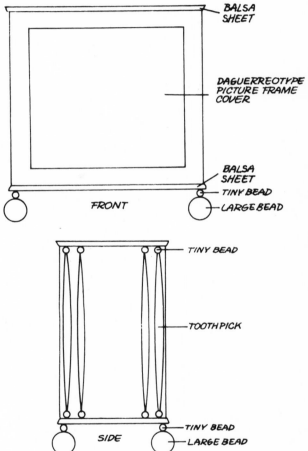

BOOKS AND BOOKENDS
(Georgian bedroom, library)

For leatherbound books, cover ½″ sq. or 1″ sq. ceramic tiles with leather or suede cloth and glue to secure. (If you can't find tiles, use ¼″ balsa sheet and cut to book sizes.) Streak top and front edge of book with gold paint, and add a few gold stripes across the binding edge to simulate lettering.

For bookends, use a small pair of decorative earrings, such as the ivory elephants shown in diagram. For a base, cut a ½″ × 1¼″ piece from ⅛″ balsa sheet; stain and varnish. Glue earrings to ends of balsa base, and glue books to base between earrings.

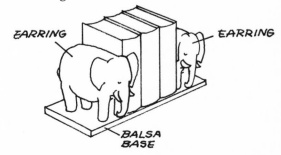

DEED BOX
(Georgian bedroom)

To have a deed box, or strong box, use a small gold metal pillbox as is.

DESK ACCESSORIES
(Georgian library)

To make a blotter and blotterholder, cut a piece of thin balsa sheet to desired size. Cover one side of balsa with green velour paper, cover underside and top, side edges with leather or suede cloth, and secure velour paper and leather with glue; see diagram. Make an inkstand from a flat or box-type jewelry clasp; make two inkwells from one- or two-faceted crystal beads ¼" in diameter. Make quill pens from the very tip of a bird feather or feather duster, cut to the tiniest possible size and glued to inkwells.

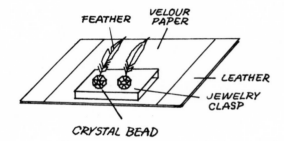

DRESSING TABLE ACCESSORIES
(Georgian bedroom)

Various perfume bottles and cosmetic jars can be made by gluing together bits and pieces of broken costume jewelry; see diagram for ideas. The back of a case on a broken watch makes a dressing table tray. Paint accessories with enamel paint in desired colors, or leave them the color they are.

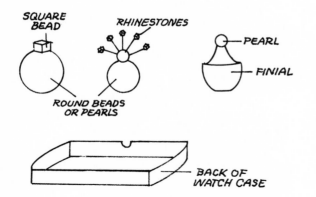

FAMILY CREST
(Georgian library)

To make a family crest or coat of arms, use a piece of the heraldic-style costume jewelry popular several years ago. Crest should measure 1" × 1" if it stands, or larger if it hangs on wall. If crest is to stand, cut an easel from balsa wood, glue to back of jewelry at right angle to it, and paint easel to match edge of jewelry piece.

FIGURINES
(Georgian library)

Figurines can be made from charms on a charm bracelet. Cut off loop at top of charm with wire cutters. Make a stand for the charm out of balsa and paint it black; glue charm to the stand. Our charm is real coral, but you could use an inexpensive charm and paint it the color of coral or jade.

Our pair of ivory figurines are actually earrings glued to the wall—screw-type backs and all—but you could remove earring backs and mount figurines on balsa bases painted black.

FLOWER VASE
(Georgian library)

Make a fluted vase by painting a toothpaste cap in gold, silver, or some other color with enamel paint. Fill center of cap with a small amount of floral clay and insert tiny artificial flowers in clay; see diagram.

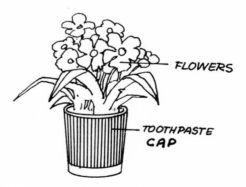

FOLDING SCREEN
(Georgian dining room)

To make a three-paneled folding screen, you need the following: ¼″ balsa sheet, black paint, Oriental print from magazine, rubber cement, burnt umber, four decoupage hinges, and wire cutters. Cut three 2″ × 7″ panels from balsa sheet. Paint one side and all edges of panels black. Cut Oriental print in three pieces to fit panel and glue to panel with rubber cement; see diagram. Antique panels on print side with burnt umber; wipe off excess and let dry. Varnish panels with one light coat. Cut decoupage hinges with wire cutters to smallest possible size and attach two to each fold of screen on back about 1½″ from top and bottom; see directions under hardware for hinging.

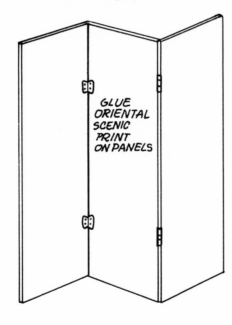

GLUE ORIENTAL SCENIC PRINT ON PANELS

FRETWORK SHELF
(Georgian bedroom)

To make this shelf, you need the following: ½″-wide embossed paper picture frame with openwork design, ¹⁄₁₆″ balsa sheet, two tiny round beads, and woodtone paint. Cut two matching pieces, each 2½″ long, from embossed paper, and paint with woodtone paint to match stain you will use on shelf. Cut the following pieces of wood from balsa sheet on lengthwise

grain: two ½″ × 2″ pieces, two ½″ × 1⅞″ pieces, two ³⁄₁₆″ × 1⅞″ pieces, two ⁵⁄₁₆″ × ½″ pieces. Sand and stain all wood pieces.

The ½″ × 2″ wood pieces are open shelves to be glued between embossed paper sides; see diagram. Glue one shelf ¼″ from top of paper sides and glue second shelf ¾″ from top shelf. The rest of the wood forms a drawer to be assembled as follows: Glue front and back pieces (³⁄₁₆″ × 1⅞″) between top and bottom pieces (½″ × 1⅞″) so the long edges of top and bottom pieces are flush with outside surfaces of front and back pieces; glue drawer side pieces (⁵⁄₁₆″ × ½″) to assembly. Glue drawer between embossed paper sides ¼″ from bottom of sides.

Shellac and varnish shelves and drawer, but not paper sides. For drawer knobs, paint beads with woodtone and glue to front of drawer. Attach fretwork shelf to wall, using glue along back edges and double-faced masking tape behind drawer. Six tiny seashells, measuring about ¼″ × ½″, make an attractive display on the two shelves.

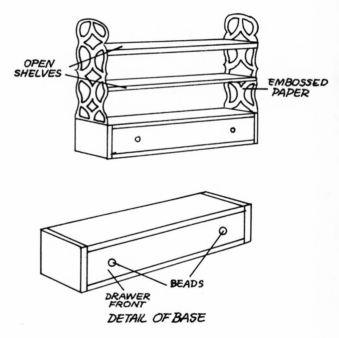

OPEN SHELVES

EMBOSSED PAPER

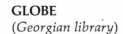

DRAWER FRONT

BEADS

DETAIL OF BASE

GLOBE
(Georgian library)

For this project, you need to purchase a metal globe pencil sharpener mounted on a plastic stand, which is sold in stationery stores. You also need the following: ³⁄₃₂″ and ¹⁄₁₆″ balsa sheets, ¹⁄₁₆″ × ³⁄₁₆″ balsa strip, ³⁄₁₆″ sq. balsa strip, ³⁄₁₆″ dowel, hat pin or long sewing needle, four round beads ¼″ in diameter, a tiny bead, burnt umber, gold paint, woodtone paint.

Remove globe pencil sharpener from its plastic stand and discard stand. String globe on stiff wire and paint it with burnt umber, then brush the paint with dry bristles of a bushy paint brush to give an antiqued look. Cut a ring 2¼″ in diameter and ³⁄₁₆″ wide out of ¹⁄₁₆″ balsa sheet, and paint ring gold. Mount globe inside ring with hat pin or sewing needle cut ⅛″ longer than inside of ring; before inserting pin into ring, place tiny bead on pin at South Pole end of globe so that globe can revolve.

For a standard for the globe, cut four 1⅜″ legs from dowel and eight ³⁄₁₆″ cubes from ³⁄₁₆″ sq. balsa strip; stain wood and glue a cube to ends of each leg. Paint four beads with wood-tone paint to match stain and glue to underside of bottom cubes. Cut a second ring ¼″ wide and 2⅜″ in diameter from ³⁄₃₂″ balsa sheet and stain ring. Glue four legs, spaced evenly, to underside of ring; see diagram. Cut two 2″ crossbars from ¹⁄₁₆″ × ³⁄₁₆″ balsa strip and stain them. Glue one crossbar between two opposite legs near bottom edge of bottom cubes; cut other crossbar in half, and fit and glue between first crossbar and other two opposite legs in same manner as you glued the first crossbar.

Make two ¹⁄₁₆″ wide cuttings in standard's ring directly opposite each other and exactly between two pairs of legs; see detail in diagram. Insert globe and gold ring assembly into cuttings in standard's ring, and glue gold ring to this at its own diameter and with globe tilted slightly on an axis. Shellac standard only with one coat and varnish it.

JEWELRY BOXES
(*Georgian bedroom*)

Make an ornate jewelry box with a rectangular, rhinestone and pearl, box-style clasp from a large string of pearls or beads. Make a ring box with a small round or oval, filigree clasp from a necklace; some of these clasps have mother-of-pearl tops. Separate clasps from beads and use as is.

KNIFE CASE
(*Georgian dining room*)

To make a knife case in the Hepplewhite style, you need ¹⁄₁₆″ and ¹⁄₃₂″ balsa sheets, a lipstick tube, and woodtone paint. From ¹⁄₁₆″ balsa sheet, cut bottom of knife case following outline of pattern in diagram; cut ¾″ × 1″ piece for back of case. Stain both pieces. Glue back piece perpendicular to straight edge of bottom piece so bottom edge of back piece is flush with underside of bottom piece.

For sides and curved front of knife case, cut a 1¼″ × 2¾″ piece of wood on crosswise grain from ¹⁄₁₆″ balsa sheet. Soak wood in warm water for five minutes. Then bend carefully around lipstick tube and hold in place with a wide elastic band (don't let elastic band indent the soft wet wood); dry wood at room temperature or in low oven for ten minutes. Remove wood from mold and stain. Glue molded wood to side edges of back piece and to sides and curved front edges of bottom piece so molded piece covers these edges; you may have to trim side edges of molded piece to make them flush with back surface of back piece. Hold assembly with hands until glue begins to set.

Draw a line near top edge of molded piece ac-

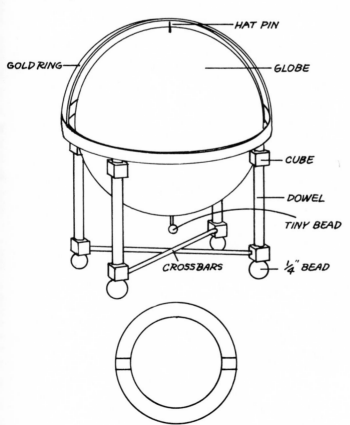

GOLD RING — HAT PIN
GLOBE
CUBE
DOWEL
TINY BEAD
CROSSBARS
¼″ BEAD

cording to broken line in diagram; this is tricky to draw because it is a straight, but angled line on a curved surface. Begin the line ¼" in from back corners and draw it slanting downward to the curved front of the knife case, where the line should be 1" up from bottom. Cut on line very carefully.

From ½₂" balsa sheet, cut top for knife case following outline of pattern in diagram; sand and stain. Cut away a ¼" × ¾" rectangular piece from straight edge of top piece, and glue rectangle to top edge of back piece and ¼" straight top edges of molded piece. Glue remaining top piece to slanted top edge of molded piece.

Shellac and varnish knife case. With woodtone paint and a tiny artist's brush, draw a second line ¼" down from top piece and parallel to line you cut; this line indicates where the knife case could be opened.

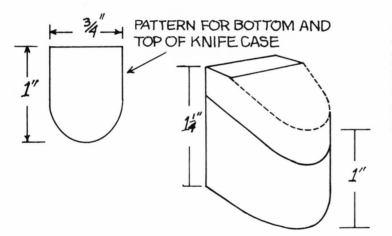

PATTERN FOR BOTTOM AND TOP OF KNIFE CASE

ORIENTAL URNS
(*Georgian library*)

One of our oriental-looking urns is actually a reproduction of a snuff bottle. The pair of Far East imports is made from two 1½" oblong beads that have some carving on them. For lids, glue rounded shank-type buttons to tops of the beads. If necessary, paint beads and buttons in desired colors with enamel paint. You can also use round beads for urns, which require mounting on balsa bases painted black, or square beads, which need no bases.

SILVER TEA SERVICE
(*Georgian dining room*)

Teapot, sugar, and creamer are made from metal perfume bottle tops; use a top ¾" in diameter for teapot and tops ½" in diameter for sugar and creamer. All three tops should be shaped identically; see diagram.

Make a spout for the teapot by attaching part of a drapery hook to it with liquid solder; liquid solder another part of the drapery hook to teapot for a handle. Make a spout for the creamer by bending a bit of the top edge with long-nose jewelry pliers. Glue flat buttons for bases to bottoms of teapot, creamer, and sugar; glue rounded button to top of teapot for a lid and glue a round bead to center of lid. Cut handles for creamer and sugar from thin picture hanging wire and attach with liquid solder, or cut handles from plastic acetate and glue in place.

For tray, cut an oval, round, or square piece from balsa sheet on which the teapot, sugar, and creamer will fit; cut same size piece from clear plastic acetate. Glue acetate onto balsa. Cut piece from ¼"-wide embossed paper to go around edge of tray, and glue to tray to create a gallery. For handles, glue two sewing loops to short ends of tray. For feet, glue four small beads to bottom of tray.

Paint entire tea service with silver paint.

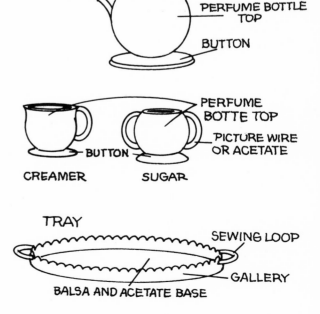

TEAPOT

DRAPERY HOOK

PERFUME BOTTLE TOP

BUTTON

CREAMER

SUGAR

PERFUME BOTTE TOP

PICTURE WIRE OR ACETATE

BUTTON

TRAY

SEWING LOOP

GALLERY

BALSA AND ACETATE BASE

THROW PILLOW
(*Georgian bedroom*)

Our throw pillow is actually an antique button covered with embroidered silk. But you can use any fabric-covered button made with a covered button kit. A lightweight to medium fabric works best.

VERMEIL BASKET
(*Georgian dining room*)

Make a lacy basket from a costume jewelry pin with a filigree setting. Remove stone from setting with tweezers, if there is one, and remove pin back with wire cutters. Cut a handle from picture wire and attach to basket with liquid solder; see diagram. Paint basket gold to resemble vermeil, or paint it silver, or paint it with enamel paint in a desired color to resemble porcelain.

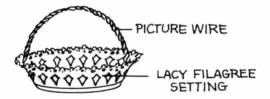

VERMEIL COMPOTE
(*Georgian dining room*)

To make this compote, you need a flat metal disc from either a costume jewelry pin or earring. Remove pin or earring back with wire cutters. Also with wire cutters cut off a screw to within three turns from the bottom. Liquid solder pin to screw and screw to flat metal, non-shank-type button; see diagram. Paint compote gold to resemble vermeil, or paint it silver, or paint it with enamel paint in a desired color to resemble porcelain.

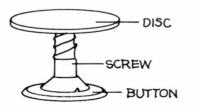

½ BUTTON (FROM COVERED BUTTON KIT)

VERMEIL DISH
(*Georgian library*)

This unusual little dish is actually a metal button ½" in diameter—the kind of button to be covered with fabric; see diagram. Paint it gold to resemble vermeil, or paint it silver, or paint it with enamel paint in a desired color to resemble porcelain.

ART GLASS DOGWOOD VASE
(*Victorian living room*)

Tiny clear glass vases are available in most gift and souvenir shops. With a tiny artist's brush and shiny model paint, paint small pink flowers and green leaves on such a vase to resemble dogwood.

BISQUE FIGURINE
(*Victorian living room*)

Paint a tiny figure—from a game, a train model set, an old charm bracelet, etc.—with a coat of flat white paint to resemble bisque.

BOOT FLASK
(*Victorian living room*)

Our boot is an old-time crackerjack prize. For the same effect, paint a tiny plastic doll's shoe from the dimestore in a desired color.

CAKES
(*Victorian kitchen*)

Make a layer cake from a white plastic medicine bottle cap; see diagram. Leave the cake white, or paint it another appropriate color. Glue cap to a round flat button that looks like a plate.

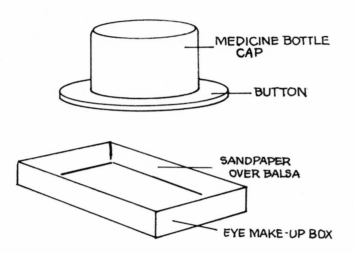

For a sheet cake, you need a small rectangular, plastic eye make-up box, silver paint, some balsa sheet, and fine grain tan sandpaper. Discard top of eye make-up box, and for cake pan, paint bottom half of box silver. Cut balsa sheet and sandpaper to fit inside pan, glue balsa and then sandpaper in place; see diagram.

CANNISTERS
(*Victorian kitchen*)

You can make many different cannisters and cannister sets from bottle tops or caps and from thimbles; see diagram. Glue flat or rounded buttons on top of cannisters, and if you want, glue tiny beads to center of lids. The thimble cannister needs a flat button glued to bottom to steady it. Paint cannisters in desired colors.

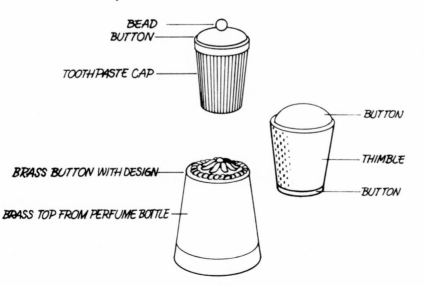

COFFEEPOT
(*Victorian kitchen*)

To make a coffeepot, use liquid solder to attach part of a drapery hook to a metal perfume bottle top to form a spout and another part of drapery hook to form a handle; see diagram. Glue a slightly rounded button to coffeepot to form a lid. Paint entire coffeepot with black enamel paint or any desired color.

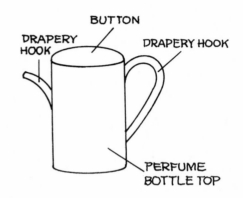

COLLANDER
(*Victorian kitchen*)

Make a collander with the small metal top to a salt or pepper shaker. Glue sewing eyes or loops to the sides for handles, and glue three tiny round beads to the bottom; see diagram. Paint entire collander with silver paint.

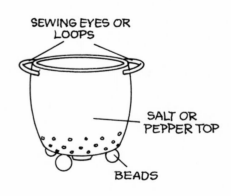

COPPER LUSTER WARE
(Victorian living room)

Glue together the parts of any or all of the designs in diagram, and paint with copper-colored model paint to simulate copper luster ware.

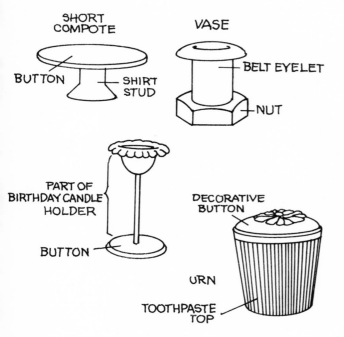

COOKING POT AND LADLE
(Victorian kitchen)

Make a cooking pot with the cap of an after-shave lotion bottle, and paint in desired color. Make a ladle from a screw-type earring. Paint with silver, gold, or woodtone paint.

CORN HUSK MILK GLASS VASE
(Victorian living room)

To make this vase, use glue or liquid solder to attach the tiny metal end of a pull chain on a light to a belt eyelet or tiny electrical socket; see diagram. Paint vase with flat white paint to resemble milk glass.

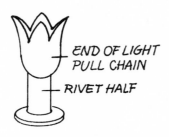

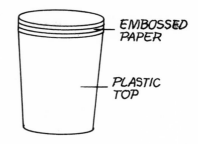

CUT GLASS VASE
(Victorian bedroom)

Make a cut glass vase with the tall, clear plastic top that protects the spray nozzle on a bottle of hairsetting lotion. Glue some gold embossed paper around opening for a decorative edge; see diagram. Fill vase loosely with tiny artificial flowers, if you wish.

DECANTER
(Victorian dining room)

To make a decanter, you need a small flat, non-shank-type button; a round bead ½" in diameter; a flat-head screw; a thin drapery hook. Bend drapery hook into the shape shown in diagram and glue or solder decanter parts according to same diagram.

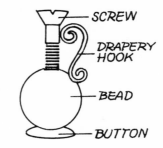

DOILIES
(Victorian living room)

Fine doilies, or antimacassars, for furniture can be cut from lace trimming. Be sure to pick a pattern that can be cut apart into pieces ¾" to 1" in diameter.

DECORATED EGGS
(Victorian living room)

To make one egg, glue a small, egg-shaped button to a flat button base, so the egg doesn't roll around on the shelf, and paint egg in pattern and colors of your choice; see diagram.

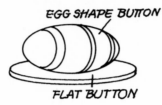

EGG SHAPE BUTTON

FLAT BUTTON

DRESSER SET
(Victorian bedroom)

Cut out mirror, brush, and comb from gold embossed paper according to patterns in diagram; make tiny cuts in paper for comb teeth. Using same patterns, cut out mirror and comb, and brush handle only, from $1/16''$ balsa sheet; cut brush head from $1/8''$ balsa sheet. Glue balsa pieces to underside of corresponding embossed paper pieces for reinforcement.

MIRROR BRUSH COMB

GARBAGE CAN
(Victorian kitchen)

A garbage can is made from a perfume or after-shave lotion bottle top, and the lid is a slightly rounded button; see diagram. Paint can in desired color. Top can be omitted.

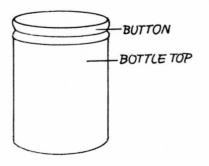

BUTTON

BOTTLE TOP

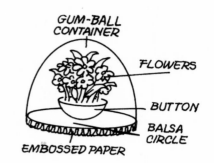

GUM-BALL CONTAINER

FLOWERS

BUTTON

BALSA CIRCLE

EMBOSSED PAPER

GLASS DOME
(Victorian dining room)

To make this, you need one half of a plastic gum ball container (the kind that dispenses prizes to children), a thin balsa sheet, a small slightly rounded button, gold embossed paper, and tiny artificial flowers. Cut a circle from the balsa sheet to fit opening of gum ball container; stain the balsa mahogany. Glue button to balsa and stick flowers into holes of the button; see diagram. Place gum ball container over flowers and glue to edge of balsa circle. Trim bottom edge of glass dome with embossed paper.

END OF LIGHT PULL CHAIN

EARRING SCREW

GOBLETS
(Victorian dining room)

Each goblet is made with the tiny metal end of a pull chain on a light and the screw part of an earring; see diagram. Attach the two parts with liquid solder and paint with gold, silver, or pewter-colored paint.

INKWELL AND INKSTAND
(Victorian living room)

For an inkwell, glue a tiny rhinestone or pearl to a round bead $3/8''$ in diameter; see diagram. For an inkstand, glue a square button to the inkwell.

RHINESTONE OR PEARL

BEAD

BUTTON

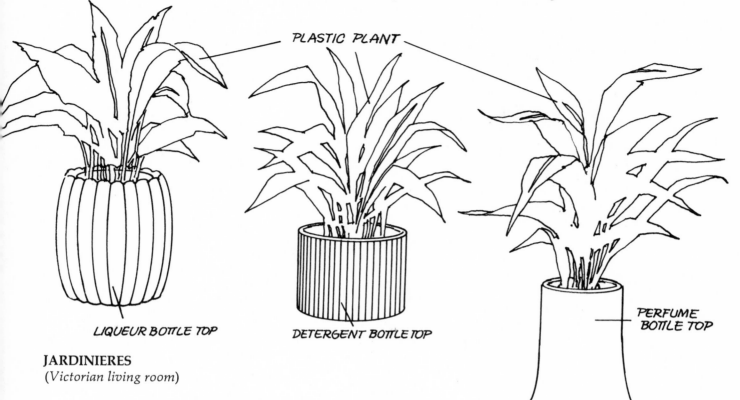

PLASTIC PLANT

LIQUEUR BOTTLE TOP

DETERGENT BOTTLE TOP

PERFUME BOTTLE TOP

JARDINIERES
(*Victorian living room*)

Jardinieres for holding potted plants can be made from a variety of fairly large liqueur, perfume, after-shave lotion, and dish detergent bottle tops; see diagram. Many of these tops can be used as is, but others—like dish detergent tops—need to be painted. Fill bottle tops with small amounts of floral clay and insert miniature plastic plants in the clay; you can find these plants at a pet store where they are sold for use in fish tanks.

MILK CAN
(*Victorian kitchen*)

The smallest size bottle of Bufferin makes a perfect tin milk can when painted with a coat of pewter-colored paint; see diagram.

BUFFERIN BOTTLE

HATBOX
(*Victorian bedroom*)

Make a hatbox by gluing together two checkers (these can come from a set that is already incomplete); see diagram. Decorate hatbox sides and top with a floral print from gift wrap paper or a magazine picture.

CHECKERS

MIXING BOWL
(*Victorian kitchen*)

For a mixing bowl, use one half of a plastic gum ball container (the kind that dispenses prizes to children) and paint in desired color.

NAPKINS AND NAPKIN RINGS
(*Victorian dining room*)

To make napkins, cut tiny pieces from white bias tape and fringe ends just a little. Roll each piece into a tiny gold circle that comes from a broken jewelry chain; see diagram.

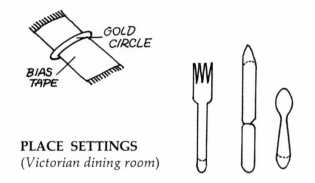

PLACE SETTINGS
(*Victorian dining room*)

You can buy gold embossed paper with knives, forks, and spoons drawn on it. Simply cut out as many place settings as you need. You may have to trim knife blade and fork handle so they are properly scaled; see broken line in diagram.

PLATTERS
(*Victorian kitchen*)

Make a set of matching platters with four flat buttons in same color and style but with different diameters; see diagram. Cover button-holes with four flat decorative buttons in the same size or graduated sizes. If button colors do not match, paint them in desired color to match. If you wish, you can paint the bands a different color.

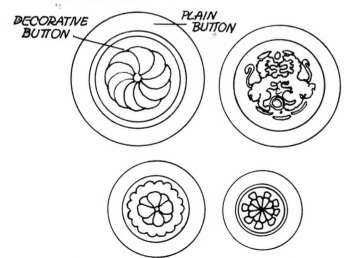

PORCELAIN BIRD
(*Victorian living room*)

Perhaps you have an old or odd cufflink on hand to be turned into a tiny figurine. We painted the bird on a cast-off cufflink in two colors, but otherwise used the cufflink as is; see diagram.

SÈVRES VASE
(*Victorian dining room*)

To make this impressive vase, glue together the following items in the order given: a flat button, a round bead ¾" in diameter, two nuts from the hardware store, a slightly rounded button, a tiny round bead; see diagram. Paint vase in desired color, glue gold embossed paper around rim of top button, and paint tiny flowers on bowl of vase.

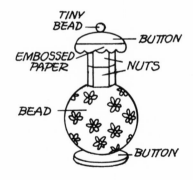

SOUVENIR BELL
(*Victorian living room*)

This bell is actually a Christmas package trim. Use it as is or paint in desired color.

TOWEL AND TOWEL RACK
(*Victorian kitchen*)

For the towel, fringe the short ends of a tiny scrap of fabric. For the towel rack, use one half of a small linking belt buckle. Drape towel over rack and glue rack to wall where indicated in diagram.

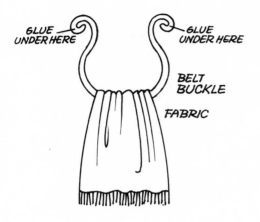

UMBRELLA AND UMBRELLA STAND
(*Victorian kitchen*)

To make an umbrella, wrap a tiny piece of fabric around one end of a decorative hors d'oeuvre pick and glue to secure; see diagram. For an umbrella stand, use the top of a lipstick tube, which may be silver or gold, painted with flowers, or have a fretwork design. Put a small amount of floral clay inside tube to weight it, then put in umbrella.

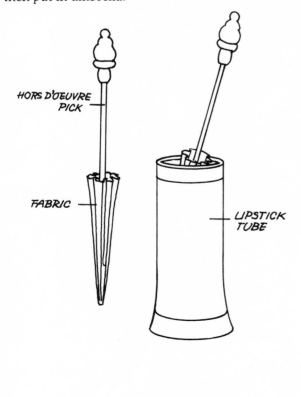

VEGETABLE DISHES
(*Victorian dining room*)

Covered vegetable dishes can be made from two earrings or two buttons glued together or from a lady's empty wrist watch case; see diagram. Attach a tiny round bead to lid of each dish, using liquid solder if lid is metal. Paint dishes in desired colors.

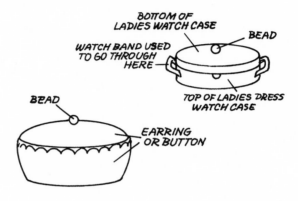

WASHBOARD
(*Victorian kitchen*)

To make this you need a $\frac{1}{16}$" balsa sheet, a $\frac{1}{8}$" sq. balsa strip, and a small piece of corrugated balsa. Cut a $1\frac{3}{8}$" $\times$ 2" piece from balsa sheet; cut two pieces, each $2\frac{3}{8}$" long, from balsa strip; cut one $1\frac{1}{8}$" piece from balsa strip. Stain wood pieces pine or another light color. Glue longer balsa strips to 2" sides of balsa sheet so outside edges on three sides are flush; see diagram. Glue short balsa strip along top edge of balsa sheet between longer balsa strips. Cut piece of corrugated balsa $1\frac{1}{2}$" long to fit between washboard sides, paint it silver, and glue in place.

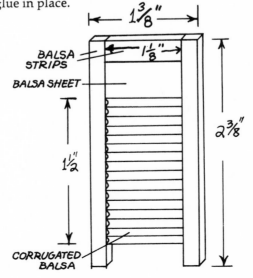

CHAPTER **30** *Paintings and Mirrors*

ALPHABET SAMPLER
(Colonial bedroom)

To make this sampler, you need the following: small embroidery needle, one strand of embroidery floss, 4″ sq. piece of bandage gauze or other white loose-weave fabric, $\frac{1}{16}$″ balsa sheet, $\frac{1}{4}$″ × $\frac{1}{8}$″ balsa strip.

If bandage gauze is your fabric, treat it with two coats of spray starch to stiffen it. With light pencil, mark off $2\frac{1}{2}$″ × $2\frac{3}{4}$″ work area on fabric. Stitching begins with the top middle letter D; see diagram. Stitch the top row with tiny cross stitches, completing letters to the right of D and then letters to the left of D; count threads of the fabric as you stitch to make sure the letters are the same size and spaces are even. Complete remaining rows of sampler in the same manner, always following the diagram.

Cut two $2\frac{1}{2}$″ pieces and two $2\frac{3}{4}$″ pieces from balsa strip. These pieces are the frame for your sampler; miter the corners. Stain or paint frame before gluing together.

Cut piece of balsa sheet large enough to include sampler frame. Glue sampler to balsa sheet piece after trimming away excess fabric. Glue frame to balsa sheet around sampler. Attach assembly to wall with glue or double-faced masking tape.

FLOWER PRINT
(Colonial dining room)

Our flower print is one of the "Twelve Months of Flowers" by the English artist, Robert Furber; we cut it out of a Colonial Williamsburg publication, but any small flower print is suitable for this project. Cut a frame to fit the print from a $\frac{1}{4}$″ × $\frac{1}{8}$″ balsa strip. Miter the corners and paint frame with flat black paint. Cut a piece of $\frac{1}{16}$″ balsa sheet large enough to include picture frame. Glue print and frame to balsa sheet; see diagram. Attach assembly to wall with glue or double-faced masking tape.

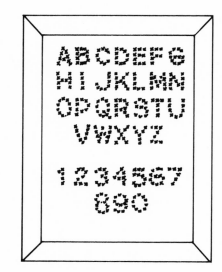

GLUE
FLOWER PRINT
HERE

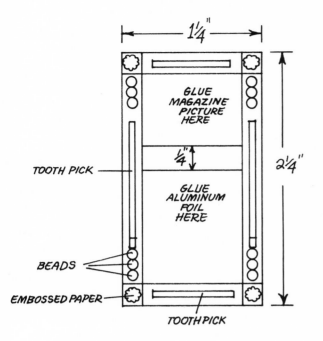

HITCHCOCK MIRROR
(*Colonial bedroom*)

To make this mirror, you need the following: $1/16''$ balsa sheet, $1/16'' \times 1/4''$ balsa strip, small decorative scene from a magazine, aluminum foil, clear plastic acetate, four round wooden toothpicks, gold embossed paper, six small round beads.

Cut a $1\frac{1}{4}'' \times 2\frac{1}{4}''$ piece from balsa sheet. Cut two $1\frac{1}{4}''$ pieces and two $1\frac{3}{4}''$ pieces from balsa strip; miter corners of strips. Stain all wood pieces. Glue strips together to form frame and glue frame to piece of balsa sheet; see diagram. Score corners of frame.

With rubber cement, glue magazine picture inside frame at the top, and glue aluminum foil inside frame at bottom; cut picture and foil so there is a space of $1/4''$ between them. Cut a piece of acetate the same size as the foil and glue over foil around edges to provide a glassy look. Cut off ends of toothpicks, stain midsections, and glue each piece to center of each frame piece to resemble spindles. Paint beads with woodtone paint and glue to vertical frame pieces above and below toothpicks. Shape four small rosettes out of embossed paper and glue to corners of mirror. Carefully apply a coat of shellac or varnish to mirror frame. Attach mirror to wall with glue or double-faced masking tape.

PORTRAITS
(*Colonial living room, dining room*)

To create portraits of the master and the mistress of the house, you need magazine pictures in color of people in old-fashioned costume. Our pictures came from *Antiques* magazine. You can also find such pictures in certain mail order catalogs under the headings of "Prints" or "Frames."

To make one portrait, glue picture to $1/16''$ balsa sheet cut large enough to include a frame around the picture. Paint picture with burnt umber, then brush the paint with dry bristles of a bushy paint brush to give an antiqued look. Give picture several coats of Mod Podge, an instant decoupage finish sold in craft stores.

Cut frame pieces from $1/4'' \times 1/8''$ balsa strip and miter corners. Stain frame before gluing together, then give it a coat of satin or eggshell finish varnish. Glue frame around picture and attach entire assembly to wall with glue or double-faced masking tape.

SEASCAPE PAINTING
(*Colonial living room*)

Follow preceding directions for making a portrait and substitute a picture of an appropriate sailing vessel on the water.

CHIPPENDALE MIRRORS
(*Georgian dining room, bedroom*)

For a large mirror, glue a $2\frac{1}{2}'' \times 3\frac{1}{2}''$ thin pocket mirror to a piece of $1/16''$ balsa sheet cut the same size as the mirror. Frame the mirror with gold embossed paper, gluing paper to mirror $1/8''$ in from mirror's edge; see diagram. With paint brush, apply two coats of glue to back of paper to stiffen it. If you want a less shiny finish, give paper a coat of dull gold paint before gluing to mirror. Attach mirror to wall with glue or double-faced masking tape.

For a smaller mirror, glue a $2'' \times 2\frac{1}{2}''$ thin pocket mirror to a piece of $1/16''$ balsa sheet cut the same size as the mirror. Frame the mirror with gold embossed paper, shaping paper into a crest at the top, and glue paper to mirror $1/8''$

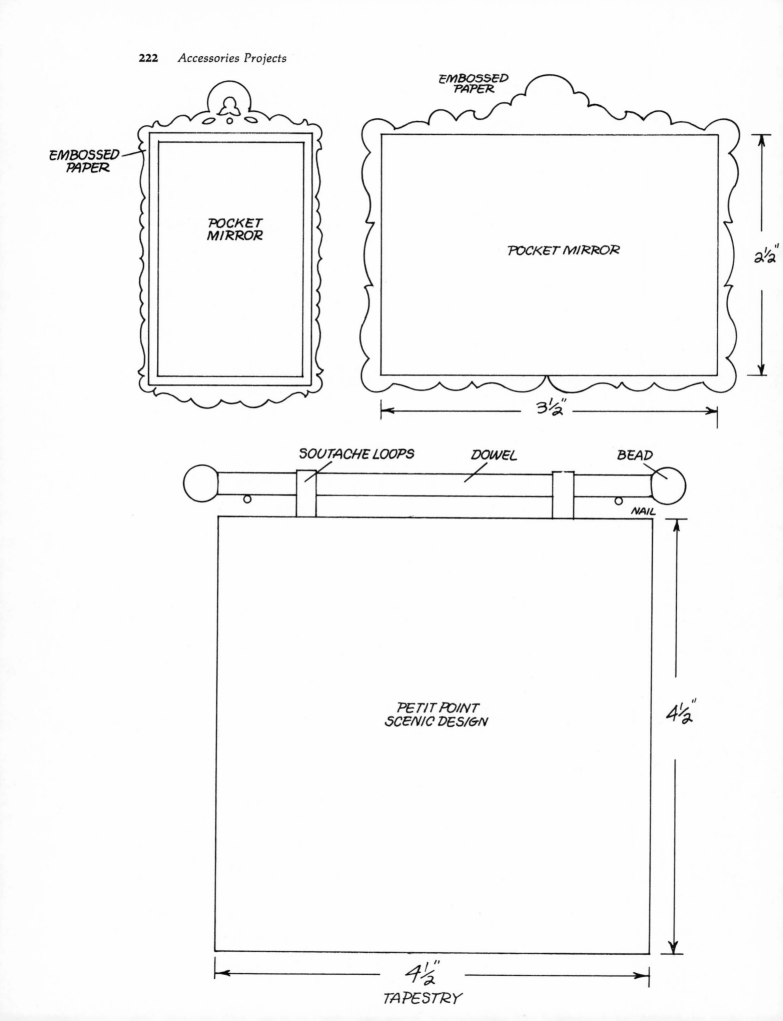

EMBOSSED
PAPER

POCKET
MIRROR

EMBOSSED
PAPER

POCKET MIRROR

2½"

3½"

SOUTACHE LOOPS   DOWEL   BEAD

NAIL

PETIT POINT
SCENIC DESIGN

4½"

4½"

TAPESTRY

in from mirror's edge; see diagram. Paint frame brown to simulate mahogany and highlight frame with gold paint to simulate gilding. Give frame a coat of stain or eggshell finish varnish. Attach mirror to wall as above.

PORTRAIT
(Georgian library)

Find a magazine picture in color of a noble man or woman of the day; our picture of Queen Anne is from *Antiques* magazine, but you can also find such pictures in certain mail order catalogs under the headings of "Prints" or "Frames."

Glue picture to $\frac{1}{16}$" balsa sheet cut large enough to include a frame around the picture. Paint picture with burnt umber, then brush paint with dry bristles of a bushy paint brush to give an antiqued look. Give picture several coats of Mod Podge, an instant decoupage finish sold in craft stores.

Cut frame pieces from $\frac{1}{2}$"-wide, $\frac{1}{4}$"-thick decorative molding, prefinished in blue and gold or another combination of colors; miter corners and glue frame around picture. Attach entire assembly to wall with glue or double-faced masking tape.

TAPESTRY
(Georgian dining room)

For this hanging tapestry, you need a $4\frac{1}{2}$" × $4\frac{1}{2}$" piece of petit point in a scenic design (ours was machine-embroidered petit point cut from an old evening purse), two thin soutache loops, two small round beads, and a $\frac{1}{8}$" dowel cut to $4\frac{1}{2}$". Finish any raw edges of petit point with zig zag stitch on a sewing machine, or by hand with tiny overcast stitches. Glue soutache loops to top of tapestry, run dowel through loops, and glue beads to ends of dowel; see diagram. Hang tapestry by driving two tiny nails into wall to support dowel.

BEADED PICTURES
(Victorian dining room, bedroom)

Make an ornate picture by framing a scrap of bead work or petit point with a gold plastic frame sold as gift package trim in gift and card shops. Glue bead work to piece of balsa sheet cut to fit it, and frame. Attach to wall with glue or double-faced masking tape.

DAGUERREOTYPES IN FRAMES
(Victorian living room)

You may have on hand an actual photograph of a turn-of-the-century individual, but if not, you can find old-fashioned photographs in magazines or as gift wrap paper motif. Such a photograph can be mounted in several ways; see diagram. One is to put it in the metal liner of an antique daguerreotype frame. Another is to use either an oval or rectangular embossed paper picture frame. For a tabletop picture frame, use a costume jewelry pin with a flat mounting. Remove pin back and stone and glue an appropriate photograph where the stone was. Make an easel out of a small piece of balsa sheet and glue to back of pin mounting to make it stand upright; paint easel the same color as the mounting.

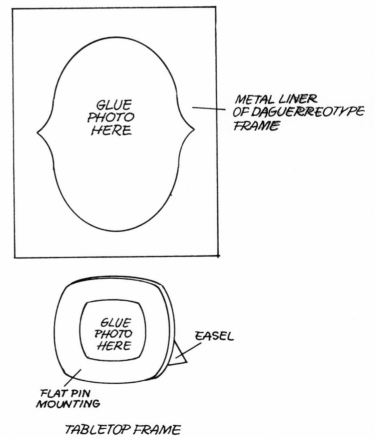

TABLETOP FRAME

FIREPLACE MIRROR
(*Victorian living room*)

Remove the glass from an old oval or rectangular metal picture frame that is about 5″ tall. Give the frame a coat of gold or brass paint and insert a piece of mirror cut to fit inside the frame. Attach mirror to wall with glue or double-faced masking tape.

FRAMED MOTTO
(*Victorian kitchen*)

To make this you need the following: small embroidery needle, three strands of embroidery floss in two colors, a 1¾″ × 3¼″ piece of white loose-weave fabric, ¹⁄₁₆″ balsa sheet, ¼″ × ⅛″ balsa strip. Stitch motto onto fabric, counting threads as you go to make sure the letters are the same size and spaces are even; see diagram.

Cut two pieces, each 2½″ long, from balsa strip, making cuts on a slant in the same direction; cut two pieces, each 4″ long, from balsa strip, making cuts on slant in same direction. Stain the pieces, then glue longer strips over shorter strips to form frame.

Cut piece of balsa sheet large enough to include frame. Glue stitched fabric to balsa sheet and glue frame to balsa sheet around fabric. Shellac or varnish frame, if you wish. Attach assembly to wall with glue or double-faced masking tape.

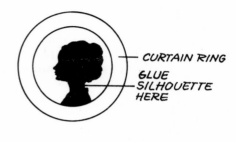

SILHOUETTES
(*Victorian bedroom*)

Silhouettes can be cut out of certain mail order catalogs; check the headings "Prints" or "Frames." Glue each silhouette to the back of a plastic curtain ring 1″ in diameter which you have painted gold; see diagram. Attach silhouette to wall with glue or double-faced masking tape.

SCENIC PAINTINGS
(*Victorian living room, dining room*)

Cut a scenic picture in muted colors from a magazine. Frame it with decorative molding according to directions for portrait in Georgian library, or with a gold plastic frame sold as gift package trim. Or you can frame a scenic picture with a decorative cover designed to conceal two electrical light plug outlets; see diagram. The latter can be found in many styles, but be sure to choose one with ornate edging. Glue picture to center of cover *over* the two outlets. Hang scenic paintings from ceiling molding with rope and tassel, or attach to wall with glue or double-faced masking tape.

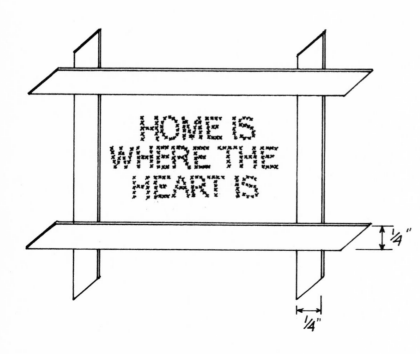

PICTURE HANGERS AND TASSELS
(Victorian living room, dining room)

A rope-like picture hanger can be made from either a strand of gold drapery tassel or from a piece of string dyed gold. To make a tassel, wrap a piece of gold embroidery floss around your finger ten times, then remove from finger. Tie a 2″ piece of gold floss around top of the wrapped floss and knot; see diagram. Tie another 2″ piece of floss around wrapped floss ¼″ down from top and knot. Cut across bottom of wrapped floss (see broken line in diagram), then trim to even bottom of tassel.

Glue rope hanger to back of picture frame at top corners and hang on wall with tiny finishing nail; see diagram. Push tassel onto nail.

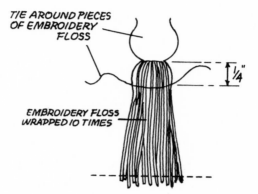

TIE AROUND PIECES OF EMBROIDERY FLOSS

¼″

EMBROIDERY FLOSS WRAPPED 10 TIMES

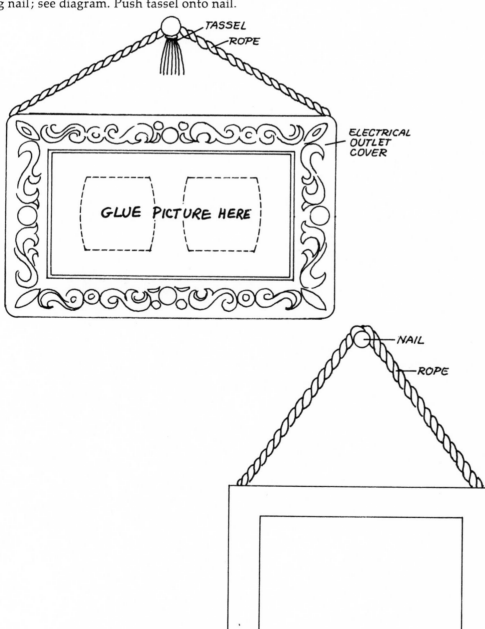

TASSEL

ROPE

ELECTRICAL OUTLET COVER

GLUE PICTURE HERE

NAIL

ROPE

BRAIDED RUG
(Colonial dining room)

SIZE: 7½″ × 9″

To make this oval rug, you need 5-yard packages of double-fold cotton bias tape in the following colors: one package *each* of brown, tan, and beige; one package of one shade of green (or blue, or red); one package of another shade of green (or blue, or red). If you can't find double-fold bias tape in the colors of your choice, buy single-fold tape and fold in half by pressing with an iron. You need transparent thread for this project, also.

Cut tape as follows (you will use all the brown and beige tape, and will have some of the other tapes left over):

Row 1 2 pieces brown, each 41″; 1 piece #1 green, 41″

Row 2 2 pieces brown, each 40″; 1 piece tan, 40″

Row 3 3 pieces tan, each 35″

Row 4 3 pieces beige, each 28″

Row 5 2 pieces beige, each 28″; 1 piece tan, 28″

Row 6 2 pieces #2 green, each 26″; 1 piece #1 green, 26″

Row 7 2 pieces #2 green, each 20″; 1 piece brown, 18″

Row 8 2 pieces beige, each 20″; 1 piece #1 green, 20″

Finished size is 7½″ × 9″.

Finished size is 4″ × 4¾″.

Braid each row fairly loosely, keeping the full ¼″ width of the tape as flat as possible and the folded side on the bottom. For best results, anchor one end of the braid to your work surface while braiding it. When the eight rows are braided, pin braids on a terry cloth towel in an oval pattern so you can see how the rug will look when sewed together. The shortest row, 8, is at the center of the rug, row 7 is next, and so on until row 1, which forms the outside edge. All the braids should go in the same direction; see photograph below.

Using transparent thread, sew the rug from the back side. Beginning with row 8, make the very center row 2½″ long and sew remainder of row 8 down one side of center row and back up other side of center row; this makes a tiny oval rug about 3¼″ long. Sew row 7 to outside edge of oval formed by row 8; you should now have an oval rug about 4″ long. Sew row 6 to outside edge of row 7, and proceed in the same manner for remaining rows. At the end of each row, cut the braid and tuck the three end pieces into the beginning of the new row of braid to achieve the appearance of one continuous oval braid. When the rug is completed, press with a steam iron, using a pressing cloth, so it lies flat.

BRAIDED YARN RUG
(Colonial bedroom)

SIZE: 4″ × 4¾″

To make this little rug, you need scraps of Persian yarn or thin-ply yarn in many colors, plus transparent thread. To begin, take three 15″–20″ strands of yarn in three different colors and knot them together two inches from one end. Place knotted end under a heavy weight and braid until you are one inch from the other end of the strands; knot to secure the braiding and set this piece aside. Repeat with other colors for five to six more braids.

To assemble rug, follow directions for the braided rug, making sure all knots fall on underside when you join one section of braiding to another. See above photograph.

HOOKED RUG
(Colonial bedroom)

SIZE: 8″ × 10″

To make this rug, you need the following: a wooden picture frame (buy a cheap one at the dimestore); a crochet hook; a 10″ × 12″ piece of #10 or #12 Mono canvas; an 8″ × 10″ piece of thin cotton fabric; 16 windings of Persian yarn—10 windings in the rug's primary color, four windings in one contrast color, and two windings in another contrast color. A winding is a pre-cut length of about 10–12 strands of Persian yarn sold in craft and needlework stores (if your yarn is not pre-cut, cut it to lengths of about 20″). Because the tension used in hooking a rug differs from person to person, you should purchase a little more yarn than called for here (most stores will let you return extra yarn for credit); also, dye lots can vary slightly in color, so it's best to err on the side of too much yarn rather than too little.

To begin, tack canvas to wooden frame with staple gun or tacks. Hold frame taut in your lap while working and keep your left hand (if right-handed) under frame to guide the yarn.

Work the pattern in the following order, and according to photograph: first, the border; second, the dividing lines of the squares; third, the flowers; last, the area around flowers inside the squares. Insert crochet hook and one strand of yarn from top side of canvas through a mesh to the underside and bring up a loop of yarn, leaving a 1″ tail underneath; repeat with the next mesh, and so on across the row, working from right to left. The loops won't ravel unless you pull very hard. When you run out of yarn, pick up a new strand, leaving a 1″ tail.

When hooking is completed, carefully remove canvas from frame and trim canvas to within ½″ of the work. With pressing cloth and steam iron, turn under raw edges of canvas. Glue cotton fabric to underside of rug and press rug for a short time under suitable weight.

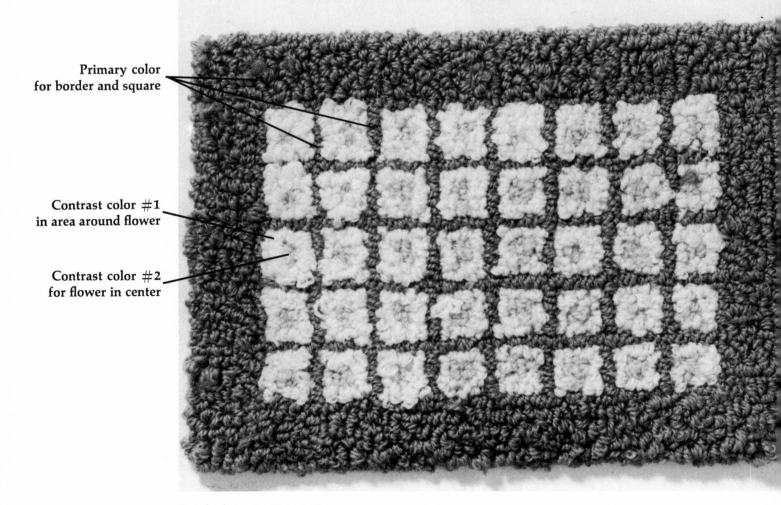

Primary color for border and square

Contrast color #1 in area around flower

Contrast color #2 for flower in center

Finished size is 8″ × 10″.

NEEDLEPOINT ORIENTAL RUG
(Colonial living room)

SIZE: 8½″ × 13″

To make this rug, you need to buy a kit for a needlepoint doorstop with a pre-worked design. Thus, all you have to do is fill in the background and even out the corners, as seen in the shaded areas of the diagram; keep the corner design similar to the rest of the design, or make the corners part of the background. Kits for needlepoint doorstops are reasonably priced and come in a wide variety of designs and colors.

When you have completed the needlepoint, have it blocked professionally, if possible. Or block it yourself with a pressing cloth and steam iron, tacking the edges with small tacks or a staple gun to a piece of plywood so it will dry as a perfect rectangle; the work should be tacked about every inch. When dry, trim the canvas on all sides to within ½″ of the work. Then turn under all edges ½″ and press them in place with pressing cloth and steam iron.

Next, take a tapestry needle and beige yarn and make ¼″ loops in each mesh of the canvas on the short edges, staying as close to the needlepoint as possible. Secure loops across the top by sewing machine or by hand; then cut loops open with scissors and trim them to ¼″ to form fringe. Cut a piece of felt in a neutral color to fit underside of rug, excluding fringe, and glue to secure. Place rug under weight to dry.

NEEDLEPOINT CANTON RUG
(Georgian library)

SIZE: 9″ × 12″, photograph on page 232.

To make this rug, you need the following: tapestry needle, #12 Mono canvas measuring 11″ × 13″; permanent color magic markers in various colors; 9″ × 12″ piece of thin cotton fabric; 11 windings of Persian yarn in the primary, or background, color; 4 windings of yarn in the secondary color; 1 winding of yarn in each other color. A winding is a pre-cut length of about 10–12 strands of Persian yarn sold in craft and needlework stores (if your yarn is not pre-cut, cut it to lengths of about 20″). Your primary color should be beige or white; your secondary color (for the two rectangular borders) should be blue or green; the other two or three colors should complement the primary and secondary colors and should be subdued shades.

Bind raw edges of canvas with masking tape. Transfer the pattern in diagram to canvas with felt tip pens in colors approximating your yarn colors. Work the pattern on your canvas, following photograph, until rug is completed. Have the rug blocked professionally, if possible. Or block it yourself with a pressing cloth and steam iron, tacking the edges with small tacks or a staple gun to a piece of plywood so it will dry as a perfect rectangle; the work should be tacked about every inch. When dry, trim the short edges of the canvas to within ¼″ of the work, and the long edges to within ½″. Turn under long edges for ½″ and press down with pressing cloth and steam iron.

Fringe the short edges of the rug by pulling away ¼″ of the horizontal canvas threads, except for the thread right next to the work on both edges. Glue cotton fabric to underside of rug, excluding fringe.

NEEDLEPOINT SCATTER RUGS
(Georgian hall)

SIZES: 3″ × 4″ and 7″ × 9″: photographs overleaf.

These small scatter rugs are coordinating. To make them, you need the following: tapestry needle; two pieces of #12 Mono canvas, one measuring 4″ × 5″ and the other 8″ × 10″; permanent color felt tip pens in various colors; some thin cotton fabric; leftover bits of Persian yarn in various colors.

Bind raw edges of each piece of canvas with masking tape. Transfer patterns in diagram to canvas with felt tip pens in colors approximating your yarn colors. You should have one primary color and one secondary color, as shown in the photographs, plus three other colors that complement to fill in rest of patterns. Work the patterns on each piece of canvas, until rugs are completed. Block rugs with a pressing cloth and steam iron, then dry them under suitable weight. Trim short edges of each canvas to within ¼″ of the work, and the long edges to within ½″. Turn under long edges ½″ and press down with pressing cloth and steam iron.

Fringe the short edges of the rugs by pulling away ¼″ of the horizontal canvas threads, except for the thread right next to the work on both edges. Cut cotton fabric to fit the underside of each rug, excluding fringe, and glue in place.

LARGE NEEDLEPOINT SCATTER RUG

Finished size is 7″ × 9″.

SMALL NEEDLEPOINT SCATTER RUG

Finished size is 3″ × 4″.

NEEDLEPOINT CANTON RUG

Finished size is 9″ × 12″.

RAG RUG
(Colonial keeping room)

To make a rag rug in whatever size you want, you need a sample of thin cotton upholstery from an upholstery sample book; most furniture and interior decorating shops will let you have samples when they are ready to discard a sample book. Remove sample from book with single-edged razor blade. Trim edges to desired measurements. Fringe ¼" on short edges by pulling out horizontal threads with a straight pin and discarding them.

ORIENTAL RUG
(Georgian dining room)

To make this rug, you need a sample of upholstery, which is tapestry cloth, in an Oriental design; most furniture and interior decorating stores will let you have upholstery samples when they are ready to discard a sample book. Remove sample from book with single-edged razor blade and trim to the size you need. Turn under edges ¼" and press down with pressing cloth and steam iron. Cut a piece of felt to fit underside of rug, glue in place, and dry under suitable weight. Glue ½"-wide cotton fringe to short edges of rug; try to butt fringe against the edges without any overlapping of fringe and fabric. Trim ¼" off fringe.

VELVET RUG
(Georgian bedroom)

Cut a scrap of velvet or velveteen fabric to correct size. Do not turn under the edges, but instead rub a little glue along edges with a toothpick; when glue is dry, glue ½"-wide silk fringe to the short edges of the rug.

LINOLEUM FLOOR
(Victorian kitchen)

Make a linoleum floor with a piece of oilcloth cut to fit the dimensions of your dollhouse kitchen. Glue down and place suitable weight on floor while it dries. You can also use samples of heavy, textured vinyl wallpaper.

ORIENTAL CARPET
(Victorian bedroom)

To make this Oriental-type carpet, use the material of half a beaded purse (or needlepoint or petit point purse). Separate half the purse from the other half with manicure scissors and trim to desired size. Cut a piece of felt to fit underside of carpet, glue in place, and dry under suitable weight. Glue ½"-wide cotton fringe to short edges of carpet; try to butt fringe against the edges without any overlapping of fringe and fabric.

BRUSSELS CARPETS
(Victorian dining room, living room)

The simplest rugs are made with a sample of upholstery; most furniture and interior decorating stores will let you have upholstery samples when they are ready to discard a sample book. For each rug, remove sample from book with single-edged razor blade and trim to desired size. Overcast the edges by hand or by the zig zag stitch on the sewing machine; do not turn under edges because rug will look lumpy.

THROW RUGS
(Victorian kitchen)

Make a small, round throw rug by using a crocheted drink coaster as is. For a larger round throw rug, dye a crocheted doily in a color.

Index